Palgrave Studies of Entrepreneurship and Social Challenges in Developing Economies

Series Editor
Rajagopal, EGADE Business School, Tecnológico de Monterrey, Mexico City, Mexico

This series explores the role of entrepreneurship in managing social challenges comprising poverty, gender inequality, sustainability and climate change, income disparity, social healthcare, community housing and homelessness, and clean food and water supplies across Asia, Africa, and Latin America.

Entrepreneurship in developing countries has an economic motivation and it is taken up as a survival occupation. The books in this series discuss various attributes of social enterprises, innovation, technology, and the role of leadership in meeting the recurring social challenges. The discussion on entrepreneurship in this book series is central to social entrepreneurship, family enterprises, entrepreneurial business models, disruptive innovation, consumer behavior, marketing-mix, branding, profit and performance, market expansion, new product development, operations and supply chain, manufacturing, and servitization. In addition, the volumes in this book series also address the PESTEL (political, economic, social, technological, environmental, and legal) perspectives that support socio-economic development.

Rajagopal

Rebuilding Entrepreneurship at the Grassroots

Converging Divergent Factors of Society and Economy

Rajagopal
EGADE Business School
Tecnológico de Monterrey
Mexico City, Mexico

ISSN 2731-6874 ISSN 2731-6882 (electronic)
Palgrave Studies of Entrepreneurship and Social Challenges in Developing Economies
ISBN 978-3-031-43269-9 ISBN 978-3-031-43270-5 (eBook)
https://doi.org/10.1007/978-3-031-43270-5

© The Editor(s) (if applicable) and The Author(s), under exclusive license to Springer Nature Switzerland AG 2024

This work is subject to copyright. All rights are solely and exclusively licensed by the Publisher, whether the whole or part of the material is concerned, specifically the rights of translation, reprinting, reuse of illustrations, recitation, broadcasting, reproduction on microfilms or in any other physical way, and transmission or information storage and retrieval, electronic adaptation, computer software, or by similar or dissimilar methodology now known or hereafter developed.
The use of general descriptive names, registered names, trademarks, service marks, etc. in this publication does not imply, even in the absence of a specific statement, that such names are exempt from the relevant protective laws and regulations and therefore free for general use.
The publisher, the authors, and the editors are safe to assume that the advice and information in this book are believed to be true and accurate at the date of publication. Neither the publisher nor the authors or the editors give a warranty, expressed or implied, with respect to the material contained herein or for any errors or omissions that may have been made. The publisher remains neutral with regard to jurisdictional claims in published maps and institutional affiliations.

Cover illustration: Maram_shutterstock.com

This Palgrave Macmillan imprint is published by the registered company Springer Nature Switzerland AG
The registered company address is: Gewerbestrasse 11, 6330 Cham, Switzerland

Paper in this product is recyclable.

...to my wife Arati

Preface

This book builds thematic convergence through the discussions on interconnected perspectives across chapters. It addresses multi-layered topics between the broad domains of entrepreneurship and social challenges through various contemporary strategies with a focus on changing business dynamics. Social challenges in generating continuous income, employment, sustainability, and infrastructure have been growing complex with economic transitions and technology growth. Historically, entrepreneurs face a lack of desire to grow amidst social challenges, which causes decision conflicts for artisans. However, the increasing demand for artisan-made goods and services in emerging markets implies that artisans face a seemingly challenging dilemma toward upholding artisanal values and resisting growth or embracing it.[1] the interrelationship between the topical discussions across chapters reveals that entrepreneurship, social challenges, marketing strategies, and entrepreneurial behavioral are aligned linearly in the book.

Chapter 1 discusses the introduction to the concept of promoting entrepreneurship as a key driver to meet the social challenges in farm and non-farm sectors, housing, community health, education, and sustainability. The future perspectives have been conceptualized in this chapter in

---

[1] Solomon, S. J. and Mathias, B. D. (2020). The artisans' dilemma: Artisan entrepreneurship and the challenge of firm growth. *Journal of Business Venturing*, 35 (5), in Press. https://doi.org/10.1016/j.jbusvent.2020.106044.

view of the conventional entrepreneurial practices and discuss the possibilities of scaling entrepreneurship to upstream markets. This chapter thematically complements the discussion in Chapter 2 which focuses on entrepreneurial ecosystem embedding the social systems and family businesses. Chapter 2 establishes backward and forward entrepreneurial linkages in view of the public policies which play significant roles in improving innovation, technology, and skills among entrepreneurial activities. Chapter 1 also connects thematically to Chapter 7 which focuses on developing new entrepreneurial ventures as reshaping the future to meet the existing social challenges. Chapter 7 discusses the future perspective of the incubating innovation and technology start-ups through entrepreneurial accelerators. Both chapters discuss a future prolific shift in entrepreneurship by taking a long leap from the conventional practices through efficient mentoring, skills development, and social dynamics. These chapters argue that crowdsourcing and crowdfunding are the new domains to nurture entrepreneurship in the future to grow along innovation, technology, and market competition.

Similarly, Chapters 3 and 5 have symbiotic discussions on entrepreneurial behavior and crowd-based entrepreneurship respectively. Chapter 3 discusses artisanal pedigree by analyzing the impact on entrepreneurial trade and skills over the generational transcend. Such transition entrepreneurial philosophy is affected by the leadership, crowd effects, and the boom of open innovations (Chapter 5). Chapter 3 discusses various perspectives of entrepreneurship contextual to the gender and economic dependencies while Chapter 5 supplements this discussion with decision-making and exploring new opportunities within the regional markets. In another paired discussion, the reverse entrepreneurship and upstream business modeling are divulged in Chapters 4 and 6 respectively, which synthesize the growing trend of reverse migration (from far-home destinations to the home destination) with the intention to invest in local enterprises and developing upstream market branding, internationalization, and behavioral shifts in business.

This book categorically reviews the sociological and economic theories on entrepreneurship, social intervention, collective intelligence, decision-making, and stakeholder values. It also examines previous researches and analyzes the strategic and tactical stewardship of firms in managing neurobehavioral responses of consumers and designing demand-led entrepreneurial business models. The book discusses new strategies suitable for co-creating entrepreneurial business models in association with the market players, stakeholders, and social leaders. This book significantly contributes to the existing literature and serves as a learning post and a think tank for students, researchers, and business managers. The book argues the rationale of inclusivity in business and marketing agility to increase customer-centric focus in business organization and co-create agile marketing strategies to stay competitive. It focuses on design-to-society as the pivot of marketing and argues that the commitments of customers and stakeholders on advocating the agile marketing approaches. The book argues that firms can make a high impact on competitive leadership by meticulously exploring problems, needs, and solutions (PNS factors) to drive social and emotional impact on consumers. The book discusses new strategies suitable for the companies to develop an agile marketing model suitable for the emerging markets and how to co-create strategies in association with the market players, society, stakeholders, and customers. This book significantly contributes to the existing literature and serves as a learning post and a think tank for students, researchers, and business managers.

Some of my research papers on business modeling and customer-centric marketing in the emerging markets have been published in the international refereed journals that have driven new insights on the subject. Accordingly, filtered and refined concepts and management practices that are endorsed with applied illustrations and updated review of literature on managing business in overseas destinations have been presented in the book. The principal audience of this book are working managers, students of undergraduate and graduate management studies, research scholars, and academics in different business-related disciplines. This book has been developed also to serve as principal text for the undergraduate and graduate students who are pursuing studies in managing people, agile marketing, brand socialization, corporate governance, and new-generation marketing studies. Besides serving as principal reading in undergraduate and graduate programs, this book would also inspire working managers, market analysts, and business consultants to explore various solutions for international business management. This book fits into the courses of Entrepreneurship Management, New Venture Management, Marketing, Entrepreneurship in Emerging Markets, Entrepreneurial Business Modeling, and Innovation Management in various universities and business schools.

I hope this book will contribute to the existing literature and deliver new concepts to the students and researchers to pursue the subject further. By reading this book, working managers may also realize how to converge agile marketing practices with corporate strategies in managing business at the destination markets while students would learn the new dimensions of marketing strategies.

Mexico City, Mexico Rajagopal
September

Acknowledgments

Rebuilding entrepreneurship has become a big challenge at the grassroots of the economy after the pandemic and business recession since early 2020, which has set the new normal to maintain the business continuum and survive the social, economic, and business challenges. Agility in business, open innovation, branding of entrepreneurial products, and customer reorientation have become significant for niche enterprises to stay competitive in the market. This book is an outgrowth of research analysis and steering of new concepts to meet the emerging challenges during the post-pandemic business recovery. As institutional resources for reviving firms were confined during these critical times, the crowd dynamics were found remotely active. I have been teaching collective intelligence in M.B.A. program as a practice course at EGADE Business School in the past couple of years. The emerging storyboards on the agile marketing modeling practices at the niche and macro-economic levels have given many insights to me, which have been central to this book. I have significantly benefitted from the discussions of my colleagues within and outside the EGADE Business School and Boston University. I would like to acknowledge the support of Dr. Ernesto Amoros, Associate Dean, EGADE Business School, and Dr. Claudia Quintanilla, Director, Marketing and Business Intelligence Department of EGADE Business School, who have always encouraged me to take up new challenges in teaching graduate courses, develop new insights, and contribute to the existing literature prolifically. I am thankful to Dr. Vladimir Zlatev, Associate Professor of Practice, and Dr. Marcus Goncalves, Associate Chair of the Administrative Sciences Department, Metropolitan College of Boston University for giving me teaching assignments, which enabled me to apply the research output on entrepreneurial business modeling in the classes for past several years.

I am thankful to various anonymous referees of our previous research works on globalization, consumer behavior, and marketing strategy that helped in looking deeper into the conceptual gaps and improving the quality with their valuable comments. I express my sincere thanks to Marcus Ballenger, Senior Editor, Scholarly Business, Palgrave Macmillan, for his cooperation and support during the development of the manuscript of this book. Finally, I express my deep gratitude to Arati Rajagopal who has been instrumental in completing this book. I acknowledge her help in copy editing the first draft of the manuscript and for staying in touch until the final proofs were crosschecked and the index was developed.

Contents

Part I Dissecting the Core

1 Entrepreneurial Transitions   3
   Traditional Entrepreneurship   4
   The Driving Head   13
   Capabilities and Competencies   23
   Business Scaling   27
   Challenges in Research and Business Planning   33

2 Entrepreneurial Ecosystem   37
   Social Ecosystem and Entrepreneurship   39
   Exploring Inside Market   47
   Driving Entrepreneurial Innovations   55
   Human Element in Operational Linkages   60

3 Entrepreneurial Behavior   67
   Artisanal Pedigree   69
   Leadership   78
   Human Element in Enterprise Management   82
   Entrepreneurial Mindset, Decisions, and Strategies   86

Part II The Transition

4 Reverse Entrepreneurship   93
   Reverse Entrepreneurship   93

Investments in Local Enterprises	104
Developing Local Markets	108

5 **Crowd-Based Entrepreneurship** — 117
   Crowdsourcing — 118
   Open Innovation — 129
   New Product Development — 137
   Niche Marketing Strategy — 142

6 **Alternate Business Modeling** — 147
   Agility in Marketing — 148
   Brand Architecture — 155
   Proximity, Relationship, and Optimism — 162

Part III Thematic Fusion

7 **Synthesis: Managing Enterprises at the Grassroots** — 171
   The Bottom-line — 172
   The Transition — 177
     Sustainable Entrepreneurship — 180
   The Convergence: Market, Society, and Values — 184
     The Quadruple Bottom-line in Business — 186
     Behavioral Analysis — 189
   Profiling Innovations — 191
     Digital Media and Markets — 193
   Thematic Convergence — 195

Index — 199

About the Author

Rajagopal is Distinguished Professor of Marketing and Business at EGADE Business School of Technologico de Monterrey, Mexico City Campus, and Life Fellow of the Royal Society for Encouragement of Arts, Manufacture and Commerce, London. He is also Fellow of the Chartered Management Institute and Fellow of the Institute of Operations Management, UK. Dr. Rajagopal has been serving as Visiting Professor at Boston University, Boston, Massachusetts, since 2013 and is also engaged in teaching courses at the UFV India Global Education of the University of the Fraser Valley, Canada.

He has been listed with biography in various international directories. He offers courses on Competitor Analysis, Marketing Strategy, Advance Selling Systems, International Marketing, Services Marketing, New Product Development, and other subjects of contemporary interest to the students of undergraduate, graduate, and doctoral programs. He has imparted training to senior executives and has conducted over 75 management and faculty development programs. Dr. Rajagopal holds post-graduate and doctoral degrees in Economics and Marketing respectively from Pandit Ravishankar Shukla University in India. His specialization is in the fields of Marketing Management, Rural Economic Linkages, and Development Economics.

He has to his credit 71 books on marketing management and rural development themes and over 400 research contributions that include published research papers in national and international refereed journals. He is Editor-in-Chief of *International Journal of Leisure and Tourism Marketing* and International *Journal of Business Competition*. Dr. Rajagopal served as Regional Editor of *Emerald Emerging Markets Case Studies* (2012–2019), published by Emerald Publishers, UK. He is on the editorial board of various journals of international repute. Currently, Dr. Rajagopal holds the honor of the highest level of National Researcher-SNI Level- III. He has been awarded UK–Mexico Visiting Chair 2016–2017 for collaborative research on 'Global-Local Innovation Convergence' with the University of Sheffield, UK, instituted by the Consortium of Higher Education Institutes of Mexico and UK.

Dr. Rajagopal has been conferred the Overseas Indian Award (*Pravasi Bhartiya Samman Award*) in January 2023 for his outstanding contribution in the field of Education. This is the highest honor conferred by the President of India. This award has been conferred in acknowledgment of outstanding achievement in the field of Education in India, Mexico, and the USA.

List of Figures

Fig. 1.1	A comparative framework of conventional and contemporary entrepreneurship (*Source* Author)	9
Fig. 1.2	Future growth of entrepreneurship (*Source* Author)	17
Fig. 2.1	Taxonomy of ecosystems and the factors affecting their functionalities (*Source* Author)	42
Fig. 2.2	Exploring market and building enterprise (*Source* Author)	51
Fig. 3.1	Outgrowth of entrepreneurship from the family pedigree (*Source* Author)	73
Fig. 3.2	Human element in entrepreneurship (*Source* Author)	84
Fig. 4.1	Reverse entrepreneurship and business perspectives (*Source* Author)	100
Fig. 5.1	Crowd power and its contributions to business (*Source* Author)	125
Fig. 7.1	Synchronizing entrepreneurship with business and societal ecosystems (*Source* Author)	196

PART I

Dissecting the Core

CHAPTER 1

Entrepreneurial Transitions

Entrepreneurship has evolved from most family firms with homogeneous stereotypical attributes such as leadership control, resistance to change, stagnant approaches, and myopic growth-ideology. However, the existing literature often focuses on the dichotomy between family firm and nonfamily firm from economic and managerial perspectives, which affected P3 factors of entrepreneurship comprising productivity, profit, and performance.[1] This chapter discusses the attributes of conventional entrepreneurial philosophy and practices, and the strategies required for reshaping the future of micro and small enterprises. The thematic discussion on the state of the art in micro and small enterprises is central to the chapter. The discussions also envelop the effects of contemporary transitions in the entrepreneurial practices in the context of entrepreneurial leap, technology, and hybridity affecting the scaling of enterprises with

---

[1] Uhlaner, L. M., Kellermanns, F. W., Eddleston, K. A., & Hoy, F. (2012). The entrepreneuring family: A new paradigm for family business research. *Small Business Economics*, 38 (1), 1–11.

© The Author(s), under exclusive license to Springer Nature Switzerland AG 2024
Rebuilding Entrepreneurship at the Grassroots, Palgrave Studies of Entrepreneurship and Social Challenges in Developing Economies, https://doi.org/10.1007/978-3-031-43270-5_1

technology-supported research and development. This chapter argues that the potential opportunities have become the principal driver for the pursuit of entrepreneurial ventures that are changing rapidly.[2]

Traditional Entrepreneurship

Conventionally, entrepreneurship is carried out in family-oriented businesses as a legacy. The product-mix, technology, employee engagement, and marketing patterns emerge out of the entrepreneurial pedigree in family businesses. Such enterprises barely change their path of entrepreneurship and adapt to the changing market needs and reinvent business models to derive benefits at the competitive edge. Thus, cocreation of new products may work on interrelated actions. This shows that the relations among the players are not predefined but constructed during the process. A result derived by an actor performing a development task may result in the necessity that another actor needs to make an interactive loop.[3] A product development manager should closely observe the activities of various teams during their regular meetings by taking notes about the most important issues concerning communication about the design content. During the regular face-to-face meetings with the separate actors, which are now mostly about planning and monitoring issues and design problems or changes, the project leader could use the notes as the input for discussing the collaborative aspects with the actors. This form of storytelling will provide the project leader with knowledge about the collaborative aspects of the design process. A project leader should also learn to distill the barriers and enablers from these conversations.[4]

Entrepreneurship in developing economies conventionally grows as a family legacy. Family businesses have several distinctive traits such as traditional designs in manufacturing, low-technology services, confined business operations, focus on tactical approaches of marketing than

---

[2] Foss, N. J., & Klein, P. G. (2017). Entrepreneurial discovery or creation? In search of the middle ground. *Academy of Management Review*, 42 (4), 733–736.

[3] Weick, K. E., & Roberts, K. H. (1993). Collective mind in organizations: Heedful interrelating on flight decks. *Administrative Science Quarterly*, 38 (4), 357–381.

[4] Maaike, K., Buijs, J., & Valkenburg, R. (2010). Understanding the complexity of knowledge integration in collaborative new product development teams: A case study. *Journal of Engineering and Technology Management*, 27 (1–2), 20–32.

strategic vision, low resources, and low investment in innovation and technology. These attributes of family business prevent external collaborations and focus on research and development. Leadership in these enterprises grows within the family with resistance to inducting external leaders and adapting to change management practices. Often, succession of leadership within the family business often creates conflicts which affect significantly the business operations of the firm. The size of the family, number of children, and claims on the successions jeopardize the growth of the company. Many children of family business owners and stakeholders, being close relatives of owners, tend to launch their careers inside the company thinking they could be encouraged to build a substantial career outside the firm and boomerang as change agents. Conventional entrepreneurial firms need to plan ahead to explore potential roles they can serve beyond just taking over the firm as family leaders or chief executives.[5]

Though the term *family business* quickly relates to the local mom-and-pop firms, which have grown largely as a family-controlled companies that contributes enormously on the global stage. Not only do these firms refer to the extensive business giants like Walmart in the USA and Tata Group in India, but they also account for over one-third of all companies with sales in excess of one billion US Dollars. However, strategically the financial performance of these firms exceeds to that of several traditional public companies. Family-controlled companies supersede their peers because they stay resilient on strategic transitions over the short-term results. During economic booms, this approach led these firms to oversee the next generation opportunities but it puts them back to a strong enough during business recessions, when they tend to shine. Among various attributes, family-run enterprises demonstrate the following business traits:

- Frugal strategically but may not tactically to gain quick benefits
- Set high control on capital expenditures
- Avoid carrying debt
- Selective in mergers and acquisitions
- Operate in diversified sectors, so often fail to achieve economies of scale

---

[5] Bruehl, S., & Lachenauer, R. (2018). *How family business owners should bring the next generation into the company*. Harvard Business Review Digital Article, June 24, Cambridge, MA: Harvard Business School Press.

- Grow faster in niche markets as compared to competitive marketplaces
- Work with loyal employees with long trajectory of T-5 attributes comprising task performance, timeliness, target-oriented, thrust absorbers, and trustworthy

Though these practices come more naturally to executives who feel an obligation to be stewards for the next generation, executives at any corporation can adopt them. The researchers have uncovered several nonfamily-controlled companies that mimicked the behaviors of family firms and saw very similar patterns of performance.[6]

Technology-led innovations and business models can be successful provided they are user oriented. The agile use of technology, however, can erode customer care. Firms must listen empathetically to the requirements of consumers to cater the technology to them, managers, and front-line employees. However, impulsive innovations targeted primarily at lowering costs and increasing use values have made many companies impervious to their customers. Such a situation drives estrangement of employees from customers, and firms face difficulty in diffusing, launching, and serving the technology to the consumer segments. Several innovation-driven firms have shown intricate relations between businesses and the consumers they serve. These firms enrich consumers by upholding their commitment, empathetic involvement with consumers, understanding the ways in which current technology is valued by consumers, and co-promoting technology-led products through social networks and informal ways to help consumers in developing sustainable storyboards, and inculcate trust on the firm and technology service providers.[7]

Innovation and its commercialization are the top priorities for every emerging enterprise, and to achieve success through frugal and radical innovations, firms must put as much energy and investment into marketing new offerings as they do in generating them. Commercializing the innovation and marketing the innovative products and services are central to strategic decisions and sustainable approaches rather than merely tactical functions of acquiring and retaining customers, as many

---

[6] Kachaner, N., Stalk, G., & Bloch, A. (2012). What you can learn from family business. *Harvard Business Review*, 90 (11), 103–106.

[7] Gorry, G. A., & Westbrook, R. A. (2011), Once more, with feeling: Empathy and technology in customer care. *Business Horizons*, 54 (2), 125–134.

firms tend to practice today. The full, business-growing power of the marketing strategies for both frugal and radical (disruptive) innovations are penetrated ambidextrously in the upstream and downstream markets through social media and collective intelligence. Nonetheless, the major focus in commercializing the innovation is to co-create and coevolve markets by engaging customers and stakeholders. Such a marketing strategy would help firms in developing value-based stakeholder-led decisions to gain benefits over the competitors. Understanding the PNS factors and consumption drivers, identifying customers, and working with the go-to-market approach offer several competitive benefits to the firms to market innovative products irrespective of their scale of business. It is also important to explore and analyze the consumption ecosystem congruent to the innovations, especially those that support the breakthroughs. Marketers, therefore, need to be included in development discussions earlier in the innovation process and must be engaged in implementing the tasks of project charter.[8]

The frugal innovation with a focus on PNS factors and economies of scale has significantly contributed to the social and economic development within the niche. Consequently, disruptive innovation has increasingly become a core attraction to the large firms to collaborate, converge, and commercialize (C3 factors) not only to motivate business alliances but also to build the business strategy cube. The business strategy cube has triadic business strategies comprising design-to-market, design-to-society, and design-to-value perspectives. Such micro–macro business alliances within various social development sectors including health, housing, energy, transportation, machinery, and robotics have bridged economics to engineering and technology. This change is occurring as most firms in the world are facing contemporary challenges such as intense global competition, rising market volatility, constantly changing consumer demand, and shortened product lifecycles. Such socioeconomic and business conditions have driven disruptive innovation and disruptive innovation-based entrepreneurship to resolve social challenges, which are increasingly becoming a strategic means for achieving sustainable

---

[8] Yohn, D. L. (2019). *Why great innovations need great marketing*. Harvard Business Review Digital Article. Cambridge: Harvard Business School Press.

company growth and competitiveness.[9] The concept of disruptive technology can be either radical, frugal, or superior to the existing technology. A challenge-based research design is generated through a process of social, economic, and political negotiation and value-based stakeholder focus. Accordingly, low-cost technologies with high-perceived use value and ease of use perception influence the social and economic needs, survive, and prosper. However, penetration of social innovation and technology is slow, which causes delay in adoption and jeopardizes their success.[10] There is a wide gap between conventional and contemporary entrepreneurship. Advancement of technology and the rapid pace of market-centric innovations have transformed the entrepreneurial practices today, which appear to be at a far reach of conventional enterprises operating at the grassroots. Strategic and operational differences between these types of enterprises are illustrated in Fig. 1.1.

The conventional enterprises emerge commonly as an outgrowth of family businesses, which face challenges of low resources and resistance to change management due to risk-averse behavior in investing in innovation and technology projects. Figure 1.1 illustrates 14 attributes of each conventional and contemporary entrepreneurship practice. Limited financial and human capital entwined with the inadequate infrastructure often develops high resistance among these enterprises, besides low awareness of the benefits of transforming to an improved operations culture. Most family-business oriented enterprises operate in a niche market, which creates low optimism for growth and adapting to changing innovation and technology environment. Due to organizational and cultural barriers, continuous learning and the zeal to explore new initiatives are largely absent among these firms. Consequently, the cost, time, and risk factors in addition to the lifecycle risk of innovative products often discourage local firms from adapting to innovation, technology, and systems thinking perspectives. Among many, one of the principal reasons that restrict the conventional entrepreneurial firms to transform is due

---

[9] Si, S., Zahra, S. A., Wu, X., Jeng, D. J. F. (2020). Disruptive innovation and entrepreneurship in emerging economics. *Journal of Engineering and Technology Management*, 58 (in Press). https://doi.org/10.1016/j.jengtecman.2020.101601.

[10] Si, S., & Chen, H. (2020). A literature review of disruptive innovation: What it is, how it works and where it goes. *Journal of Engineering and Technology Management*, 56 (in Press). https://doi.org/10.1016/j.jengtecman.2020.101568.

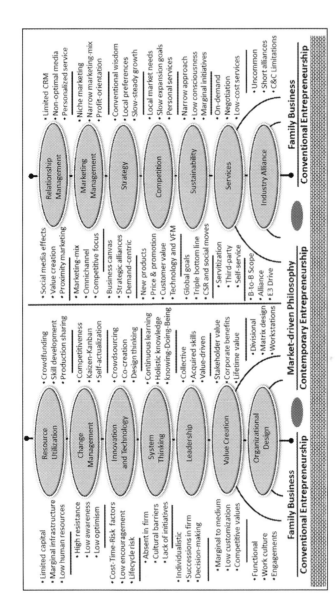

Fig. 1.1 A comparative framework of conventional and contemporary entrepreneurship (*Source* Author)

to individualistic leadership, successions within the family, and centralized decision-making process. Therefore, these enterprises operate at functional level with traditional work culture and low stakeholder engagements. Such entrepreneurial practices in family business firms drive low customizations and competitive values among the internal (employees) and external (consumers and key partners) stakeholders. Conventional enterprises are relatively weak in managing relationship with the internal and external stakeholders by delivering values consistently as compared to the contemporary technology-driven start-ups which make optimal use of social media. Because of low involvement in social media, the conventional enterprises experience low customer outreach and proximity to the changing market dynamics. Low-proximity market and customers confine these firms into a niche, where firms focus on optimizing profit through limited marketing-mix strategies based on conventional wisdom, local preferences, and slow growth drivers. Firms in niche markets are commonly protected from the wider competitive tactics as they cater to local needs with a low threat of market expansion due to marginal initiatives. Sustainability in business is not an active business goal for these firms, as the firms focus on conventional and low-cost creativities. Industry alliance is almost absent in conventional family-owned firms which operate in a niche market.

Contemporary entrepreneurial firms invest in acquiring skills in resource management and tend to exploit resources using both conventional and digital channels. These firms tend to enhance their resource base (financial, human resources, and intellectual capital) through crowdfunding and crowdsourcing. Small and medium entrepreneurial firms also use production-sharing approach to involve neighborhood artisans or contract manufacturers available locally to support cost-effective production strategy. These firms focus on designing and implementing market competitive strategies and encourage employee engagement through Kaizen and Kanban approaches. Both internal and external stakeholders of the firm are encouraged in continuous learning on market trends and dynamics to effectively contribute to design thinking, co-creation, strategy development, and business operations. Continuous learning and holistic knowledge of innovation, technology, management skills, and value-creation help both the internal and external stakeholders of the firm to achieve the state of *knowing, doing, and being* in the firm. Contemporary micro-, small-, and medium-size enterprises largely follow collective leadership with a value-driven approach to enhance stakeholders' perceived value, lifetime value, and derived corporate benefits. To implement business strategy meticulously, these companies refine their organizational design by implementing digital workstations, functional divisions, and product-service-territories matrix to conduct business operations with precision and cost-effectively. As exhibited in Fig. 1.1, a well-developed organizational design helps in value-creation through marketing-mix, business canvas, strategic alliances, and demand-centric competitive focus. Nonetheless, the intensive involvement of contemporary entrepreneurial firms on social media has enhanced the outreach of these firms to stakeholders. In addition, the proximity marketing strategies of these firms significantly motivate the customer value and help them gain a competitive advantage through the development of price-sensitive new products and generating the value for money perception among the customers. Some firms with a focus on sustainability goals adapt to the concept of triple bottom-line integrating people, planet, and profit strategies. There is a growing trend of micro, small, and medium firms to develop business linkage with large firms within the industry adapting to E-3 drive comprising engagement, enhancement, and engineering business strategies.

Breakthrough innovation in markets is a continuous process backed by the distribution, retailing, and services industry. Innovations leading to commercial breakthroughs demonstrate a highly skewed distribution of the use value of inventions explaining that some are useless, a few are of moderate value, and there is rarely one that qualifies as a breakthrough. Those breakthroughs embed the long tail of innovation, and distribution plays a key role in the breakthrough process. It is necessary for the firms to account for the total number of inventions a company generates and the average score of the inventions and track the number of successful breakthrough inventions. Such corporate awareness may help in developing a strategic balance between individual innovation workers and teams. Greater team diversity stimulates firms to build higher involvement in working with breakthrough innovations. Thus, it is first and foremost requirement for the companies to introspect within the organization and identify how they want to improve their innovation process; take appropriate measures to drive the innovative products and services as breakthrough, and contrary to that, address any deficiencies in the process. Such dynamism in innovation process would allow the companies to improve their competencies and capabilities to innovate in ways that make the best sense for the organization and market.[11] Innovation and enterprise integration are two compelling sources of growth in a dynamic competitive marketplace. The ability to coordinate across organizational boundaries largely appears as a critical factor in determining the speed and lifecycle of a market-driven innovation. Innovations need to be integrated into the larger operations of the corporation at a sufficient scale to show a prolific impact on business and sustainability in the marketplace. Many large businesses spend huge resources on innovations but fail to capitalize on them. There is a variety of innovations driven by firms in the global marketplace. Innovations are not limited to consumer-centric or market-oriented products and services. Categorically, most of the large firms possess trajectories of innovation and technological change in reference to the consumer requirements. While the market today is very unpredictable, small firms are thrusting more resources to increase innovation to compete with the large industries and commercial brands.[12]

Firms in many industries have immense pressure to improve their ability to innovate consumer-centric products and services. However, managers know that the best ideas don't always come out of their own research and development laboratory. Hence, a growing number of companies are exploring the idea of open-market innovation, an approach that uses tools such as licensing, joint ventures, and strategic alliances to bring the benefits of free trade to the flow of new ideas.[13] Disruptive innovation is linked to reverse innovation that drives the firms back to the consumers' buying behavior in reference to 4As paradigm comprising awareness, acceptability, adaptability, and affordability. Reverse innovation refers to developing ideas in an emerging market and persuading them in the existing markets, which drives tough challenges. Such innovation requires a company to overcome the institutionalized thinking that guides its actions and acquires ideas through social media. Firms following reverse innovation develop a radically simpler and cheaper way of creating

---

[11] Farzaneh, M., Wilden, R., Afshari, L., & Mehralian, G. (2022). Dynamic capabilities and innovation ambidexterity: The roles of intellectual capital and innovation orientation. *Journal of Business Research*, 148, 47–59.

[12] Rajagopal. (2014). Architecting enterprise: Managing innovation, technology, and global competitiveness. Basingstoke, UK: Palgrave Macmillan.

[13] Rigby, D. K., & Zook, C. (2001). Open-market innovation, *Harvard Business Review*, 80 (10), 80–89.

products in emerging markets and then position them in the desired consumer segments.[14,15]

THE DRIVING HEAD

In the growing competitive markets today, micro, small, and medium enterprises are developing strategies to move into the provision of innovative combinations of products and services as 'high-value integrated solutions' tailored to each customer's needs than simply 'moving downstream' into services. Such enterprises are developing innovative combinations of service capabilities such as operations, business consultancy, and finance required to provide complete solutions to each customer's needs in order to augment the customer value.[16] Market-driven behavior for innovations is different from a firm's market orientation, which emphasizes the competitive dynamics among firms conducting identical business such as automobile sales. It is argued that the firm's market orientation on innovation-led products interacts with other strategic orientations, in the process determining how they are manifested and implemented. Furthermore, market orientation plays a critical role in determining transitions among various strategic orientations over time among the firms engaged in identical business products and services. A strong market-oriented strategy of the firm alleviates the possibility of using coercive influence strategies by the competitors and offers an advantage to the customers over competitive market force.[17] Integrating a global strategy involves the following key approaches:

- Selecting markets of global strategic importance

---

[14] Nooyi, I. K., & Govindarajan, V. (2020). *Becoming a better corporate citizen.* HBR Web Article, Harvard Business School Press, March–April Issue. https://hbr.org/2020/03/becoming-a-better-corporate-citizen.

[15] Rajagopal. (2016). *Innovative business projects: Breaking complexities, building performance (Vol.2)-Financials, new insights, and project sustainability.* New York: Business Expert Press.

[16] Rajagopal. (2007). *International marketing: Global environment, corporate strategy, and case studies.* New Delhi: Vikas Publishing House.

[17] Chung, J., Jin, B., & Sternquist, B. (2007). The role of market orientation in channel relationships when channel power is imbalanced. *International Review of Retail, Distribution and Consumer Research,* 17 (2), 159–176.

- Standardizing products
- Locating value-adding activities in a global network
- Using uniform marketing techniques
- Integrating competitive moves across countries

Business expansion is a stage when firms explore additional means to generate profit above the normal and continue to strive in the competition within the industry. Expansion in business drives the business growth, which is simply a function of a business life cycle. Entrepreneurs face challenges as growth trends of an industry and entrepreneurs' desires are often not congruent to create equity in values. However, a growing business can expand in diverse ways that have the strongest influence on global trade. The application of global strategy in industries with high globalization potential improves business performance. Local enterprises constantly search for opportunities to achieve the benefits of business expansion and globalization by taking a zero-based productivity view. Zero-based productivity is a comprehensive approach that extends zero-based-budgeting principles in determining the operations cost and spending in the entrepreneurial process. Adapting to the zero-based principles can catalyze MSMEs toward transformative idea generation as to how an enterprise be organized. In addition, the zero-based philosophy helps these enterprises to create a culture of innovative solutions that move beyond conventional work. Such an approach drives the enterprise to be a more agile and responsive organization that is better positioned to pursue new opportunities. With the increasing adaptation to the technology, MSMEs are flouting conventional wisdom and established technology-driven practices that are able to systematically analyze the business ecosystem, develop market-oriented strategy, and redesign organizational linkages within the industry. Local enterprises are acquiring competencies on forward business strategies, which assume that entrepreneurial strategies should be global but implemented locally.[18]

The Marketing 4.0 generation focuses on IoT, digitization in business, and e-commerce as the principal tools for industrial marketing. The success of e-commerce in business-to-business segment has given

---

[18] Yip, G. S., & Johansson, J. K. (1994). *Global marketing strategies of US and Japanese Business*, Report 93–102. Boston: MA, Marketing Science Institute.

an up-thrust in industrial marketing by offering convenience and cost-effective transactions. The virtual business platforms are supported largely by lean process management practices toward the client decision-making, ordering, order processing, delivery of products, and post-sales services. Accordingly, the terms of reference in business-to-business marketing have also become easier and more favorable to clients. Deploying e-commerce resources in industrial marketing provides distinct and specialized consumption capabilities for the clients. Industrial marketing is critical to buyer–seller relations to sustain the market uncertainties in the competitive marketplace. The importance of e-commerce resources and marketing capabilities illustrate how distribution and promotion efficiencies can mediate capability-performance matrix in industrial firms (Leonidou and Hultman, 2019).

Firms face challenges in positioning new products in the target market segments and follow market-driven approach to product development as they thrive on continuous innovation. Another pertinent challenge the companies face is avoiding the innovator's dilemma of bringing successful technology or protecting the new products against disruptive technology. Firms engaged in product innovations and improvements should develop a set of design and technical features, strategies for consumers' purchase benefits, and alliances with potential brands to sustain market competition and ensure high market share. However, as the consumer value and market share of firms are largely interrelated and generic in nature, the technology-driven innovations provide scope for new products in the market, which guarantees uploading of value for money over time. By focusing their efforts on generic as well as hybrid technologies, firms can be unconventionally innovative and remain sensitive to customer needs and simultaneously focus on market-driven strategies to lead the market competition. Firms that seek to develop successful and sustainable strategies for innovation must identify generic technologies with unique product designs and competitive marketing strategies.[19]

Integrating an entrepreneurial strategy involves five key dimensions comprising business modeling for local markets, standardizing products for cost advantage, implementing value-added activities in a competitive marketplace, using frugal innovation and low-cost technology, and developing strategic alliances with large companies. The application of global

---

[19] Glazer, R. (2007). Meta-technologies and innovation leadership: Why there may be nothing new under the sun. *California Management Review*, 50 (1), 120–143.

strategy in industries with high globalization potential improves business performance. Micro, small, and medium enterprises are constantly exploring opportunities to achieve benefits of the changing customer preference and shift in market demand, take a zero-based view of existing activities, flout conventional wisdom and established practices, systematically analyze industry, strategy, and organizational linkages, and make multiple reinforcing changes in strategy, entrepreneurial system, and organization. They assume that the strategy should be global but implemented locally.[20] The changing business ecosystem and global perspectives on entrepreneurial success have brought into focus new drivers to guide the entrepreneurship and business process ahead. Figure 1.2 exhibits the transformational drivers of entrepreneurial growth.

The future perspectives (P) of entrepreneurial growth have been discussed in the context of the six-branched growth strategy in Fig. 1.2. They are categorically illustrated under organizational and functional philosophy of the firms. Industry 4.0 (P_1) evolution has significantly motivated micro, small, and medium enterprises (MSMEs) to explore the possibilities of market expansion through developing strategic alliances with the technology firms on automation and creation of self-service platforms. Such technology integration will help MSMEs to grow faster and develop congruence with contemporary market trends to achieve competitiveness and proximity. Future growth of these firms also encourages them on zero-based management (P_2) in budgeting, planning, productivity, and net-zero strategies. Zero-based management encourages incremental growth in both large and small firms. A zero-based approach helps firms establish organizational visibility and consistency, benchmarking, refining organizational design, and linking business alliances to strategic priorities by exploring internal capabilities and competencies. Zero-based organization significantly contributes to the incremental improvements in existing operations and enhances the scope to create a fit-for-competition business design. Moving with better operations design, MSMEs can follow transparency in the strategy development process by understanding overall budgets, compare them with other firms in the industry, and highlight opportunities to apply approaches such as shared services, process redesign, and automation to reduce costs.

---

[20] Yip, G. S., & Johansson, J. K. (1994). *Global marketing strategies of US and Japanese Business*. Report 93–102. Boston: MA, Marketing Science Institute.

1 ENTREPRENEURIAL TRANSITIONS 17

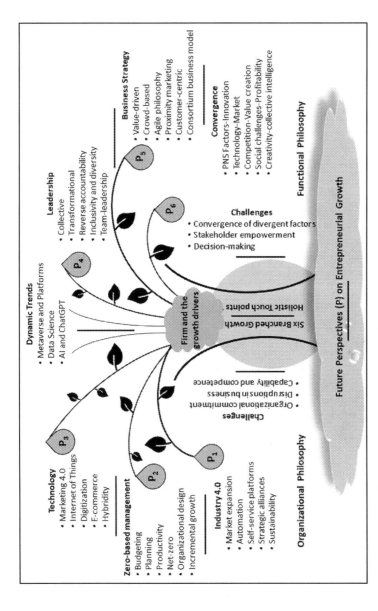

Fig. 1.2 Future growth of entrepreneurship (*Source* Author)

Figure 1.2 illustrates the scope of technology (P_3) adoption in marketing such as Radio Frequency Identification (RFID), artificial intelligence (Metaverse and ChatGPT), and Internet of Things to gain competitive advantage in the changing market dynamics. Adapting to hybrid business is a strong option for MSMEs to transform to fit into the rapidly changing business and market dynamics to conduct business on ambidextrous platform with an Internet-front-end (E-commerce) as well as its bricks and mortar premises (physical stress). However, to drive organizational change, transformational leadership (P_4) at the grassroots of the organization needs to be changed, which can be assimilated through collective voices (leadership drive), reverse accountability (stakeholder engagement), and team leadership. Collective leadership in teams is an innate behavior, which is provides team leaders with a roadmap to diagnose and solve business problems. It is a systematic approach that helps team leaders identify the cause of team issues and take corrective action to improve team performance. The changing conventional leadership style to transformative approach leverages entrepreneurs to explore technology alliances with large companies within the industry to enhance their performance. The reforms of public administration and democratic approach to social enterprises have led to decentralization of power and redistribution of responsibilities to the lowest possible level of administrators. Therefore, social governance has become closer to the citizens and stakeholders to make appropriate decisions locally.[21]

Inclusivity and diversity in business is also a growing trend, which is important to follow for the MSMEs to stay competitive in the industry and market. Entrepreneurial performance can be optimized by encouraging inclusivity and diversity to gain competitive advantages in the long run. The change-driven future perspectives (P_5) in business can be focused on creating stakeholder values to develop agile and crowd-based business strategies, which can help firms in enhancing their social proximity and outreach to customers and external stakeholders. Firms adapting to the consortium business model also help them grow horizontally. In consortium business modeling, firms develop complementary skills and expertise and develop collaboration to share resources, knowledge, and risks in pursuit of a specific objective. Consortiums are often

---

[21] Benites-Lazaro, L. L., & Mello-Théry, N. A. (2019). Empowering communities? Local stakeholders' participation in the clean development mechanism in Latin America. *World Development*, 114, 254–266.

formed to increase production, expand markets, develop technology, and improve skills to achieve competitive advantage. In managing the future growth perspectives, firms should develop effective convergence (P_6) between various business factors as stated below:

- *PNS Factors-Innovation*: Firms must explore the problems, needs, and expected solutions of stakeholders to invest in innovations to develop new products or manage vertical improvements.
- *Technology-Market*: Both technology and market trends are dynamic and competitive in nature. Firms need to evaluate the lifecycle of technology and the CTR (cost, time, and risk) factors to invest in acquiring new technology to improve the business performance of the firm.
- *Competition-Value Creation*: Brand value-creation among stakeholders is one of the many competitive challenges among the MSMEs. Customer values are associated with both economic and social perspectives. Economic value is measured by the perceived value, willingness to pay, and value for money associated with the products or services. Firms must also invest in building corporate image through both social and market penetration of brands.
- *Social challenges-Profitability*: Some firms at the grassroots level address the social challenges such as sustainability in agriculture, construction, consumer products, transportation, and energy, which helps in building the corporate image. These hybrid value chains blending digital and interpersonal actions to resolve social challenges are engaging firms in exploring new ways to serve consumers by redefining socio-psychological values. Gujarat Cooperative Milk Marketing Federation in India, which is the owner of AMUL brand of dairy products and chocolates, works with dairy farmers and coffee growers, which has changed both its supply chain and its relationship with customers. In both cases, citizen-sector organizations and social entrepreneurs have a critical role to play.
- *Creativity-collective intelligence*: Creativity, open innovation, and collective intelligence are symbiotic with each other. Collective intelligence (CI) is the shared knowledge emerging from the collaboration, collective efforts, and competition of many individuals, and it appears in consensus decision-making. CI is derived from an open public platform (digital or interpersonal), which encompasses

sociopsychological, political science, creativity and innovation, and crowdsourcing applications.

Entrepreneurship with active business modeling helps to meet several social challenges in agricultural and agribusiness-, public health-, housing-, sustainability-, public education-, and non-farm income-generating activities. There are many prominent attributes of social challenges and entrepreneurship, which serve as drivers in improving social and economic growth. Besides public health, education, and housing for all challenges at the bottom of the pyramid socio-demographic segment, poverty alleviation requires an integrated entrepreneurial approach within the social and economic ecosystem. The social challenges are dynamic and changing continuously over time from rural to urban needs and across the markets. The broad underlying challenges in entrepreneurship include sustainability, manufacturing, and proximity marketing by enhancing the customer outreach. Broadly, the sustainability in enterprises is associated with the renewable energy, organic cultivation, and management of conscious practices among the farming communities. Management of natural resources and their conservation has been one of the major challenges besides the public health education and housing. Such transition and social challenges often change the priorities of entrepreneurship, which affects entrepreneurship and business across the geo-demographic consumer segments and markets.

Transforming social challenges must be understood from the perspectives of PNS factors comprising embedded problems, needs, and solutions within the society in the context of cost–benefit-profit and cost-time risk factors associated with innovation and technology. To meet the social challenges at the grassroots, entrepreneurs adapt to frugal innovations while large companies tend to explore opportunities to commercialize innovations that have been developed and experimented successfully at the bottom of the pyramid entrepreneurial segment. The reverse innovation process can be explained as connecting global markets with innovation at the niche level. The low-cost technology is preferred by the entrepreneurs at the niche level to develop high-value utilitarian products and attract large industries to explore opportunities to commercialize the innovation lying at the bottom of the pyramid. Consequently, large companies are engaged in the transfer of technology to small enterprises and developing entrepreneurial consortiums by industry and by region to improve the quality and performance of the product. Such streamlining of entrepreneurial products between upstream and downstream markets facilitates quick movement of products and services at a macro level. However, micro and small enterprises are critical at adapting to low-cost technology and long technology lifecycle in manufacturing products.

Client relations play a significant role in acquiring new clients and retaining them. Industrial marketing companies extend care for customers through client-specific key-accounts managers. Technology-led business-to-business marketing companies affirm their commitment of active and empathetic involvement with customers to understand the ways in which business interactions can be co-created. The deployment of social networks and digital client-services technologies helps clients and stakeholders in experience sharing and constructing a common workplace.[22] Technology-oriented companies create the digital drive for ensuring effective client management. Strategies that support such drive range from building niche business strategies for entrepreneurs to market competitive strategies to converge ideas, strategies, policies, and customer voices. Workspaces are evolving rapidly along with technology applications, which can introduce a seamless work culture moving from conventional styles to collaborative working patterns. Empowering clients to co-design processes and co-create new service models is a high-impact approach for industrial marketing firms that motivates clients to customize their products and services with suppliers. The workstations integrating entrepreneurs, suppliers, vendors, service providers, and clients are constructed as 'containers' that embrace new ways of collaboration. Such entrepreneur-marketer setups not only redefine the expectations of a workplace but also empower the customer and help them reinforce confidence in suppliers.

Marketing technologists play a critical role in navigating the ecosystem to create effective solutions that deliver high-use value to the clients. They effectively serve as a bridge between the industrial clients and the marketing companies. The success of innovative products and services often requires cooperation between market players, organizations, and stakeholders in marketing through conventional and digital platforms. Thus, the networking aspect of commercialization is crucial for any innovation, especially in the mass and bottom of the pyramid market segments. Broadly, customers and users, distributors, investors, associations, public

---

[22] Gorry, G. A., & Westbrook, R. A. (2011). Once more, with feeling: Empathy and technology in customer care. *Business Horizons*, 54 (2), 125–134.

organizations, and policymakers and regulators can support commercialization by facilitating innovation, adoption, and diffusion process within the existing market, or help in creating new markets.[23] Such strategic thinking helps firms in carrying out innovations and business projects beyond commoditization, and fend off disruptive competitive threats to pave the path to enter new markets successfully. Innovative business projects lead to transformational growth by engaging with customers and market players. Firms develop innovation projects with unique concepts to attain higher profit, brand image, and customer value to customers.

Marketing new technology-based products to consumers is associated with the emotions and social consciousness, which are shared through digital networks. People are increasingly purchasing tangible products like food, medicines, apparel, and technology-based virtual products like movies and video games online. Conventionally, the sensory interaction has mostly been limited to visual inputs, and less to auditory inputs. However, other sensory interfaces (*e.g.*, including touch screens, together with a range of virtual, and augmented solutions) are increasingly being made available to people to interact online. This expansion coincides with an increasing engagement with the consumer's more emotional senses like touch or haptics, and possibly even olfaction. Therefore, forward-thinking marketers and researchers need to appropriate the latest tools and technologies in order to deliver richer virtual experiences for the next generation consumers.[24] Social media interactions and user-generated contents influence consumer emotions for adapting to new technology-led products and create perceived use value. Positive emotions among consumers create a pull effect and develop attitudes toward experimentation and evaluation of new products.

---

[23] Aarikka-Stenroos, L., Sandberg, B., & Lehtimäki, T. (2014). Networks for the commercialization of innovations: A review of how divergent network actors contribute. *Industrial Marketing Management*, 43 (3), 365–381.

[24] Petit, O., Velasco, C., & Spence, C. (2019). Digital sensory marketing: Integrating new technologies in to multisensory online experience. *Journal of Interactive Marketing*, 45 (1), 42–61.

Capabilities and Competencies

Firms tend to acquire skills from both internal (capabilities) and external (creativity and practices) sources by exploring the supporting technology and managerial competencies in the industry and market. Competencies in an organization build key competitive advantages to make it stronger internally and competitive externally. The organizational competencies must be continuously explored in relevance to the changing marketing dynamics and match with the strategic intent of the firm. The required competencies in MSMEs in manufacturing, marketing, innovation, technology, resource planning, and services can be mapped and prioritized. Delving more deeply, competencies in the operations management category include communication skills, team-based decision-making and tasks management. However, to match with the leadership and business administration practices, firms must motivate employees to develop listening, reasoning, and performance skills through community knowledge, regulatory knowledge, and leadership savvy. The strategic perspective on acquiring capabilities and competencies in a firm focuses on systematic planning at an organizational level and delivers the skill development process as the convergence of needs, resources, and capabilities. Firms should respect personal competencies as contributions to a team culture and refine them by delivering advanced knowledge, skills, abilities, and experience, and rebuild the personality of employees. Capabilities and competencies in a firm are a blend of corporate and individual efforts. The synergy and synchronization of individual competencies build the corporate competencies, and the assimilation of personal competencies can form a way of work culture and inculcate a feeling of *knowing, doing, and being* among peers. In addition, corporate attributes determine the type of personal competencies that will motivate employees to consider the best work fit in the organization.[25]

Employee competencies are one of the critical success factors of the firm and determine the overall performance of the firm. These characteristics manifest organizational behavioral patterns, which contributes a positive difference in the performance and competitiveness of the firm. The knowledge, skills, and abilities (KSA) critically examine employee profiles in a firm to match the T-5 perspective of business projects comprising

---

[25] Cardy, R. L., & Selvarajan, T. T. (2006). Competencies: Alternative frameworks for competitive advantage. *Business Horizons*, 49 (3), 235–245.

team, tasks, target, thrust, and time factors that contribute to its success. The KSA model helps firms to assign qualified people to specific tasks. These underlying characteristics have been referred to as below-the-waterline characteristics, which are iceberg (hidden) attributes of an organization comprising beliefs, assumptions, perceptions, attitudes, feelings, and real-time values on specific business scenarios.[26] It has been observed that firms are unable to successfully implement well-conceptualized and well-stated strategies without the needed competencies. Competencies of employees and key partners (suppliers, service providers, and relationship managers) put the concept of strategic intent in order to be operationalized. VRINE factors comprising value (organizational and stakeholders), rarity (uniqueness), inimitability (high switching costs and difficult to fit in all sizes of firms), non-substitutability (difficult to be overridden by other strategies), and exploitability (optimization of yield or returns) strengthen the core strategies and business model of MSMEs and large firms. From a strategic perspective, competencies can be identified as functions, processes, and routines in an organization. However, from the human resources perspective, competencies can be viewed as the capabilities of people.[27]

The observable behavior of employees includes competencies across personality traits, values, motives, and the like, which determine the organizational culture over time. The behavioral pattern is related broadly to the organizational performance, while competencies largely refer to KSAs. However, firms face the challenge to transform the conventional KSA to a contemporary pattern. Digital transformation has been a recent leap of firms of all sizes, which has significantly driven a paradigm shift among the firms to enable competitive advantage. While the effects of digital transformation and their analytics, along with platform technologies, are yet to exhibit performance results for the firms at the grassroots, there is still a need to examine their implications as a business continuum. In such a paradigm shift, small firms need to drive balance across capability,

---

[26] Hofrichter, D. A., & Spencer, L. M. (1996). Competencies: The right foundation for effective human resource management. *Compensation and Benefits Review*, 28 (6), 21–24.

[27] Cardy, R. L., & Selvarajan, T. T. (2006). Competencies: Alternative frameworks for competitive advantage. *Business Horizons*, 49 (3), 235–245.

competency, and decision-making to support innovation and competitiveness.[28] General Electric Company (GE) started manufacturing low-cost countries through local joint ventures and outsourcing to some extent. However, as the products of the firm moved to the growth stage of lifecycle, both local and overseas competitors emerged in developing markets. Consequently, the behavior of factors of production has changed and significantly affected the comparative advantages in production and marketing. In this scenario, the core competency of the firm is critical to the competitive downslide in the market when speed to market had been the prime concern, adapting the local manufacturing at low cost appeared to be a questionable decision. However, GE built in-house innovation capability, lean manufacturing, and a new approach to triadic labor-production-cost relations with local collaborations to revert the low performance caused by competitive aggression.[29]

Technological upgrading, in the form of introduction of new machinery and improvement of technological capabilities, provides a firm with the means to be successful in competition. In the process of introducing better technologies, new lower-cost methods become available, which allow the firms to increase labor productivity, i.e., the efficiency with which it converts resources into value. Firms adopt these newer methods of production if they are more profitable than the older ones. The ability of a firm to take advantage of technical progress is also enhanced if the firm improves its entrepreneurial and technological capabilities through two competitive strategies: learning and adaptation, and innovation. The latter is a process of searching for, finding, developing, imitating, adapting, and adopting new products, new processes, and new organizational arrangements. For many companies, developing innovative products does not occur as a chance or coincidence, but through careful attention to many important criteria. Firms should analyze their innovation practices and capabilities to become more effective in driving innovation as a breakthrough and to gain a competitive advantage.

---

[28] Jackson, N. C. (2019). Managing for competency with innovation change in higher education: Examining the pitfalls and pivots of digital transformation. *Business Horizons*, 62 (6), 762–772.

[29] Immelt, J. R. (2012). The CEO of General Electric on sparking an American Manufacturing Renewal. *Harvard Business Review*, 90 (3), 43–46.

Besides the conventional hierarchical management style or stakeholder-based reverse accountability (bottom-up approach), barriers toward capability and competence include unclear strategy, conflicting priorities, ineffective team culture, poor vertical communication, poor coordination across functions, and inadequate functional leadership skills. These factors broadly affect the organization's quality decision-making, vertical communication, quality of learning, and weak implementation due to the absence of stage-gate work breakdown structure, monitoring, and evaluation linearity.[30] Samsung Electronics, in its early days, manufactured inexpensive, imitative electronics for other companies but the firm improved its capabilities and competencies to the global level as the corporate leaders valued speed, scale, and reliability to match with the global market challenges and needs. The company created a committed, resourceful corps of designers who overcame internal resistance by deploying the same tools they use in pursuing innovation, which included empathy, visualization, and experimentation in the marketplace.[31]

It has been argued that firms improve their marketing capabilities and competencies by experimenting with various strategies in the predetermined minimum viable segment. This is a learning process for companies, in which they experiment with the development of pro-competition marketing strategies and improve product attributes. They do so through co-ideation and co-designing as parts of co-creation by engaging stakeholders. The continuous learning process helps to track failures and modify product attributes to serve the needs of the consumers. The learning process improves innovation capability across innovation types, which also improves the organizational performance.[32] In the long run, marketing strategy may also involve intermediaries and multi-channel operations to integrate the logical function of delivering products and services within and outside minimum viable segments. The increasing competition in the marketplace has driven innovation among firms. Most firms recognize that they should invest resources in building ideas and capabilities for innovation. Consumer-centric companies, who fail to build

---

[30] Beer, M., & Eisenstat, R. A. (2000). Silent killers of strategy implementation and learning. *MIT Sloan Management Review*, 41 (4), 29–40.

[31] Yoo, Y., & Kim, K. (2015). How Samsung became a design powerhouse. *Harvard Business Review*, 93 (9), 72–78.

[32] Govindarajan, V., & Trimble, C. (2005). Building breakthrough business within established organizations. *Harvard Business Review*, 83 (5), 58–69.

and sustain consumer-centric business models, collaborate with larger companies on business-to-business prospects. Such shift in the focus does not always pay companies in a competitive marketplace. Co-creation skills are important capabilities for companies, essential to manage agile processes, quick test-and-learn cycles, and perceived values of customers. Co-creation-focused companies gain value rapidly by delivering high-quality products and service innovation.[33]

Business Scaling

Scaling the business has two major concerns, which include reducing the total cost spread across manufacturing, marketing, business administration, innovation, and technology while increasing the volume of production and sales simultaneously. Economies of scale fundamentally provides the cost advantage to the firms when production becomes efficient, and the break-evens are usually achieved in a short time. Companies can achieve economies of scale because costs are spread over a larger number of goods because of optimization of both product-mix and product-line with the product categories. The full costs include both fixed and variable factors upon accounting for activity-based costing (ABC) and achieve more cost savings and higher production levels to gain the state of economies of scale at both internal and external levels. Internal economy is influenced by the micro-factors within the firm, which include resources, innovation, technology, and all elements of a business canvas,[34] while external factors affect the entire industry including macro factors (political, economic, social, technological, environmental, and legal). By integrating strategic business plans into tightly connected, distributed production systems, a firm can explore and capture the opportunity for a new manufacturing scale advantage.[35]

Most MSMEs visualize regional expansion as a potential growth opportunity by implementing a single business model as widely as possible to

---

[33] Rajagopal. (2020). *Transgenerational marketing: Evolution, expansion, and experience*. Cham: Switzerland (A Palgrave Macmillan Imprint).

[34] Business canvas comprises nine elements, which include key resources, key activities, key partners, value propositions, relationship management, segmentation, channels, cost structure, and revenue stream.

[35] McGrath, M. E., & Hoole, R. W. (1992). Manufacturing's new economies of scale. *Harvard Business Review*, 70 (3), 124–132.

maximize economies of scale. Consequently, the key strategic challenge faced by these companies is to quantify the cost, production, and sales (also market share), and adapt to local preferences to achieve economy of scale. However, firms oversee the real opportunities while focusing on business niche as a platform for attaining the business scale. Strategically, firms can yet gain from exploiting as wide, as they are able to maintain the competitive differentiators and establish their brand uniqueness. The growth of MSMEs can be divided into cultural, administrative, economic, and geographic clusters, which could prompt the firms to attain the economies of scale and competitive advantage. In each category, old opportunities persist, and new ones are arising. Most firms work on purely economic wage differentials that stimulate the business scaling process.[36]

Most consumer-centric companies work with dynamic marketing-mix, as strategies often need to be revised either by introducing temporary elements of marketing strategies or by laying emphasis on specific marketing-mix elements to develop marketing strategies specific to geo-demographic segments. The widespread adoption of marketing technology driving e-commerce trends, and social media leveraging peer interactions to share their consumption experiences has dramatically altered the set of products consumers compare before making a purchase decision. Marketing through social channels in the twenty-first century has succeeded in connecting consumers with companies, brands, and destinations by highlighting peer evaluations, consumer preferences, and motivations toward buying decisions. However, the contribution of marketing technology in establishing both product and customer inter-connectedness across markets prompts companies to make the dynamic decisions based on the market competition trends. The dynamic marketing decisions often develop inconsistencies in the consumer policies of the company, and the deliverables of brands are affected.[37]

Successful companies are selective toward developing strategies systematically, to create and lead new markets. Marketing-mix strategies need to be appropriately designed for acquiring new consumers and retaining those existing, by providing competitive leverage and customer value.

[36] Ghemawat, P. (2003). Forgotten strategy. *Harvard Business Review*, 81 (11), 76–84.

[37] Dass, M., & Kumar, S. (2014). Bringing product and consumer ecosystems to the strategic forefront. *Business Horizons*, 57 (2), 225–234.

Developing marketing strategies for new customers with unfamiliar brands is challenging for the companies. An appropriate marketing-mix also guides companies in minimizing cost-time-risk convergence in marketing and optimize market share and profitability. The opportunity to create and dominate a new market offers the prospect of working with right marketing-mix to gain competitive leverage in the marketplace and enhance the scope of business performance and profitability. Marketing-mix in a company is evolved over the existing business environment and government policies in a destination market. Marketing-mix consists of eleven elements spread across the taxonomic distributions of basic elements (4P's), extended functional elements (5P's), and design elements (2P's) of a company. The basic elements integrate product, price, place, and promotion elements with varied attributes of each element in this category of marketing-mix.

Products in the contemporary marketplace are consumer-driven and are developed as a solution to the consumer needs. The intangible factor of perceived use value and tangible preference of consumers determining the value for money of products governs the decision-making process for products, among consumers. Products with high-perceived value and longevity, and delivering expected value for money among consumers, stay as top-of-mind products. Therefore, in a dynamic competition, companies periodically offer programs on improvements of product designs to deliver continuous improvement in the product quality. Product attractiveness is largely driven by the product design, competitive leverages, and consumer preferences. Hence, most consumer-centric companies are engaged in co-creating product designs. Companies engage consumers to share their experiences, while the consumers offer solutions to the companies in the form of product designs, services, and expected values. Companies deliver these co-created tangibles in the competitive marketplace. Product differentiation is another major challenge for consumer-centric companies to stay ahead of marketplace competition. Most companies believe that successful product differentiation allows the consumer brands to enter the mass market in the emerging markets. Product differentiation needs to be supported by the attributes of price competitiveness and product promotions and exhibit unique product features. Companies in the global markets generally believe that product differentiation appeals to potential consumers who want their needs satisfied over the existing product advantages. Product lifecycle determines the longevity of the product in the market, its perceived use value, and associated value for money. The consumer thus prefers to measure the quality–price relationship in products considering the longevity and competitive advantages.

Product lifecycle determines the longevity of the product in the market, its perceived use value, and associated value for money. Consumer thus prefers to measure the quality–price relationship in products considering the longevity and competitive advantages. Pricing is one of the most complex decisions facing any company. Along with a lack of academic interest (especially among marketing academics) in the field of pricing, this complexity has contributed to the dominance of simplified, cost-based formulas when levying prices. Nevertheless, pricing cannot be determined in isolation from the other elements of the marketing-mix. The goal of the marketing-mix is to satisfy customers by offering the right product with the right promotion and place (i.e., distribution channels) at the right price in order to satisfy customers' needs better than competitors, and thus achieve the firm's objectives.[38] The increase in market competition has provided increasing choices of products and services altering the consumption patterns frequently. Such marketplace situation has developed a consumer philosophy of *touch, feel,* and *pick,* which makes consumers product-loyal instead of brand-loyal with instantaneous switching behavior. Hence, to prevent consumers from switching brands, most consumer products companies tend to continuously replenish inventory on the retail stacks in retail outlets. The emergence of e-commerce has prompted consumer-centric companies to adapt to 'direct-to-customer' (DTC) distribution strategy. This strategy has been successful over the years as it helps companies in minimizing the cost, time, and risk (CTR) effects in managing distribution. Lowering the CTR effects results in increasing the consumer value, brand loyalty, market share, and profitability of the company. The promotional strategies are evaluated by the companies in reference to its impact on the volume of sales, market share, and their contribution to the profit specific to the products and services. Among the fashion-oriented brands, promotions are largely driven by the word-of-mouth and interactions on social media with other consumers. Sales promotions need to be reviewed in reference to economic viability, informational aspects that consumers use to make

---

[38] Indounas, K. (2006). Making effective pricing decisions. *Business Horizons*, 49 (5), 415–424.

purchase decisions, and affective aspects that help in generating consumer experience.[39]

Packaging and marketing affect the business performance of production-led, sales-led, and marketing-led companies. Ergonomics of packaging today plays a significant role in establishing the product attractiveness, developing consumer preferences, defining the market, determining price, and the brand values. Packaging industry is growing innovative to add value to the brands and develop unique selling proposition for most consumer products companies (Farmer, 2012). In recent development, Novel food packaging technologies arose as a result of consumer's desire for convenient, ready-to-eat, tasty, and mild processed food products with extended shelf life and maintained quality. Companies, as first-movers, manage the market pace by investing resources to attract consumers and position their brands, which tends to lower the profit rate. However, efficient companies try to minimize the cost, time, and risk (CTR) factors in launching and delivering products in the marketplace. Many companies believe that the first company dealing in a new product category gets a significant breakthrough in the markets and gets long-lasting benefits. However, it does not happen always. To ensure the advantages of the pace strategy, companies should monitor the gradual evolution in both the technology and the right opportunity to move in the market, which could provide a first-mover by influencing the consumers and creating demand in the neighboring markets.

People in the marketing-mix constitute front-liners in markets, who manage sales of products and services. Selling is an art largely associated with the behavioral skills of the sale personnel of a sales organization. In a competitive marketplace, selling is performed using scientific methods of product presentation, advertising, and various approaches drawn to take the customer into confidence. A firm begins to sell its products in a competitive marketplace and thrives continuously on acquiring new customers and launches new product lines or services in order to gain competitive advantage, retain the existing customers, enhance customer value, and gain competitive lead in the market. To compete in a dynamic and interactive marketplace environment, firms must shift their focus from just selling the products and services to value-added sales management,

---

[39] Raghubir, P., Inman, J. J., & Grande, H. (2004). Three faces of consumer promotions. *California Management Review*, 46 (4), 23–42.

to maximize customer lifetime value and encourage repeat sales. Performance in the marketing-mix is considered as a hybrid element. This element is evolved through various factors comprising all basic elements of marketing-mix, innovation and continuous improvement, organizational culture, employee engagement, and consumer involvement in co-creating products to enhance consumer value. To thrive in the competitive open markets, companies need to map their strategic choices on the business performance matrix in reference to various vital variables such as cost, price, innovation, differentiation, distribution, technology, promotion, customer value, and psychodynamics. Companies need to adapt to new roles as low-cost entrants, focused segment marketers, and providers of shared utilities. They must also be prepared to make new strategic choices as the structure of the industry changes.

Positive psychodynamics among consumers creates pull effect for specific brands in the market. The pull effect generates high consumer demand, which benefits companies in increasing market share and profit by reducing the marketing costs. Such costs for brands are spread across advertisements, in-store promotions, price discounts, and point-of-sales incentives to the consumers. The psychodynamics also generates referrals and brand advocacy behavior among consumers, which helps companies acquire new consumers at relatively low cost. Most firms involving social media as a marketing communication channel tap the knowledge and expertise of consumers for mutual benefit and brand-building process more than a traditional knowledge management approach where people dump their information in a giant database that nobody reads. Posture of the company and its path of business proliferation by diversifying the business operations to new markets and expanding the product portfolios constitute the design elements in the marketing-mix of a company. Corporate image develops the posture of a company within the industry and among the consumers in the marketplace. Consumer confidence is built through the corporate image which develops brand association and brand loyalty among consumers. Proliferation of business activities is commonly grown around product and market diversifications exploring new consumer segments for existing and future products developed using advanced technologies. Consumer-centric companies planning for business proliferation might face the risk of disruptive innovation and gray market competition. However, business proliferations are often challenging for companies to manage the desired operational efficiency and profit levels.

Challenges in Research and Business Planning

The challenge-based research to cater to the social and economic developmental needs of stakeholders is largely nurtured within the social and cultural ecosystems, which catalyzes significantly the industrial and consumer marketing practices of local enterprises. In addition, global concerns on entrepreneurship in the context of sustainable development goals motivate both manufacturing and marketing competencies of entrepreneurs. Accordingly, the social innovations are driven by the PNS factors and sustainability-led ideation for developing cleaner utilitarian products. Some enterprises with the competencies to manufacture and market radical products, also stimulate demand in the competitive markets, while most enterprises at the bottom of the pyramid are engaged in frugal innovations manufacturing low-cost and utilitarian products, which tend to create high-perceived value and demand. Innovations driven by challenge-based research are focused on social needs, social development, and economic growth. The basic motivation for micro, small, and medium enterprises is to grow competitively by exploring market opportunities for disruptive products to transform the value chains associated with the existing products in the marketplace. Such an approach of these enterprise helps in developing synergy in business modeling and performance.

Sustainable products with low-cost technology with a long lifecycle ensure both affordability and inculcating a sense of value for money among consumers. Such strategies of local enterprises encourage vertical growth in upstream or downstream markets and planning the outreach of embedded technologies in the products. Consequently, consumers develop a perception on ease of use of products and derive high-perceived use value. In a holistic view, these strategies increase the marketability of technology-led sustainable innovative products. In a socially sensitive and technologically advanced enterprises, the business model is architected with design-to-market, design-to-society, and design-to-value perspectives. Many micro and small enterprises have also been benefitted by the crowd-based business modeling, which are significantly supported by collective intelligence. Crowd business models are agile and collaborative. Nonetheless, the consortium business models designed by integrating many micro and small enterprises within the same industry strengthen their bargaining power and negotiation skills and help in standardizing the cost, time, and technology application by reducing the risk and uncertainty in manufacturing and marketing processes.

It is yet debatable to determine the governance pattern of social enterprises and whether they should be led by the conventional leaders, progressive stakeholders, or the state authorities (government). Alternative reasoning prompts that partnerships such as consortiums and corporate collaborations may also provide strong governance to the agglomeration of enterprises within an industry. The strategic alliances with large firms in production, innovation, technology, marketing, and resource pooling would also help in developing joint governance of local and sponsoring firms. In addition, social institutions such as the community and self-help groups have also emerged as efficient governance. The digital drive in the enterprises has significantly stimulated the hybrid management by combining the brick and click marketing strategies. Some social enterprises like housing, health, and energy in the developing countries are successfully managed through public–private partnerships. An appropriate governance system helps entrepreneurs to develop a positive mid-set and drive both individual and group behavior to inculcate progressive reasoning and entrepreneurial motivation.

The challenge-based research diffused through social institution has higher outreach among the stakeholders and customers. This has been evidenced during the COVID-19 pandemic as the social institutions took the lead in creating awareness about the sanitation regulations and personal and public protection norms. In response to societal grand challenges, professors have unique opportunities to effect change, repurposing their expertise to deploy relevant, timely, practical, and research-backed knowledge for the betterment of communities. Incubation of innovations has emerged as a new model of start-up facilitation in most developing economies. Venture capitalists review the incubators and assess the projected growth and profitability of businesses to invest. The venture capitalists review the incubators to diversify risky investment portfolios, while the prospecting entrepreneurs approach the incubators to review the economically viable and technologically feasible support for start-up projects. Entrepreneurial incubators face both challenges and opportunities to grow competitive enterprises considering the embedded investment and entrepreneurial risks. Broadly, there are five incubator archetypes such as the university incubator, the independent commercial incubator, the regional business incubator, the company-internal incubator, and the virtual incubator.[40] Innovations of local origin are attracted to the global companies as they plan to bring back the local innovation, which is largely frugal in nature, to the mass-market. Therefore, the relational embeddedness of large companies with the external enterprises appears to be essential for the evolution of local innovations to the global scale. Hybrid enterprises working with the social and economic development objectives tend to develop entrepreneurial ideas both through face-to-face interactions and on social media platforms.[41] Turning local innovations into global brands can be identified as innovativeness evoked by large companies or their subsidiaries at the bottom of the pyramid. However, in this process, the transfer of reverse knowledge in the functional areas is a critical perspective.[42] The contemporary research on social entrepreneurship has consistently focused on the benefits and challenges of designing hybrid organizations, which integrate the competing institutional reasoning to tackle social problems using market-based methods, especially in developing economies.[43]

Most studies reveal that the relationship between innovation efficiency and the size of the firm play a significant role in improving market performance and exploring the prevailing and new market opportunities. Marketing and product innovation strategies are the key contributors to market performance, while the competitiveness has become an indispensable factor for both social and commercial enterprises to survive the marketplace rivalry.[44] In an open-market competition, firms of different

---

[40] Carayannis, E. G., & von Zedtwitz, M. (2005). Architecting gloCal (global–local), real-virtual incubator networks (G-RVINs) as catalysts and accelerators of entrepreneurship in transitioning and developing economies: lessons learned and best practices from current development and business incubation practices. *Technovation*, 25 (2), 95–110.

[41] Bacq, S., Geoghegan, W., Josefy, M., Stevenson, R., & Williams, T. A. (2020). The COVID-19 virtual idea Blitz: Marshaling social entrepreneurship to rapidly respond to urgent grand challenges. *Business Horizons*, 23 (6), 705–723.

[42] Isaac, V. R., Borini, F. M., Raziq, M. M., & Benito, G. R. G. (2019). From local to global innovation: The role of subsidiaries' external relational embeddedness in an emerging market. *International Business Review*, 28 (4), 638–646.

[43] McMullen, J. S., & Bergman, B. J. (2018). The promise and problems of price subsidization in social entrepreneurship. *Business Horizons*, 61 (4), 609–621.

[44] Blocker, C. P., Flint, D. J., Myers, M. B., & Slater, S. F. (2011). Proactive customer orientation and its role for creating customer value in global markets. *Journal of Academy of Marketing Science*, 39 (2), 216–233.

types and sizes use up-front marketing strategies and tactics to pull down the competing firms. Such competition forces small firms to struggle for existence against relatively large firms, while large firms strengthen their marketing strategies to sustain the competition and stay fittest in the competitive marketplace. However, large firms at the early maturity stage of their business attempt to consolidate their product-line to stay abreast with market competition and develop product portfolio in tune with the market demand. To gain a suitable competitive position in the marketplace, firms pump enormous resources into innovation, technology, advertisement, communication, and sales activities. The low returns on investment build sunk cost over time.

CHAPTER 2

Entrepreneurial Ecosystem

The intrinsic factors within the social ecosystem, which stimulate the co-creation process of social entrepreneurs, customers, and stakeholders, include social responsibility-led self-esteem, voluntary behavior, social leadership, and active involvement in social media. This chapter argues that social entrepreneurs focus on reaching milestones that improve social welfare. However, far from family firms, the growing upstream enterprises work on profit-oriented strategic business projects that create sustainable social value.[1] This chapter discusses the shifts in entrepreneurial practices due to behavioral swings, availability and utilization of resources, upstream evolution of social and customer values, technology, innovation, and transformation in business practices because of changing social ecosystem. Innovation, technology, and skills matrix are largely driven by the problems, needs, and expected solutions within the social system. The opportunity recognition and exploitation are the core preconditions for generating and implementing innovative social business ideas.[2] In

---

[1] Hoogendoorn, B. (2016). The prevalence and determinants of social entrepreneurship at the macro level. *Journal of Small Business Management*, 54, 278–296.

[2] Halberstadt, J., & Spiegler, A. (2018). Networks and the idea fruition process of female social entrepreneurs in South Africa. *Social Enterprise Journal*, 14, 429–449.

© The Author(s), under exclusive license to Springer Nature Switzerland AG 2024
Rebuilding Entrepreneurship at the Grassroots, Palgrave Studies of Entrepreneurship and Social Challenges in Developing Economies, https://doi.org/10.1007/978-3-031-43270-5_2

addition, the backward linkages (resources, infrastructure, skills, and technology) and forward linkages (relationship management and marketing) contribute significantly to the entrepreneurial ecosystem.

The social business models include sustainability strategy and leadership, mission, communication and learning, social care and work life, and loyalty and identification. Companies and stakeholders intending to proactively manage social sustainability need to undertake participatory projects with key partners and stakeholders on cultural change and development initiatives toward sustainability.[3] Circular design thinking is a continuous process, which connects society and business with learning on R-3 factors comprising acquiring knowledge on resources, recycling technology, and reusability of products from consumers' perspectives. Most companies engaged in CE applications remain as learning organizations and invest in collective intelligence, prototyping, and feedback loops. Social values are built on cultural dimensions and ethnicity. Egalitarianism and embeddedness of consumers in the society affect the business environment. Companies, thus, develop social welfare policies as corporate social responsibilities and build consumer values. Moreover, social values affect the individual ideological orientation on consumer attitudes toward industry, government policies, and consumer behavior.[4] Technology shows a significant positive impact on economic growth, while both human capital and technology are important determinants of growth in developing countries and emerging markets. Therefore, improvement of the educational sector and more funding for research and development among developing countries are prominent considerations to monitor and measure business growth. Such conditions encourage innovations needed to facilitate sustained economic growth.[5]

---

[3] Schönborn, G., Berlin, C., Pinzone, M., Hanisch, C., Georgoulias, K., & Lanz, M. (2019). Why social sustainability counts: The impact of corporate social sustainability culture on financial success. *Sustainable Production and Consumption*, 17, 1–10.

[4] Arikan, G., & Bloom, P. B. (2014). Social values and cross-national differences in attitudes towards welfare. *Political Studies*, 63 (2), 431–448.

[5] Adelakun, O. J. (2011). Human capital development and economic growth in Nigeria. *European Journal of Business and Management*, 3 (9), 29–39.

Social Ecosystem and Entrepreneurship

Social capital, which is a valuable asset in improving the knowledge of stakeholders, positively affects their purchase intention toward organic foods and stimulates actual purchase behavior. Contemporary knowledge and experience sharing among women in interpersonal or digital platforms help in developing trust in the acquired knowledge. Trust significantly mediates relationships between available information, perceived knowledge, and organic purchase intentions. Attitudes toward organic foods and subjective norms also significantly influence organic food choices among women consumers.[6] Social influence and perceived knowledge develop cognition in the form of beliefs, utilitarian attitudes, and behavior toward consumption of organic products. Women also feel hedonic pleasure in paying premium price for organic products to cater to health and family wellness needs.[7] The successful adaptation and creation of sustainable entrepreneurial ventures are significantly influenced by the interactions within social networks (tradition and digital), which augment the ability to create collective intelligence, and environmentally and socially integrated economic systems. Sustainable business models are largely driven by the social networks and stakeholders at the mature stage of businesses, as they rely more on social patronage and values than corporate sponsorship. However, the development of sustainable business models is a complex process that requires a supportive entrepreneurial and social ecosystem.[8]

Social impact theory (SIT) also explains the contextual association of an individual's decision-making within the social values and influences behavioral perspectives of entrepreneurship. Major behavioral theories, therefore, focus on proximal influences on behavior that are instrumental

---

[6] Teng, C. C., & Wang, Y. M. (2015). Decisional factors driving organic food consumption: Generation of consumer purchase intentions. *British Food Journal*, 117 (3), 1066–1081.

[7] Lee, H. J., & Goudeau, C. (2014). Consumers' beliefs, attitudes, and loyalty in purchasing organic foods: The standard learning hierarchy approach. *British Food Journal*, 116 (6), 918–930.

[8] Neumeyer, X., & Santos, S. C. (2018). Sustainable business models, venture typologies, and entrepreneurial ecosystems: A social network perspective. *Journal of Cleaner Production*, 172, 4565–4579.

in developing cognitive attributes within the social context.[9] Attributes of SIT delineate how emotions shift the focus of individual decision-making to the wider context of social relations and guide the subjective norms such as hedonism, anthropomorphism, and self-esteem among individuals.[10] Social interactions embedded in social commerce sites and media channels influence the purchase intention. Positive interpersonal communication and user-generated content on digital platforms significantly affect consumers' intention to buy a product. Intention to purchase driven by social interaction facilitates the likelihood of actual buying and sharing information with peers.[11] Eco-innovations, on the other hand, approach problems with the question as are we integrating the social values in the prototype and building the right solution in the first place? Combining imagination, insights, and impact in providing a right ecological solution emerges as a major challenge to the companies.

Social value on sustainable projects is delivered by the non-governmental organizations with varied performances in alliance with the companies. Most companies implement CSR projects in association with the informal social groups, known as self-help groups (SHG). Women's self-help groups in India provide an interesting and concrete example of an intervention that is well aligned with theoretical ideas about development as a process of capability expansion. These groups contribute to the policy priorities of gender empowerment laid in the global sustainability development goals. The JEEVikA (livelihood) program in Bihar, India, finds that economically and socially marginalized groups have been benefited from SHG membership through a reduction in reliance on high-cost sources of borrowing.[12] These SHGs have helped to increase the participation of women in household decision-making and delivered positive impacts on human development in rural areas. Similarly, another SHG

---

[9] Burke, N. J., Joseph, G., Pasick, R. J., & Barker, J. C. (2009). Theorizing social context: Rethinking behavioral theory. *Health Education & Behavior*, 36 (5-suppl), 55S–70S.

[10] Gilbert, T., & Powell, J. L. (2010). Power and social work in the United Kingdom: A foucauldian excursion. *Journal of Social Work*, 10 (1), 3–22.

[11] Wang, Y., & Yu, C. (2017). Social interaction-based consumer decision-making model in social commerce: The role of word of mouth and observational learning. *International Journal of Information Management*, 37 (3), 179–189.

[12] Rajagopal. (2021). Sustainable businesses in developing economies: Socio-economic and governance perspectives. Cham, Switzerland: Springer.

in Andhra Pradesh, a southern state in India, has evidenced the impact on enhancing social capital as the organization has motivated program members on higher savings to move freely within their village and interact within their caste. Protein and energy intake, and consumption of sustainable food increased among members of the group as income or asset changed. These groups establish sustainability in human development and rural wealth generation.[13]

Broadly, there are social, cultural, and market ecosystems, which are supported by social capital and values, and cultural integration. The taxonomy of ecosystems and the factors that affect these ecosystems have been exhibited in Fig. 2.1.

There are multiple ecosystems that interact within the social, cultural, and economic scape and affect the entrepreneurial pattern, process, and performance within a spatial and temporal domain as illustrated in the Fig. 2.1. The social, cultural, and ethnic ecosystems are interdependent and significantly influence the factors of the market ecosystem. The elements architecting the socio-cultural and ethnic ecosystems also interact with knowledge and value ecosystems. Besides the relational effects of these ecosystems, market ecosystem has proximity to the entrepreneurial ecosystem. Social ecosystem is a complex adaptive system delimiting spatial and functional boundaries that include demographic structure, economic layers, leadership, community infrastructure, and education. Economic layers in social ecosystem exhibit occupation (entrepreneurship), income distribution, and allocation of resources. Cultural and ethnic ecosystem benefits people by gaining value through interactions with different social workspaces, ecological activities such as cultural parks learn and conserve cultural heritage and values. Entrepreneurship evolves within this ecosystem encompassing art, music, cinematography, and marketable souvenir products. The principal driver of knowledge ecosystem is the creation of knowledge which claims to foster the dynamic social and personal networks of collaboration. The elements of ecosystems discussed above help in generating social capital, people, and networks that build leadership and social networks. The major contribution of social networks boosts collective intelligence and transforms social values, philosophy of work, and lifestyle of entrepreneurs.

---

[13] Anand, P., Saxena, S., Gonzalez, R., & Dang, H. H. (2019). *Can women's self-help groups contribute to sustainable development? Evidence of capability changes from Northern India* (Policy Research Working Paper #9011). Washington, DC: World Bank Group.

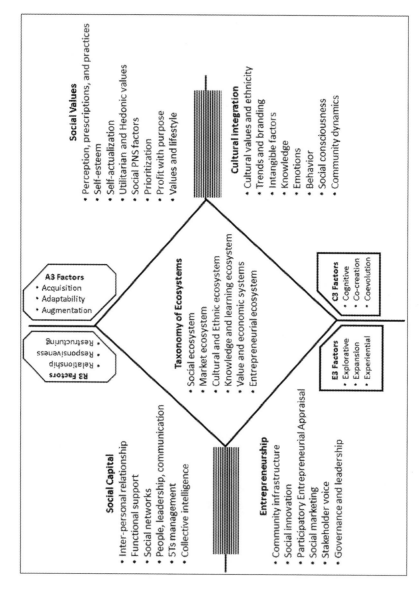

Fig. 2.1 Taxonomy of ecosystems and the factors affecting their functionalities (*Source* Author)

The 5T work-based social philosophy includes task (work charter), time (projections), target (beneficiary segment), thrust (PNS factors), and trust (commitment). The formation and contributions of social capital generate social value founded on social perceptions, market prescriptions, and entrepreneurial practices. Social perceptions are built through self-actualization while market prescriptions are based on PNS factors and utilitarian and hedonic values of consumers. Accordingly, entrepreneurial practices are set by prioritizing market plans that optimize profit in the long run.

There are many intangible factors such as acquisition of new knowledge, emotions, ethnicity, and socio-psychological behavior that embed the social and cultural values in formation of social capital as illustrated in Fig. 2.1. However, the social consciousness tends to change with the shifts in community dynamics. For example, consumers adapt to austerity measures by staying conscious of price and utilitarian values of the artisanal product, while the younger generation of consumers are attracted to the changing technology in vogue. Social medial and collective intelligence play a critical role in driving the community dynamics. These factors significantly contribute in building the prismatic entrepreneurship integrating the design-to-market, design-to-society, and design-to-value perspectives. Social capital, social values, and cultural integration along with the stakeholder voices promote social innovation and social marketing of entrepreneurial products and services. Effective governance of entrepreneurial activities in the family or cooperative business models helps in building community infrastructure to be used as entrepreneurial commons. Such governing ecosystems encourage start-up firms to conduct a participatory entrepreneurial appraisal to evaluate economic viability, technological feasibility, and operational models to stay competitive in the market. The domains of entrepreneurship (social capital, values, culture, and ethnicity) with the ecosystems of various related taxonomies are affected by the RACE factors with a triadic multiplier effect. RACE factors are driven by three variables in each segment in the following pattern:

- Social Capital—R-3 factors that include relationship (stakeholders and leaders), responsiveness (PNS factors), and restructuring (linking society, market, and entrepreneurship)

- Social Values—A-3 factors consisting of acquisition (crowd behavior and contemporary knowledge), adaptability (perceived values), and augmentation (hybrid communication and collective intelligence)
- Cultural integration—C3 factors comprising cognitive (interaction, reasoning, and analyzing), co-creating (engaging crowd and stakeholders), and coevolution (stakeholder and market-driven growth)
- Entrepreneurship—E-3 factors including explorative (market opportunities and customer values), expansion (vertical and horizontal), and experiential (knowledge entrepreneurship with the ability to exploit opportunities)

The cultural dimensions of individualism, uncertainty avoidance, power distance, and masculinity should be a useful framework to explain cross-cultural differences in customer acceptance of designer products. The personality dimensions often play a critical role in shifting the consumer culture toward brand-led buying behavior of utilitarian goods. Designer apparel brands are perceived by the consumers as prestigious brands encompassing several physical and psychological values such as perceived conspicuous value, perceived unique value, perceived social value, perceived hedonic value, and perceived quality value. Consumption patterns are largely governed by the social value of the product, which determines the purchase intentions, consumer attitudes, or perceptions of brand or advertising slogan. Consumer experience with high socioeconomic power perceptions creates qualitatively distinct psychological motives toward buying designer apparel that develop unique consumption patterns.[14] Companies need to understand the factors that drive consumer stimuli toward getting associated with new products and brands.

Social Cognitive Theory explains how variables such as self-regulation and self-efficacy direct spending behavior and determine consumer lifestyles. Product attributes influence consumer perceptions of the personal relevance of a product or service to their needs, and consumer preferences for product attributes are significantly linked to their lifestyle. The lifestyle theory suggests that the consumers' perceived hedonic attributes and social identity factors determine the shopping behavior of

---

[14] Rucker, D. D., & Galinsky, A. D. (2009). Conspicuous consumption versus utilitarian ideals: How different levels of power shape consumer behavior. *Journal of Experimental Social Psychology*, 45 (3), 549–555.

urban consumers. The social learning theory explains this phenomenon as positive reinforcement, and it occurs when a behavior (response) is followed by a favorable stimulus (commonly seen as pleasant) that increases the frequency of that behavior. In the conceptual foundations of social learning theory, respondent conditioning, and observational learning are the empirically supported approaches to understanding normative human development and the etiology of psychosocial problems. Consumer perceptions toward the innovative products include:

- Beliefs, trust, and loyalty with the store
- Home-grown and serviceable products
- Convenience and low cost to customer
- Customizable and nearer to the consumer preferences
- Relative advantages on price and quality

Brands are designed and developed considering consumer perceptions of the store image. Shopping satisfaction includes consumers' perceptions of store attributes as well as subjective evaluations of products purchased from the store by the consumers themselves or by their fellow shoppers. Brand impact is largely derived also through the word-of-mouth interaction. However, response to the store brands appears to be more complex in nature than a simple affective summary of the relative frequencies of positive and negative emotions during consumption experiences. Another factor that affects the consumer decision on brands is the recognition of the role of store sales personnel in a retail environment. It has been observed that effective salespeople influence not only the shopping process but also influence the consumers to switch their store patronage. Consumers may abandon one store brand to a new store brand to follow specific sales and service personnel.[15] Attitude toward promoted brands is characterized by positive store image, smart shopper self-perception, need for affiliation, and money attitude regarding power-prestige and anxiety. However, attitude of consumers toward store brands is determined by a

---

[15] Terblanche, N., & Boshoff, C. (2005). The in-store shopping experience and customer retention: A study of clothing store customers. *Business Review*, 4 (1), 118–125.

more positive store image, price advantage, range of products to exercise buying options, and loyalty- and trust-related factors.[16]

Most innovations grow in emerging markets around the ethnic needs of consumers and are developed at low cost considering the affordability and adaptability potentials of the consumers in the home market. As marketing has evolved over time, the associated elements of marketing like consumer behavior, supply chain, business-to-business marketing, decision-making models, and business diplomacy and corporate social responsibility strategies have also grown over generations. Social values are built on the cultural dimensions and ethnicity. Egalitarianism and embeddedness of consumers in the society affect the business environment. Companies thus develop social welfare policies as corporate social responsibility and build customer values. Thus, ethnic marketing is sometimes challenging, as several factors like consumption behavior, social and family culture, beliefs, and personal values intervene in buying decisions. The distinctiveness of cultural features like social media reviews is profoundly associated with emotional expressions that play a significant role in the buying behavior among consumers. The consumer behavior of young consumers is found homogeneous through the different ethnic consumer segments across markets. However, some generational differences among consumers exist due to technology, social media interactions, and wider experience on consumption.[17] Consumer cognition is often influenced by societal values, referrals, and peer reviews within the ethnic and cultural boundaries. Sometimes, with the strong effects of acquired culture and knowledge, consumers tend to choose the values and lifestyles beyond the ethnic and cultural boundaries of the society. Such consumer cognition radicalizes the decision-making process.

Most innovations are grown in the emerging markets around the ethnic needs of consumers and are developed at low cost considering the affordability and adaptability potentials of the consumers in the home market. Frugal innovation is based on substantial cost reduction, concentration on core functionalities, and optimized performance level. The concept of frugality is more a formative economic construct than a business model, which encompasses the following dimensions:

---

[16] Liu, T., & Wang, C. (2008). Factors affecting attitudes toward private labels and promoted brands. *Journal of Marketing Management*, 24 (3), 283–298.

[17] Rajagopal & Castano, R. (2015). *Understanding consumer behaviour and consumption experience*. Hershey, PA: IGI Global.

- Quality integrated into the product with the basic assumption of utilitarian values,
- Cost of production, consumption, and value for money concepts,
- Simplicity in product design, functions, and management, and
- Sustainability orientation of the product

The low cost and sustainability of the frugal innovation products are considered within the value perspectives of consumers. Frugal innovations promoted by the regulatory bodies and policymakers sometimes ignore the consumers within sustainable innovation, which causes the failure of innovation marketing efforts.[18]

Exploring Inside Market

Learning communities are developed by the consumer-centric companies to transfer knowledge on social consumption causes like healthy foods, green consumption, organic farm products, and the like. Such learning communities are designed primarily to increase consumer attitudes toward learning new consumption patterns, and building convergence with social, ethnic, and personal values. The community learning process prompts co-shopping and co-viewing of brands in the marketplace, which also stimulates consumers to review the referrals and conform to community decisions. Hence, most referral programs of consumer product companies focus on diffusing brand awareness among the family or community as a source of knowledge hub of consumers. Companies monitor consumer needs, perceptions, and expectations through the learning communities, and identify marketing strategies, which contribute to augmenting consumer involvement in learning new consumption experiences and perceived satisfaction. Digital consumer learning communities do attain positive outcomes; however, consumer education programs need to be developed specifically to the requirements of geo-demographic segments.[19] Consumer engagement in companies not only builds high-perceived values among consumers but also helps in developing social

---

[18] von Janda, S., Kuester, S., Schuhmacher, M. C., & Shainesh, G. (2020). What frugal products are and why they matter: A cross-national multi-method study. *Journal of Cleaner Production*, 246, 118977. https://doi.org/10.1016/j.jclepro.2019.118977.

[19] Andrade, E. B., & Cohen, J. B. (2007). On the consumption of negative feelings. *Journal of Consumer Research*, 34 (3), 283–300.

consumption behavior. The positive psychodynamics among consumers through social media and interpersonal relations help in developing pro-brand perceptions, attitudes, and behaviors. Popular brands try to develop positive perceptions among consumers along the path to purchase, while utility brands influence consumer experience at every touchpoint.

Collective intelligence plays a significant role in the ideation process and in managing the demand for innovative products in the initial stages of the market. Crowdsourcing categorically delivers relevant knowledge in innovation and business modeling processes by addressing consumer problems and offering solutions. Previous studies suggest that three distinct types of crowdsourcing can be used to solve the problems of differing scope and complexity and to generate opportunities for innovation.[20] Many companies diagnose social problems with an engineering mindset to build it the right way and make sure it works. During this process, often the social and cultural intentions are ignored, which results in delays in adaptation to the solutions. Combining imagination, insights, and impact in providing a right ecological solution emerges as a major challenge to the companies. Concept mapping to develop consumer behavior for sustainable products and services varies based on the needs and problems of consumers and expected solutions. Self-help groups work in close proximity of consumers to know their needs and perceptions of sustainable products and services. The perceptual mapping has merged as an advantageous exercise for companies to know the cognitive semantics of consumers about their needs and problems.

Applied organizational learning is the basic philosophy that underpins the ideas of achieving competencies and capabilities in management of corporate and functional issues. Often, a positive consumption experience guarantees satisfaction, and develops brand loyalty and sustainable behavior among consumers over time. Consumers active on social media also develop knowledge, perceptions, and motivations through the user-generated contents and experience sharing. As social media is dynamic, it attributes to the variable consumer behavior. As the innovations in the business-to-consumer and business-to-business segments have shown the tendency of boom and bust, one of the major concerns for the companies

---

[20] Williams, A., Seidel, V. P., & Woolley, A. (2020). Make your crowd smart. *MIT Sloan Management Review*, 61 (2), 1–6.

Rajagopal. (2020). *Market entropy: How to manage chaos and uncertainty for improving organizational performance*. New York: Business Expert Press.

carrying out innovative business projects is to make it competitive and sustainable in the marketplace over the spatial and temporal dynamics. Learning from consumers is a grassroots expedition for researchers to explore the emotions, perception, attitude, and behavior that lead to the semantics of decision-making within the dynamic of business ecosystem. Most companies engaged in manufacturing and marketing of sustainable products and services believe in conducting design-based research with qualitative and narrative focus to know the perceptions of consumers. Consumer cognition is often influenced by societal values, referrals, and peer reviews within the ethnic and cultural boundaries. Sometimes, with the strong effects of acquired culture and knowledge, consumers tend to choose the values and lifestyles beyond the ethnic and cultural boundaries of the society. Such consumer cognition radicalizes the decision-making process. In addition, acquired knowledge, self-learning, ability to critically analyze the information, and observations based on causes and effects help consumers rationalize their cognitive frameworks. However, cognitive rationales are often disrupted by the subconscious movements and affect the conscious thinking. A refined cognitive framework helps consumers reach self-actualization over time.

Social entrepreneurship has high-value proposition and it is intended to drive societal transformations. Such entrepreneurs address social issues and problems and empower transformational progress throughout the system. The dominant factor for the rise of social entrepreneurship is the societal pressure on green recovery and sustainability governance.[21] Another successful and impactful social enterprise is ME to WE that provides Fairtrade products and global volunteer trips to a mostly millennial audience. It was launched in 2006 by two Canadian brothers and has grown rapidly. The enterprise allows consumers to enter a unique code from ME to WE products to transparently see exactly how and where the funds from their purchases are used for the needy people to transform lives by providing financial support on various vital requirements.[22]

---

[21] Gandhi, T., & Raina, R. (2018). Social entrepreneurship: The need, relevance, facets and constraints. *Journal of Global Entrepreneurship Research*, 8, Art. 9, 1–13. https://doi.org/10.1186/s40497-018-0094-6.

[22] For details on Me to We social enterprise see https://www.metowe.com/about-us/.

The global trends have driven the PNS factors through emotions, vogue, social dynamics, and peer pressure over time. Consequently, cognition and personality among consumers is influenced by collective intelligence and crowd behavior. Consumers learn by analyzing the product, market, and crowd information; and establish the competitive differentiators contextual to self-actualization and satisfaction. In addition, social and technological factors such as digitization, e-commerce, hybrid business platforms, social media, and crowd behavior have significantly shifted the consumer behavior. Knowledge-sharing, empowerment (inclusivity) and self- and social perceptions drive consumer behavior in the context of changing marketing attributes. The diffusion of business knowledge, analytical skills to determine the PNS factors, and setting up the collectivistic principles in ideation, innovation, intelligence, and information streamlining (4Is) constitute the important factors for the team stability. Convergence among the above-discussed entrepreneurial factors play an effective moderating role of team collectivism and dynamics.[23] The inclusive business model helps firms create new possibilities to serve people's latent needs and contribute to the productivity and profit of the firm. Operating with such business model, firms can reduce costs and risks associated with PNS factors and gain significant market power through customers as the 'gateway' for leveraging markets at the bottom of the pyramid. Exploring market opportunities is an underlying challenge among continuing and start-up entrepreneurs, as it is a synchronized process integrating various stages comprising preparation, incubation, innovation, marketing, and evolution as exhibited in Fig. 2.2.

Exploring markets to grow business in an enterprise is initially complex as most start-up enterprises face problems due to limitation of resources, skills, and planned strategies as illustrated in Fig. 2.2. There are in-depth challenges for micro, small, and medium enterprises to look inside the market edge and analyze the intensity of market competition, the extent of disruptive innovation and marketing threats, radical consumer behavior, and sales tactics. Such interventions affect consumer preferences and the equity of familiar brands against the infant brands and unfamiliar innovative products of micro, small, and medium enterprises. Conducting market appraisal and simultaneously exploring consumer

---

[23] Agarwal, R., Campbell, B. A., Franco, A. M., & Ganco, M. (2016). What do I take with me? The mediating effect of spin-out team size and tenure on the founder–firm performance relationship. *Academy of Management Journal*, 59 (3), 1060–1087.

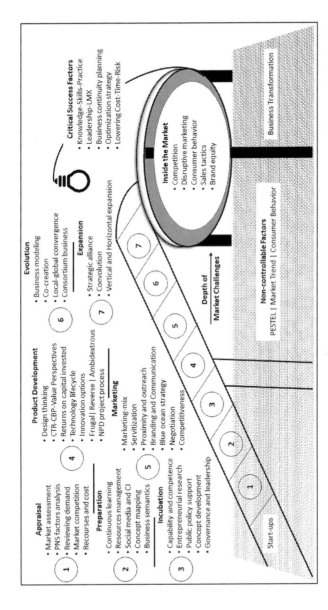

Fig. 2.2 Exploring market and building enterprise (*Source* Author)

problems, needs, and expected solutions stand a primary task for micro, small, and medium enterprises before planning the entrepreneurial activities and operations. Reviewing resources, cost structure, and demand for products and services help entrepreneurs to understand market behavior and attributes of competition to develop appropriate entrepreneurial strategy. In preparation to set-up a micro, small, or medium enterprise, leaders and employees need to adapt to continuous learning to understand the radical shifts in market, develop opportunity-driven strategies, and stay risk-averse. It is a wise practice to develop business semantics by plotting probable business focus, growth, and diversification strategies. Such exercise will help in mapping selected business concepts and planning for resource management approaches. Social media and collective intelligence significantly contribute in developing semantics and concept maps on entrepreneurial business activities. Consequently, staying abreast with social media is very helpful to the start-up entrepreneurs. Following the preparation to explore the market, entrepreneurs need to incubate their competitive business ideas and conduct pilot test to ensure the right product development for the right consumer segment in the selected market. The incubation period can be used to improve capabilities and competencies by conducting market research on innovation, new product development, and public policy programs to develop market-appropriate business concepts, resources management, and competitive strategies. The enterprise governance modalities and effective leadership styles also need to be defined during incubation period of enterprises.

The product development and marketing stages emerge at the later stage of incubation of enterprises. Design thinking is one of the major challenges in new product development in a project management approach, which must embed the analysis of CTR (cost, time, and risk) factors and CBP (cost, benefit, and profit) indicators. In the new product development process, entrepreneurs might exercise options of innovation types considering the technology lifecycle as illustrated in Fig. 2.2. However, financially, the underlying challenge in new product development process is optimizing the returns on capital invested, which can be analyzed from the perspective of marketability of the product. Most micro, small, and medium enterprises face challenges in marketing their products and services as the marketing strategies are often not competitive and customer-centric. To stay competitive in the market, these enterprises must develop strategies that support an advanced marketing-mix (11Ps) comprising product, price, place, promotion, packaging, pace, people, performance, psychodynamics, posture, and proliferation. These strategies help firms enhance their proximity and geo-demographic outreach to acquire customers and create value. Investment in branding is essential to create product-driven impact and competitiveness in the market. Start-up enterprises get into the Blue Ocean Strategy, which is of high risk and challenging, to create their uniqueness within the industry and market. Blue Ocean Strategy refers to a market for a product that has near monopolistic attributes or very less competition. This strategy revolves around searching for a business in which very few firms operate and where there is no pricing pressure in the initial stages of its lifecycle. Over time, these firms may exert in co-creating innovative products with the internal and external stakeholders and develop market-centric business models. Established firms are also engaged in developing consortium production practices by engaging other firms as partners in manufacturing and marketing. Moving to growth and maturity stages, firms are able to develop local–global convergence through strategic alliances, which helps them in carrying out both vertical (by portfolios) and horizontal (by geographic coverage) expansion. Overall, the critical success factors for entrepreneurial firms to grow in a competitive marketplace require continuous knowledge, contemporary skills, and cost-effective practices with high leadership skills and desired efficacy in leader-member exchange (LMX). Entrepreneurial firms should develop business continuity plans to overcome unexpected risks and develop optimization strategies in production and operations by reducing costs.

Social media and digital networks help firms in crowdsourcing the ideation process for innovation. The experience sharing and collective thinking is a process of psychodynamics that helps companies work with the crowd-based business model. Social learning and perceptual semantics through the crowdsourcing is used to identify PNS (problems, needs, and solutions) factors to develop the customer-centric strategies. In addition, user-generated contents and wisdom of crowds help firms in implementing crowd-based business models. The community workplace provides the scope of organic thinking among the employees and stakeholders, which helps in developing inclusivity in business. Organic thinking is like brainstorming, which emerges out of interaction with peers and proactive debates in the community workplace. Organic thoughts are born out of thematic interactions within the society, organization, and teams, when inflow of thoughts is supported by the mental space and freedom of expression. The organic thinking helps companies discover, define, and develop semantics, and deliver the concepts and applications on the problems, needs, and solutions (PNS) related to the stakeholders, customers, and society at large. Proactive learning, thematic interactions, and collective intelligence help community workplaces to serve as a vital organizational source for ideation, thought processing, innovation, commercialization, and profit making. The 4D design factors include the challenge to discover the right perspectives considering the problems, needs, and desired solutions (PNS factors) required by the users. The PNS factors can be discovered by perceptual mapping of users and through the semantics (interrelated thoughts).

Convergence of digital empowerment, design thinking, and proximity to society and business need to be laid on the quadratic P4 factors comprising Proximity, Privacy, Permissions, and Performance. The proximity of firms within society enables people to get together, converse, and prioritize the common PNS factors to guide firms to acculturate business and marketing strategies accordingly. Collective intelligence addresses the PNS factors, which include problems, needs, and solutions, to co-create innovative products through collective problem-solving approaches. Collective intelligence typically addresses the optimal design to develop new products and diffuse information through communication networks to wider consumer outreach. Accordingly, firms can streamline the flow of collective intelligence, and learn about the PNS factors and the acquired needs of the consumers to develop appropriate marketing strategies. However, as firms tend to invest resources in acquiring new customers by narrowing down the proximity gap and launching relationship programs to boost the consumer outreach campaign, there is a possibility of chaos with the predefined segments. Four A's comprising awareness (PNS factors of stakeholders), attributes (preferred solutions), affordability (cost of technology), and adaptability (technology acceptance) remain central to the development of social technology. Depending on the PNS factors, collective intelligence, and social consciousness about the products and services, firms need different partners at varying distances to collaborate and co-create products and services. For example, Nestlé in India has introduced varied options for its baby food brands Cerelac and Nestum by understanding the problems, needs, and expected solutions for mothers across the multicultural communities. The company has modified its offerings of mono-grain, milk-based baby food in both brands. The company learned the single cereal and milk-base requirements by enhancing the proximity to consumers by geographic regions in

India, which enabled the company to target specific cereals in preferred regions like Nestum Rice (southern market), Nestum Wheat (central and northern market), and Nestum Corn in the parts of the Western markets of the country.

Therefore, geographical proximity is an essential approach for the firms to explore PNS factors and possibilities to co-create innovative products. Firms can gain access to new consumer segments and markets through geographically distant partners to develop new products. However, customer-centric firms usually resort to partners with close geographical proximity. The social proximity can be used by the firms as a collective tool to discover PNS factors, design innovative solutions, develop products, services, and co-create marketing strategies, and deliver them effectively to the target consumers.

Driving Entrepreneurial Innovations

Many innovations are emerging in the market that are simplified or are scaling down on improving the existing products or services and positioning them as innovations. However, managers may align their business strategies with the competitive advantages of markets and manage innovation in emerging economies to diffuse and commercialize. Though the firms may develop efficiency with regard to the above strategic positions of product/market, knowledge, and innovation independently, they are still risk-averse with the innovation. Most companies pay attention toward stakeholder engagement to manage innovation in entrepreneurial ventures. The open innovation based on crowdsourcing and crowdfunding concept appears complementary to the prospective collaborative efforts of micro, small, and medium enterprises with their primary and secondary stakeholders. The stakeholder engagement helps companies in cost and risk control, and in streamlining the sharing of knowledge and other resources for innovation management. Stakeholder engagement is implicitly understood as an umbrella concept for communication, collaboration, mutual understanding, and partnership between the firm and the collaborators.

Thinking of an innovation is easy, but making the same work is a challenging task. A cost-effective innovation in the consumer-products sector is reaching popularity in developing countries and emerging markets, where entrepreneurs face global challenges amidst paucity of resources, but hold high market potentials. Such innovations offer low-cost solutions, but exhibit attributes of being robust, consumer-friendly, and having high sales potential at the large and bottom of the pyramid market segments. Social innovation integrates social entrepreneurship and cooperative-network by investigating the product attractiveness, technology, and process innovation investments of social enterprises on social and environmental outcomes. Social innovation is central to understanding the market, in the context of needs of different stakeholders and expected benefit from co-creation. It fosters cooperation and social engagement by the enterprises and the social actors with whom firms intend to co-create a social outcome and business impact.[24] Team culture in organizations encourages functional autonomy among the employees to express their ideas, learn voluntarily, and experiment with innovation in management on a pilot basis. However, employee autonomy needs a strict accountability for results, and for the actions and behaviors that deliver those results. Therefore, organizations enforce tough monitoring and evaluation practices with measurable objectives for the employees to work in teams and enjoy autonomy.

Integrating people with business to achieve profit-with-purpose and social values has encouraged service-led growth through practical techniques. Collective intelligence has encouraged low-cost service innovation by integrating the following elements of *services ecosystem*[25]:

4As Awareness (collective intelligence), attributes (need-based design), affordability (cost-effective services), and adaptability (social and economic stimuli to consume services)

4Cs Customer cost (tangible and intangible costs), convenience (availability and perceived ease of use), communication (transparency and clarity in user-generated contents), and conflict resolution (customer relationship management)

4Vs Value (customer and social values), validity (collective decision), venue (social marketing of services), and vogue (value and lifestyle)

---

[24] Cajaiba-Santana, G. (2014). Social innovation: Moving the field forward. A conceptual framework. *Technological Forecasting and Social Change*, 82 (1), 42–51.

[25] Rajagopal. (2021). *Crowd-based business models: Using collective intelligence for market competitiveness*. Cham, Switzerland: Springer.

4Es   Exploitability (crowd-based innovation), expansion (improvements in services and processes), experience (sharing with community), and emotions (sense of belongingness with crowd-based services design)

4Is   Interest (public interest), information (crowd-based, recurring, and strategic), image (social and personal congruence), and implementation (people-led growth)

4Ms   Marketing of services (strategic and tactical focus), mobility (geo-demographic fit), management (crowd- and social governance), and maintenance (public-private partnership)

Services are intangible and dynamic, which need periodic user intervention to improve in real time using affordable technology and design driven by the crowd. Most product innovations unlike services focus on partial dynamic attributes like pricing and promotion, which have an impact on the commercialization of innovated products. The product designs are relatively static with predetermined physical properties. Services are largely driven by the experience and emotion. In managing any innovative products in the market, the innovation value chain needs to be carefully developed and implemented for consumers, market players, and stakeholders of the company. The value chain comprises the main phases of innovation including idea generation, conversion, and diffusion. Besides determining the appropriate innovation management strategies, firms need to evaluate the consistency among the ideas and their anticipated perceived values among consumers. Therefore, selecting ideas and investing on them, and converting and marketing ideas are complex. With the advancement of human interface on social media, the trend of developing frugal innovations within organization has been reverted to open platforms, which allows the voice of customers to be analyzed. The views of customers and stakeholders on developing new products have enhanced the scope of collective growth of firms in the niche market as compared to the conventional abilities of reaching the goals through in-company efforts. Teams confined to the corporate limits are also likely to overvalue the ideas they come up with, without exploring the market from the customers' perspectives.

Collective intelligence (crowdsourcing) helps to enhance the ideation process on socially sustainable business projects and leads to frugal or low-cost innovations. Frugal innovation is often associated with sustainability (ecological and social) as it is developed with an objective of minimizing the use of resources (raw material, production resources, energy, fuel, water, waste, financial resources) and maximizing the output within the given space, time, and application limitations. Frugal innovations are affordable and easily accessible as compared to conventional innovations.[26] Frugal innovation is the process of reducing the complexity and cost by taking cost-effective measures in manufacturing and following economies of scale. Usually, this refers to removing some conspicuous features from the product, such as an automobile, in order to market it in bottom of the pyramid markets and emerging markets. Designing products for such markets may also call for an increase in the sustainability of innovative products and selling through modern routes to market. However, profits earned on frugal innovations are much lower than high value–high technology innovative products targeted to the up-front or premier markets.

Managing frugal innovations through crowdsourcing is critical to the success of the competitive growth of the firm in the niche marketplace. The economic value of an innovation remains latent until it is commercialized in some way via a business model. Successful commercialization of an innovation leads to breakthrough in two different ways: in some instances, an innovation can employ a business model, which is already familiar to the firm; while in others, a company has a business model that can make use of the innovation by licensing to third parties. Most micro, small, and medium enterprises largely depend on the crowdsourced ideas to develop frugal innovations through crowdfunded business models to penetrate niche markets and later move to the wider competitive markets. The frugal innovations are defined as low-cost differentiators toward simplifying product attributes by optimizing its functions, components, and processes while maximizing its perceived use values. As consumers today have to live with complex products such as automobiles and smartphones, the frugal innovations do provide competitive leverage to them in view of their value for money. Consequently, the concept of frugal innovations emphasizes a relatively complex but less expensive product to cater to the unserved low-end of the mass market and bottom of the pyramid

---

[26] Weyrauch, T., & Herstatt, C. (2016). What is frugal innovation? Three defining criteria. *Journal of Frugal Innovation*, 2 (1), 1–17.

segments.[27] Innovative products tend to fail in the market not only due to technical inadequacies but also because of a lack of enough groundwork in the market.

Social innovation is driven by three principal domains comprising the social domain, entrepreneurial domain, and public domain, which determine the nature of social and business entrepreneurship and transformational leadership. The factors embedded in these domains influence the crowd-based business modeling for carrying out social innovation. The social services needed to support innovation in various sectors such as health, housing, education, and transportation call for social innovations through the support of the public domain. The social domain intends to promote sustainability-led businesses and drive bottom-up (local) economy. The public domain drives social innovation through collective intelligence (crowdsourcing) for ideation and contextual information pooling, and crowdfunding to co-create and coevolve crowd-based business models. Regulatory policies of crowdfunding and other financial regulations are implemented by the governments and central banks in developed and developing nations. Social entrepreneurship combines the resourcefulness of traditional entrepreneurship with a mission toward social development. The major concerns on resources management, frugal innovations, and their marketability approaches constitute the entrepreneurial domain, which contributes also to value chain management among the key business partners including customers. Local enterprises managing social innovations also engage in building strategic alliances with large companies. In addition, exploring community solutions and industry attractiveness attributes create pull effects for social innovation through crowdfunding, while enforcement of public policies and international funding and business trends drive the push effect to encourage social innovation under the public domain.

Advancement of information technology has been radically adapted to the social and frugal innovations. The crowdfunding process has been leveraged by such technological advancement. Over time, companies evaluate the threats and opportunities of crowdfunding, and create new business options for the more-connected future of digital ecosystems. Consequently, many social innovation companies such as Uber, Airbnb,

---

[27] Lim, C., & Fujimoto, T. (2019). Frugal innovation and design changes expanding the cost-performance frontier: A Schumpeterian approach. *Research Policy*, 48 (4), 1016–1029.

and Amazon are doing business successfully with the support of digitization, which offers opportunities for companies to leverage strong customer relationships and increase cross-selling. Simultaneously, many companies are deriving real value from social business using social media, social software, and technology-based social networks to enable relationships among people, information, and social capital. Social businesses play an important role in decision-making to maintain the quality of life in most rural and sub-urban population segments. It is estimated in some research studies that incremental improvements to the existing social business practices contribute to positive business outcomes, and deliver benefits associated with the social business at the stage of maturity. The continuous improvement in social businesses requires a substantial change.

Human Element in Operational Linkages

The bottom-line in business is shifting rapidly since the mid-twentieth century with the advancement of information technology and changing business philosophy. The bottom-line of business has moved over time from aggressive manufacturing to market competition, to supply-led business models, and to customer-centric business focus. With the extensive usage of social media by firms and people, companies have learned to follow a new pace in business led by the voice of crowd and collective intelligence. Consequently, the bottom-line of the business today is shifted to a functional combination of People, Accountability, Control, and Transformation (PACT), which has constituted the quadruple bottom-line in business. PACT has induced people (crowd comprising potential consumers, technocrats, creative business thinkers, stakeholders, potential investors, market operations players, and existing customers) to actively participate in the business processes. People tend to suggest transforming the existing businesses to profitable ventures through cocreation and coevolution. Most value-based businesses contribute effectively to the manufacturing process (engagement of farmer-members of agribusiness and dairy cooperatives in India, Japan, Israel, and other countries in production and business operations) and stimulate agile business prospects through open innovation, neurobehavioral analysis, and learning from social interventions. The social utility of trust considers that firms selling 'fair trade', 'organic', or other socially beneficial products must be congruent to the neuro-behavior of consumers based on the social stimuli. The cooperative and network marketing practices have witnessed such effects of social motivation on the neuro-behavior of consumers.[28] Refurbishing business with collective intelligence, social values, and neurobehavioral analytics helps companies to increase their business performance by introducing strategic engagement of stakeholders with the manufacturing and operational processes.[29]

Increasingly, manufacturers and customers co-create products and services to support co-marketing partnerships. Such a philosophy of involving stakeholders in manufacturing and marketing process has reflected in the concept of 'design-to-market' and 'go-to-market' in the dynamic competition. Most firms develop differentiated products efficiently, make their manufacturing processes flexible, and achieve higher market share. These firms attain higher product-marketing strength in the market as they focus on developing one product at a time, and share components and production processes across a platform of products.[30] The customer-centric strategies define co-production and co-creation as the phenomena that are key to developing integrated marketing communication. In other words, how companies deal with their customers through customer participation in the joint creation of communication value needs to be understood by the firms.[31] Major business trends such as decentralized business model, collective businesses, localized production and marketing, technological convergence, and hybrid business models have transformed the roles of companies from profit to people orientation. Business practitioners and scholars have contributed significantly to the management research on coevolved and alliances structure of organizations, consortium production and network marketing, and collaboration among companies. However, companies often ignore investment in customer relationship and co-creation perspectives and fail

---

[28] Lee, N., Broderick, A. J., & Chamberlain, L. (2007). What is 'neuromarketing'? A discussion and agenda for future research. *International Journal of Psychophysiology*, 63 (2), 199–204.

[29] Hawkins, G. (2001). Plastic bags: Living with rubbish. *International Journal of Cultural Studies*, 4 (1), 5–23.

[30] Rajagopal. (2019). *Transgenerational marketing: Evolution, expansion, and experience*. New York: Palgrave Macmillan.

[31] Vargo, S. L., & Lusch, R. F. (2004). Evolving to a new dominant logic for marketing. *Journal of Marketing*, 68 (1), 1–17.

to transform the operational system by knowing the cognitive developments among stakeholders.

Most studies on people or crowd-based business modeling focus on co-created and coevolved supply chains and production systems focusing on the agile marketing approach. Agile marketing represents a lean and flexible marketing management approach based on an array of customer-centric practices aimed at developing a compliant and acquiescent marketing approaches. Notably, agile marketing encourages the firm's inclusive teams (inducting customers and stakeholders) to work together on common objectives centered on the problems, needs, and desired solutions of customers and stakeholders. Periodical update on the customer needs, preferences, and opinions on various marketing touchpoints (marketing-mix elements, and value perspectives) help companies optimize their agile marketing operations. Accordingly, effective customer engagement, sustainable value, and higher market demand can be achieved by the firms.[32] Firms encourage stakeholder engagement in entrepreneurial manufacturing and marketing operations and use of technology in managing both manufacturing and marketing operations. Business modeling for entrepreneurial products of MSMEs largely focuses on both business-to-consumers and business-to-business activities (by serving as feeder firms to large industrial firms). Successful entrepreneurial firms knit their marketing strategies around 11Ps as detailed below:

- Product—sustainable, organic, attractive, innovation, social need-based, utilitarian
- Price—affordable, competitive
- Place—availability, backward and forward logistics, niche markets, proximity
- Promotion—diet concept, social value, value and lifestyle, ethnicity, anthropomorphic perceptions, endorsements
- Packaging—sustainable, green effect, circular economy based, recycled
- Pace—first-mover advantage, psychosocial standing, top-of-the-mind memory

---

[32] Xu, H., Guo, H., Zhang, J., & Dang, A. (2018). Facilitating dynamic marketing capabilities development for domestic and foreign firms in an emerging economy. *Journal of Business Research*, 86, 141–152.

- People—consumer education, customer advocacy, motivators, gatekeepers, community and family
- Performance—success stories, visual information, evidence-based marketing
- Psychodynamics—social networks, interpersonal communication, digital forums
- Posture—social values, social branding, sustainability, people, global values
- Proliferation—diversification in sustainability activities

It is a big challenge to develop market competitiveness in MSMEs, as it is complex to make decision along the cost-time-risk-profit matrix related to the social products and services. The buying power of customers determines the extent to which they retain most of the value created for themselves. The threat of substitutes determines the extent to which some other product can meet the same buyer's needs and places a ceiling on the amount a buyer is willing to pay for an industry's product. Consumers gain power when they have choices when their needs can be met by a substitute product or by the same product offered by another company. In addition, high buyer concentration, threat of backward integration, and low switching costs add to buyer power. Customer satisfaction is largely value-driven, and it has been observed that the values generate customer loyalty over the period. However, not all loyal customers are profitable and not all profitable customers are loyal.[33]

Most MSMEs develop design-to-market strategies in view of the lessons learned from market competition and their experience in managing niche market strategies. The design-to-market strategies over time become a common practice as entrepreneurial marketing. Accordingly, entrepreneurs follow bottom-up approach by choosing the target market or segment in the beginning and later explore the needs and demands of their targeted segment through personal relations to serve them efficiently.[34] The entrepreneurial marketing approach involves cost-effective activities by avoiding formal market research or involving mass

---

[33] Rajagopal. (2019). *Contemporary marketing strategy: Analyzing consumer behavior to drive managerial decision making.* New York: Palgrave Macmillan.

[34] Stokes, D. (2000). Putting entrepreneurship into marketing: The process of entrepreneurial marketing. *Journal of Research in Marketing and Entrepreneurship,* 2 (1), 1–16.

promotions strategies to promote business. However, entrepreneurs of small and medium business segments significantly depend on their personal networks to collect information about consumers and the market. These entrepreneurs heavily use consumer psychodynamics and interpersonal communication such as word-of-mouth to promote their products and services.[35] The social facet of entrepreneurship education has closer proximity to innovation diffusion and business modeling as compared to the formal teaching pedagogy or regulatory education to entrepreneurs. Though regulatory and social environment resources are external to entrepreneurship education, they can be purposely integrated and aligned with the entrepreneurial touchpoints to expand and enhance customers' journeys, customer experience, and marketability of their products or services in emerging markets.[36]

Going global is an easy process for firms. Firms need to simulate the impact of their business in global market in reference to their resources, target markets, and operational efficiency. Most firms concentrate on product markets considering the customers, who seek benefits or to be served with the same products, services, innovation, and technology regardless of the geo-demographic differences and cognitive behavior. There are a number of paradoxes in communicating the product-marketing strategies in the global marketplace. It is imperative to enhance the market competitiveness of micro, small, and medium enterprises, which requires enabling innovation and technology with adequate finance and institutional structures including human capital. Continuous innovation helps these enterprises stay competitive and transform into an agent of reverse globalization. MSMEs must embrace global changes in cultural norms so that they can develop market competitiveness in reference to quality, price, and services to survive and find a place for themselves in the global competitive environment.[37] Conventional MSMEs in developing countries search for businesses with low labor costs and the availability of high volume of workers to effectively reduce costs and maximize

---

[35] Copley, P. (2013). The need to deliver higher-order skills in the context of marketing in SMEs. *Industry and Higher Education,* 27 (6), 465–476.

[36] Homburg, C., Jozić, D., & Kuehnl, C. (2017). Customer experience management: Toward implementing an evolving marketing concept. *Journal of the Academy of Marketing Science,* 45 (3), 377–401.

[37] Anand, B. (2015). Reverse globalization by internationalization of SME's: Opportunities and challenges ahead. *Procedia—Social and Behavioral Sciences,* 195, 1003–1011.

their returns on investment. Such business philosophy forces these enterprises to develop their short-run business models to implement at lower costs and satisfy consumer demands, remain competitive, and retain profitability. This appears to be highly challenging, and for many MSMEs it is impossible to achieve such goals and change traditional production methods to a new manufacturing model that improves production efficiency, decreases labor costs, and solves the environmental issues.[38]

Small firms operating in niche markets often face the problems of conventional manufacturing processes, obsolete technologies, capital limitations, and lack of updated knowledge. These attributes drive firms to compromise with the product quality and stay non-competitive in the regional or global markets. Such business confinement needs small firms in emerging markets to coevolve with large firms and catch-up with them to improve the manufacturing and marketing processes, and improve productivity rather than engaging in frugal innovations for niche markets.[39] Small firms in emerging economies often face the challenge to break the *glass ceiling* to explore market competitiveness with the frugal innovation strategies and develop tactical marketing approaches to override close business rivals. MSMEs often fail in establishing the regional or global value chains and enhancing their business performance.[40]

---

[38] Tsai, W. H., & Jhong, S. Y. (2019). Production decision model with carbon tax for the knitted footwear industry under activity-based costing. *Journal of Cleaner Production*, 207, 1150–1162.

[39] Awate, S., Larsen, M. M., & Mudambi, R. (2015). Accessing vs sourcing knowledge: A comparative study of R&D internationalization between emerging and advanced economy firms. *Journal of International Business Studies*, 46 (1), 63–86.

[40] McDermott, G. A., & Corredoira, R. A. (2010). Network composition, collaborative ties, and upgrading in emerging-market firms: Lessons from the Argentine auto parts sector. *Journal of International Business Studies*, 41 (2), 308–329.

CHAPTER 3

Entrepreneurial Behavior

Artisanal pedigree is an evolutionary map of the entrepreneurs, their skill development, and the growth of entrepreneurial firm over temporal and spatial dimensions. This chapter discusses the artisanal pedigree in the context of evolution of entrepreneurship within the vertical and horizontal domains as a cause and effect of leadership, decision processes and strategies, gender perspectives, economic dependencies (on financial programs, subsidies, infrastructure, and marketing support) and impetus for exploring opportunities and growth. Entrepreneurial mindset can be understood in terms of thoughts, feelings, and actions, implying thinking, feeling, and action in entrepreneurship process. The principal elements of entrepreneurial behavioral mindset comprising business focus, creativity, effective implementation, social networking, resource leveraging, and mobilizing key partners determine the human element in enterprise management are also discussed in this chapter.

In the shopping perspective today, the term family business reminds of small enterprises with contemporary visions of mom-and-pop firms focused on a niche. Commonly, the family business enterprises possess family values, leadership pedigree, and are spread across family-owned manufacturing, marketing, and services activities at the local market. These firms operate in a minimum viable segment and are conservative in their entrepreneurial culture. Consequently, they are hard on accepting

© The Author(s), under exclusive license to Springer Nature Switzerland AG 2024
Rebuilding Entrepreneurship at the Grassroots, Palgrave Studies of Entrepreneurship and Social Challenges in Developing Economies, https://doi.org/10.1007/978-3-031-43270-5_3

change management and radical decision-making to stay competitive in the dynamic marketplace. The family-controlled companies play a significant role in both the local and global business environment. They not only include extensive corporations like Walmart and Tata Group but also account for more than one-third of firms across countries with sales of various volumes in the big-middle and bottom of the pyramid market segments.[1] Family businesses in the developing countries have grown manifold in response to the emerging competition and increasing managerial efficiency of the new generations of their management. Firms with the family business origins are focused on stakeholder value and committed to continuous innovation by involving stakeholders.[2] The combination of business functions and the family system offers family-centered behavioral choices that mediate the relationship among family, firm, and stakeholders. Involvement of stakeholder in managing business firms and developing strategies helps in building image of the family firms. Involvement of internal stakeholders in the family business company resulting from transgenerational succession rebuilds the family-centered ethics, financial goals, and skills on business operations and influences the proposal of business alliances to enhance the family firm image. These businesses face generational gaps in management as the new generations are guided by the contemporary market competition, innovation, and technology. However, limitation of resources and family's willingness to realign the business ties with new-generation companies have appeared as major obstacles in improving business performance. For example, in transitional economies such as Asia, Latin America, and Eastern Europe; technology adaptation and developing 'design-to-market' strategies are necessary for the family businesses to fit into the changing market environment. Notion of family in business management is not viewed equally positively in developed countries, where family firms have historically experienced high levels of cronyism, Powerful and wealthy family businesses are often weak in following the ethical codes as family ownership

---

[1] Kachaner, N., Stalk, G., & Bloch, A. (2012). What you can learn from family business. *Harvard Business Review*, 90 (11), 102–106.

[2] Binz-Astrachan, C., Botero, I., Astrachan, J. H., & Prügl, R. (2018). Branding the family firm: A review, integrative framework proposal, and research agenda. *Journal of Family Business Strategy*, 9 (1), 3–15.

and involvement are likely to have a strong niche of social networks.[3] The trans-generational skills in the management of family businesses usually rework on the vision, mission, and goals of the company over time.

Artisanal Pedigree

Family businesses are knitted around generations of in-family stakeholders in business, which often restrict the evolution of business philosophies and operational designs to stay competitive in the marketplace. Despite complexities in management, there has been a brisk growth in family businesses in the twenty-first century. These companies constitute a more significant part of regional economies in emerging markets. Family business firms have strong personal relationships with stakeholders, and they build value chain in the niche markets. As these enterprises operate in a niche, they have been proved to be resilient in the competition with the multinational companies. Family businesses may be advantageous in emerging markets where the conventions of commercial laws and corporate identity are less developed. The social reputation of family can signal greater accountability in business and exhibit stronger commitment. Collectivism is commonly observed in conventional cultures that express pride, loyalty, and cohesiveness in an enterprise. Such a family philosophy helps entrepreneurs to manage businesses against the odds in individualistic cultures.[4] Family ownership of large corporations is maintained today in many destinations through holding companies' agreements, equity holdings, and allocation of equities using multiple voting powers. This allows the founders of family business and their stakeholders to raise resources from financial markets. However, they keep controlling the company through ownership rights and reserves of only a small fraction of the share capital. The decision-making in family-owned companies is faster than in large corporations. An owner-manager in family business firms can move faster than an executive hired from outside. Business decisions in these firms do not pass through a long chain of command or

---

[3] Botero, I. C. (2014). Effects of communicating family ownership and organizational size on an applicant's attraction to a firm: An empirical examination in the USA and China. *Journal of Family Business Strategy*, 5 (2), 184–196.

[4] House, R. J., Hanges, P. J., Javidian, M., Dorfman, P. W., & Gupta, V. (2004). *Culture, leadership, and organizations: The GLOBE study of 62 societies.* Thousand Oaks, CA: Sage Publications.

the board. Family-owned businesses can therefore expand quickly irrespective of the quick pay off of new ventures. The owner-managers are largely relieved of the short-term benchmarks to define performance as their conventional wisdom is often stronger in doing business.

The family firms aim at expanding businesses without fragmenting ownership and allocating new equities to stakeholders or assuming big debts. In order to be successful as a company and allow the family to grow, a family business needs to meet the intertwined challenges of achieving strong business performance and keeping the family committed to, and capable of, carrying on the business in succession to the founder. As family businesses expand geo-demographically, they face challenges in achieving desired performance and corporate governance. The next generations that take over the business governance from the founder and predecessors, may deviate from the predefined goals of the enterprise. In addition, due to the exponential increase of family stakeholders across generations, with few oriented in doing business, the commitment toward enterprise deteriorates. A general assessment on family businesses found that less than 30% of family enterprises survive into the third generation of family ownership[5] A distributor of lubricants and owner of a petrol pump based in Alwar, Rajasthan, India, was a family business firm since 1953. In this firm, a family member oversaw daily operations, who had expanded the business significantly after the multinational players penetrated the Indian lubricant market. In 2013, this owner-partner was looking at ways to involve his children in the family business. Among many, the major dilemma in this family firm was about the distribution of business, governance, and building business-specific leadership. In an indecisive leadership stake, many children of family business owners launch their careers inside the firm jeopardizing the business and profit goals, and organizational design. Though it is advisable for the family firms to encourage succession appellants to build a substantial career outside the firm before they boomerang in nearer to midcareer. Firms should plan ahead to help them do this and restructure the existing

---

[5] Caspar, C., Dias, A. K., & Elstrodt, H. P. (2010). *The five attributes of enduring family business*. New York: McKinsey & Co.

organogram to their potential roles to serve other than the chief executive position. Accordingly, the family business firms should create a formal plan to help them develop the skills and talents they will need to succeed.[6]

A family business in a socioeconomic context may be defined as an owner-led business proposition within a given cultural environment. However, understanding the family and its objectives is crucial to the vision of a family firm.[7] Families and firms become so intertwined that they often cause family conflicts or disruptions in business relationships. This has been the principal cause of failure of firms and fragmentation of stakeholder equities. During the early industrialization period of the twentieth century, family businesses were confined to a niche with restricted growth opportunities. These firms were less predictable due to uncertainty and poor property rights. Such attributes of family firms became central to their performance, which led to further complexities, acquisitions by larger firms, or foreclosures. As the legislation on family rights improved by the mid-twentieth century in developing countries, their business portfolios got stabilized, and the firms could improve managerial competencies. Over time, they were equipped with resources, technology, and managerial know-how to break the niche and expand their businesses in diverse portfolios.

The transgenerational evolution in family firms is widely based on the business philosophies nurtured in the family. The first generation of family business is built on the business goals and ethos of the owner-founder. Firms of this generation own major business equities among the family members and are based on family values. Individual leadership governs the firm through the asymmetric business plans, which are outlined informally. Family firms initially grow in a niche market with high public relations and low profit-high business values domain founded on welfare business philosophies. However, individualism in leadership often turns subjective in the family firms. As the entrepreneurs take over the family firm in its second generation, they review the experience of previous generation and revise the business model from value orientation to profit-centric approach. The transgenerational gap between the first and second generations usually requires moderate changes in business

---

[6] Bruehl, S., & Lachenauer, R. (2018). *How family business owners should bring the next generation into the company*. Cambridge, MA: Harvard Business School Press.

[7] Aldrich, H. E., & Cuff, J. E. (2003). The pervasive effects on entrepreneurship: Embeddedness perspective. *Business Venturing*, 18 (5), 573–596.

processes. The immediate next generation leaders after owner-founder tend to modify family-centered control, and encourage incremental innovation to improve the market performance of products and services of the firm. Streamlining the financial flows, documentation of business activities, and decentralizing the business controls are taken up on priority by the second-generation leadership of family firms. Family and leadership play a significant role in entrepreneurship. The factors affecting the artisanal pedigree in evolving entrepreneurship and its business growth are exhibited in Fig. 3.1.

Most entrepreneurs emerge from the family businesses and outgrow as leaders in the original or diversified firms out of the family business units. Entrepreneurs evolve from the artisanal pedigree of a family business or consistent leadership over the generations as illustrated in Fig. 3.1. Alike genealogy of culture, trade and skills can also be mapped to explore entrepreneurship attributes from the family in a geo-demographic segment. Artisanal trades are nurtured over generations in a family, which can be evidenced in an occupational pedigree of a family. The occupational skills are usually evolved and adapted to the contemporary entrepreneurial ecosystem to some extent. The intervention of information and communication technology, advanced manufacturing processes, artificial intelligence, and accessibility to the Internet has significantly affected the entrepreneurial capabilities and competencies. Consequently, variability and entrepreneurial cognition, economic orientation, and business modeling exhibit variability against the artisanal genealogy within a family. This results in cultural exchange involving mobility, a stance of openness, higher proximity to market, and a sense of inter-connectedness with external resources and alliances.[8] Accordingly, shifts in the transfer of knowledge, skills, and occupational take place, which eventually override the family-based, learned culture in entrepreneurial trades. One of the principal push factors in the artisanal pedigree is leadership, which can be either patriarchic or matriarchic. Transgenerational leadership builds skills in leader–member exchange, governance, and decision-making, which not only build capabilities and competencies but also qualify the entrepreneurs in the succession of a family business.

The leadership skills imparted to the successors of family business affect both entrepreneurial operations and transformational frameworks

---

[8] Johnson, P. C. (2014). Cultural literacy, cosmopolitanism and tourism research. *Annals of Tourism Research*, 44, 255–269.

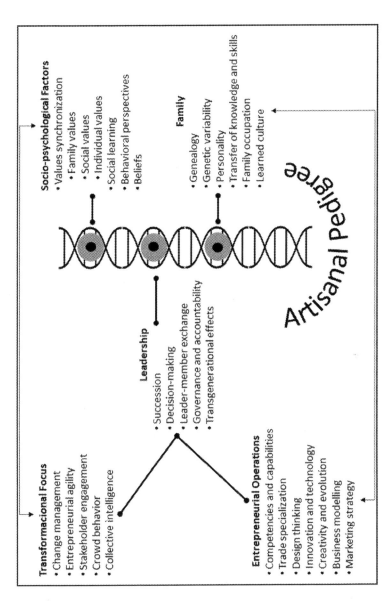

Fig. 3.1 Outgrowth of entrepreneurship from the family pedigree (*Source* Author)

as showed in Fig. 3.1. It affects trade specialization with improved design thinking process (human-centered innovation culture and processes), creativity, and market-driven business modeling. Key elements of the design thinking process include the rapid cyclicality of concepts and tests to drive early and frequent interaction with customers and reinforce agile process design with less hierarchy. Unlike conventional enterprises, entrepreneurs evolved within the changing business ecosystem and adapt to a learning-by-doing approach that involves building prototypes and creating mock-ups of any kind at the earliest in the process to stay competitive in the market.[9] Many new-generation entrepreneurs manage family businesses with a contemporary transformational view by focusing on entrepreneurial agility and stakeholder engagement to create disruptive changes in operations and process. The radical shifts in enterprise management today also rely on collective intelligence and analysis of crowd behavior. With the advancement of information and communication technology, it has been observed as a radical social phenomenon that entrepreneurial power is enhanced through the collective wisdom of crowds. It is the crowd-expressed opinions lying deep inside the firm's database, which helps in market-driven decisions overriding the managerial taboos of conventional family business. Consequently, social media- and information networking-led new tools are allowing firms to mine their data for the unconscious wisdom of crowd for effective and real-time decision marketing in the firm as well as in the marketplace.[10] However, social and psychological factors social, personal, and family values affect to adapt to unconventional changes in the firms after taking over leadership responsibilities in the family firms upon succession.

In transforming the business philosophy of a family firm to a profit-centric domain, the leaders of second-generation shuffle family stakeholders and manage business expansion by administering additional resources. As the family firms grow over generations, they become learning organizations and focus on continuous learning. During the generational transformation process between second and third generations, the successors in family firms try to reduce the family influence,

---

[9] Kupp, M., Anderson, J., & Reckhenrich, J. (2017). Why design thinking in business needs a rethink. *MIT Sloan Management Review*, 59 (1), 42–44.

[10] Ayres, I. (2008). Mining unconscious wisdom. *Harvard Business Review*, 86 (3), 21–23.

outsource human resources, and make efforts in building corporate structure. The next generation business leaders tend to be more transparent in business processes; therefore, they rely on external audits for performance improvement and control. In the following generations, business leaders of family firms make radical changes in their organizational design and business models along with the industrial-revolution over time. In this process, family firms take digitalization initiatives and build alliances with industry to serve as suppliers. The transformed generations of family firms operate on low transactional costs by outsourcing various business functions and rely on external hiring.

The leaders in the generation immediately next to owner-founder tend to modify family-centered control and encourage incremental innovation to improve the market performance of products and services of the firm. Streamlining financial flows, documentation of business activities, and decentralizing the business controls are taken up on priority by the second-generation leadership of family firms. The transgenerational gap between the second and third generation stimulates business leaders for diversifying business and adopting multi-brand, multi-market strategy in the existing and new markets. These companies also develop strategic alliances on production, distribution, technology, and finance with large companies. Transgenerational firms also carry out corporate restructuring and stakeholder management during transitions in business. On a broader business canvas, family businesses reach beyond local mom-and-pop firms and perform significantly on the global stage. Family businesses include also extensive corporations like Walmart (USA), Samsung (South Korea), and Tata Group (India), which account for very high market shares in various industrial portfolios worldwide. A streamlined leadership and strategic vision help traditional, family companies to transform into public companies. Family-controlled companies focus on resilience and strategic visions, not short-term results.[11] The family-run businesses build their resilience using the following managerial standpoints and consequences:

- Family businesses go frugal in economic booms with an objective to earn more profit at relatively low cost.
- They impose restriction on capital expenditures and carry little debt.

---

[11] Kachaner, N., Stalk, G., & Bloch, A. (2012). What you can learn from family business. *Harvard Business Review*, 90 (11), 102–106.

- They are very selective of portfolio and market expansion.
- They acquire fewer and smaller companies, and pilot test their performance in the niche.
- Family business firms are diversified as they strategically invest in building diverse portfolios to secure market share and prevent business risk.
- These companies aim to go global through a hierarchical market expansion.
- They retain talent better as compared to large competitors and manage human resources effectively with streamlined training to augment their competencies.
- Family business firms closely monitor the performance of the company.

The above-discussed standpoints are always challenging as these attributes of a family business do not set a universal pattern. Consequently, family businesses vary by family pedigree and evolution of responsibilities among the members of the family. For example, Babbitt Ranches was a fourth-generation, over a century-old family firm with extensive landholdings in Arizona. The firm has recognized responsibility and obligation to support organizational, ecological, economical, and community values through multiple bottom-line criteria complying with the new business philosophies like triple bottom-line comprising people, planet, and profit. Besides, green consumption and circular economy were also considered as the operational and performance milestones. In addition, the family's heritage has been atop the organizational culture of the firm by designing direct processes, interactions, and critical decisions engaging employees and stakeholders. However, the underlying challenge with the firm was to evaluate the current set of opportunities and to ensure the smooth transitions of real challenges faced by the business head of a fourth-generation family business due to existing fundamental differences in the business perspective.[12]

The next generation executives of family business adapt to improved business practices over time, which are highly non-conventional and different from the foundation philosophy of the family business firms.

---

[12] Majure, L. F., & Savage, K. S. (2010). *Babbitt Ranches: Governance and strategic planning in a family business*. Cambridge, MA: Harvard Business School Press.

Family businesses often face passive organizational responses during merger or acquisition with other firms. Due to wrong organizational design and lack of effective strategies and performance, family business companies often suffer from bitter power that affects its growth. Consequently, most family business firms may succumb to their organizational problems. Under such conditions, family and business transitions are managed through mediation, dialogue, and future role-building. The organizational structure and operational agenda are refurbished upon takeover of the company by merger or acquisition. Hence, adjustment to the new business environment is found to be difficult for the network of family managers, employees, relatives, and business partners. The healthiest transitions involve those old *versus* young struggles, in which both the family managers and the business change alliance partners to converge and explore hybrid path of business performance.[13]

Family-run businesses often run through interpersonal conflicts, which affect the performance of business. Exploring lucrative opportunities for improving family firms becomes a family issue, and managing conflicts on working with the identified opportunity within a family business requires coordinated efforts of stakeholders and customers. Family-based negotiation might also cause workplace disputes.[14] Most firms are shifting their marketing philosophy to customer orientation by offering quality services with the aim to acquire and retain customers in the increasing global competition. Through building personal relationships with existing and potential customers, firms look toward inculcating the customer loyalty. customer-centric firms focus on providing customer services across the table, giving access to comprehensive information that can solve the emerging issues of the customers. Such attention to detail requires well-trained and alert salespeople and efficient back-office personnel. The competitive services-marketing firms try to cultivate relationship competencies by ways of articulating their reasons for customer satisfaction, learn to build pro-customer rationale in resolving post-sales issues, build and

---

[13] Barnes, L. B., & Hershon, S. A. (1976). Transferring power in the family business. *Harvard Business Review*, 54 (4), 105–114.

[14] Sander, F. E. A., & Bordone, R. C. (2006). *All in the family: Managing business disputes with relatives*. Boston, MA: Harvard Business School Publishing.

retain alliances with more powerful customers, and excel in co-creating business culture within their customers.[15]

It has been observed historically in developing economies, family-controlled companies stay resilient to change as these firms focus on short-term gains instead of strategic growth. During economic booms, this approach led them to forgo some opportunities but made these firms stronger during recessions. Consequently, most family firms turn tactical and profit centered instead of developing a long-term business continuity approach. As most such firms are cost-conscious and focus on frugal approaches, they set a high restriction on capital expenditures, and carry small debts to stay financially manageable. As their proximity to the market and other firms within the industry is skewed and narrowed, they avoid mergers and acquisitions, though over time they might takeover smaller companies operating within the niche. Business diversification is very complex for family business firms as they operate with minimum required human resources. Nonetheless, these practices appear to be highly challenging for the stewardship of next generation executives.[16] Change management is one of the most resilient factors in family business, which needs the understanding of the PNS factors for sustained investment in organizational agility, stakeholder-centric growth, and profitability. Many of these families have operated their business under risk for decades and even centuries in emerging and frontier markets. In these situations, family businesses turn more volatile due to radical shifts in consumer behavior, innovation, and supply chain environments.[17]

Leadership

Leadership plays an important role in determining organizational culture, employee motivation, and employee engagement with the enterprise. As micro enterprises base their business model on innovation, the role of leadership has a profound impact on the growth and performance of the organization. Adequate and timely support from leaders results in

---

[15] Isenberg, D. J. (2008), The global entrepreneur. *Harvard Business Review*, 86 (12), 107–111.

[16] Kachaner, N., Stalk, G., & Bloch, A. (2012). What you can learn from family business. *Harvard Business Review*, 90 (11), 102–106.

[17] DeCiantis, D (2022). Building resilience into your family business. *HBR Web Article*. Cambridge, MA: Harvard Business School Press.

higher employee creativity and innovation, which then translates into efficiency, leading to organizational growth.[18] Family entrepreneurial firms can make a high impact on competitive leadership if the firms meticulously explore problems, needs, and solutions (PNS factors) to drive social and emotional impact on consumers. Leadership plays a crucial role in business governance and influences the best practices that are co-created and coevolved within the organization. However, the governance patterns differ with the public (state)-, crowd (community)-, and private-funded business firms. The best practices in business governance irrespective of the size of the firm are largely affected by a collaged system of organizational culture, social conventions, regulations, and a mix of public and private policies. Such governance systems in small and medium companies function with no accepted metric for determining the key performance indicators leading to measuring success. Crowd-based businesses have collective leadership involving stakeholders and externally chosen business leaders (as Chief Executive Officer), which serves as the core decision-making unit. Transformational leadership enables micro, small, and medium enterprises (MSMEs) to lead the stewardship approach. The stewardship approach helps in developing trust among the stakeholders and revises organizational goals to maximize the firm's performance. After the generations of MSMEs being successful, their leaders become the stewards of their communities and gain new economic returns by influencing organizational leadership. As enterprises change from one operational model to a more profitable entrepreneurial model in the next generation, the returns represent the transformation in the business models and leadership. As a result of this transformation, new business strategies and technologies are adopted by the firms and the organizational performance improves. Consequently, entrepreneurs gain better yields by sharing their resources and empowering employees, society, and leaders. The intrinsic and extrinsic motivation helps MSMEs in developing market-led decisions within the societal concerns, power frameworks, value identifications, and stewardship norms.[19]

---

[18] Tung, F. C., & Yu, T. W. (2016). Does innovation leadership enhance creativity in high-tech industries? *Leadership & Organization Development Journal*, 37 (5), 579–592.

[19] Mathias, B. D., Solomon, S. J., & Madison, K. (2017). After the harvest: A stewardship perspective on entrepreneurship and philanthropy. *Journal of Business Venturing*, 32 (4), 385–404.

Capabilities of the leader drive MSME toward their goals by actively involving the employees and stakeholders. The challenges faced by entrepreneurial leaders in the inception of their business include limited resources, innovative products, complications in market penetration and employee motivation, and stakeholder engagement. Additionally, they also need to identify new market opportunities to improve the organizational performance. Entrepreneurial leadership faces challenges related to the leader's decision-making capacity and promoting the collective decision-making process in MSME.[20] Innovation promoted by entrepreneurial leaders is the cornerstone in social, economic, and sustainable value-creation domains. The outlook of entrepreneurial leadership toward value generation creates value from the grassroots of the business environment through innovative products and services. Inter-organizational growth is stimulated by promoting team culture, building employee commitment, and developing positive brand–customer relationship by an effective entrepreneurial leadership style. It also adds value to the innovation-led production process, improves the efficiency of the management of capital and human resources of the MSMEs, and empowers the employees to drive better entrepreneurial performance. However, the latitudinal action of entrepreneurial leaders results in the organizational inertia, and makes complex innovative tasks easier and the decision-making process autonomous, which improves organizational performance.[21]

With the unprecedented shifts in consumer–market relationship, leaders of MSMEs are constantly looking for business models and strategies to be able to adapt to the new 'normal'. Their leaders tend to implement centralized and individualistic decision-making process, instead of decentralized leadership dynamics. The result of this myopic leadership style is obstructed and non-sustainable organizational growth. Therefore, the success of entrepreneurial growth depends on effective leadership dynamics including motivation, accountability, engagement, and value

---

[20] Chen, M. H. (2007). Entrepreneurial leadership and new venture: Creativity in entrepreneurial teams. *Creativity and Innovation management*, 16 (3), 239–249.

[21] Sarabi, A. Froese, F. J., Chng, D. H. M., & Meyer, K. E. (2020). Entrepreneurial leadership and MNE subsidiary performance: The moderating role of subsidiary context. *International Business Review*, 29 (3), https://doi.org/10.1016/j.ibusrev.2020.101672.

propositions.[22] MSMEs innovate not only their products and services but also their business model by gradually shifting their leadership style from individualistic to plural-collective-integrative-transformational leadership. Collective leadership is considered as slow and bureaucratic which hampers fast and precise decision-making.[23] It hinders the growth process instead of accelerating it, which is completely opposite to the agile business model of the MSMEs. Therefore, they adopted integrative leadership to replace the traditional leader–follower relationship with influencer–supporter relationship. Thus, a leader assumes the role of an influencer through his/her behavior, way of communication, and involving team-collaboration, which encourages collective ideas-sharing, employee engagement, and commitment. However, few leaders really become integrative leaders as it requires to maintain a balance between authoritative and collective management. The current emerging enterprises tend to implement transformational leadership style, which links knowledge-sharing and employee management to drive leader-employee communication. Based on social exchange theory, transformational leadership enables entrepreneurs to stimulate intellectual development through employee motivation and collective knowledge-sharing dynamics.[24]

The social governance in crowd-based businesses is more effective than the conventional top-down governance model. Firms experience better performance through collective or coevolved business governance model by inducting customers and crowd-led investors in decision-making and building competitive strategies of the firm. Crowd-based firms aim at motivating behavioral change through collective leadership designed in a democratic pattern with design-to-society and design-to-value business philosophies. However, it is often difficult for firms to sustain the market competition due to the lack of streamlined leadership and a predetermined business philosophy. The major challenge with the crowd-based firms is ensuring performance and competitiveness in the long-run. Most

---

[22] Liu, H., & Li, G. (2018). Linking transformational leadership and knowledge sharing: The mediating roles of perceived team goal commitment and perceived team identification. *Frontiers in Psychology*, 9, Article 1331. https://doi.org/10.3389/fpsyg.2018.01331.

[23] Quick, K. S. (2017). Locating and building collective leadership and impact. *Leadership*, 13 (4), 445–471.

[24] Rajagopal, A. (2021). *Epistemological attributions to entrepreneurial firms: Linking organizational design and operational efficiency*. Cham, Switzerland: Springer.

enterprises are engaged in building inclusiveness in business aiming at earning profit with people, purpose, and sustainability (Triple bottom-line), while some companies tend to complement the business approaches with PACT managerial approach comprising people, reverse accountability, organizational control (social), and transformational initiatives (Quadruple bottom-line). Such stakeholder inclusiveness would lead firms to experience changes in organizational behavior and encourage practices to comply with the triple bottom-line philosophy and PACT approach to coevolve business. The inclusivity approach in business largely promotes team-based work culture and transformational leadership. The social dynamics demand firms to develop businesses by reorienting their philosophy toward design-to-society and design-to-value and develop strategic partnership and corporate alliance with the local bodies to coevolve business.

HUMAN ELEMENT IN ENTERPRISE MANAGEMENT

Leadership should be agile but streamlined, and it should encourage stakeholders to participate in innovation, technology, and new product development. People-led companies adapt to collective leadership and agile business modeling to drive co-creation and coevolution initiatives in MSMEs. Accordingly, the stakeholders (*e.g.*, customers, competitors, suppliers, social organizations, and other institutions) and the key partners play an important role in determining (co-creating), implementing (coevolution), and monitoring (reverse accountability) the performance of businesses. Firms strengthen the relationships among all stakeholders associated with the business organizations, as they increasingly rely on stakeholders within the business ecosystem to co-create and capture value by redesigning inclusive and crowd-based business models.[25] Mary Kay Cosmetics, a women-centric American company, is also coevolving its business by engaging women in marketing its products to improve household income and quality of life through inclusivity in business. These strategies evidence inclusivity in the distribution of products within the community and at the bottom of the pyramid. The first-mover advantage

---

[25] Wei, Z., Song, X., & Wang, D. (2017). Manufacturing flexibility, business model design, and firm performance. *International Journal of Production and Economics*, 193 (1), 87–97.

(pace) is backed by the experience sharing of stakeholders and key business partners on social and digital media channels, while reverse accountability of stakeholders ensures performance of the company embedding the objective of profit-with-purpose. In addition, the psychodynamics (consumer-to-consumer business approach) helps in generating a pull effect in the market by augmenting the demand for the products of the company. The pull effect helps the company to lower the costs of marketing, stay customer-centric, and increase profit over time. The attributes of human elements in MSMEs and their business operations are illustrated in Fig. 3.2.

Human element in business is atop the entrepreneurship across four principal domains comprising enterprise, people, society, and business as exhibited in Fig. 3.2. Personality and attitude of entrepreneurs, relationship quality and outreach, right cognition and reasoning, self-actualization, and social consciousness are some of the distinctive attributes of entrepreneurs. Self-centered and introvert entrepreneurs may not be able to develop appropriate functional connectivity on social platforms and workplace to develop homogeneity across socio-psychological factors. A major challenge in MSMEs is co-creating stakeholder values through employee and customer engagement. Week engagements often hinder these firms from exploring appropriate PNS factors. Successful enterprises at the grassroots grow by adapting to people-centered 5Ts comprising tasks, target, time, thrust, and trust. Collective and team leadership supports to engage in and implement 5Ts which also significantly impacts the organizational culture, governance pattern, and decision-making processes. A people-centered enterprise can build a consistent identity and image to establish its posture within the industry. PACT approach encourages reverse accountability and helps in building stakeholder value. Entrepreneurial firms must develop effective social interactions to understand the crowd behavior and PNS factors and enrich people's perspectives through collective intelligence as illustrated in Fig. 3.2.

Leaders must know their employees and manage effective leader-member exchange to demonstrate a transactional leadership style. The contemporary people-oriented leadership pattern suggests entrepreneurial firms to adapt to a bottom-up approach to put the stakeholder voice first in governing enterprises. This leadership philosophy overrides the typical top-down decision-making approach through a strict hierarchy, which leaves little room for others to engage in innovative or creative

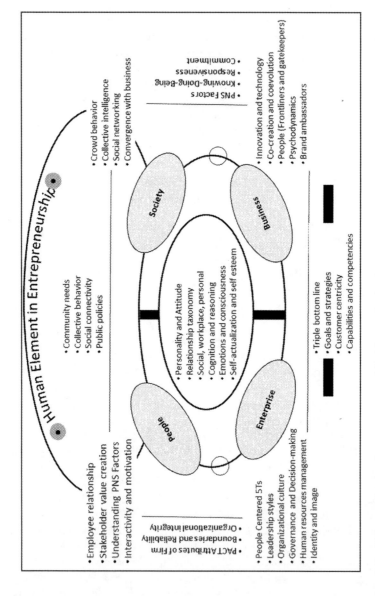

Fig. 3.2 Human element in entrepreneurship (*Source* Author)

thinking or actions. However, it is difficult for the conventional family business leaders, who are tuned to the controlling styles and who share less space with employees and stakeholders to participate in enterprise governance. A few successful entrepreneurs such as Ratan Tata (India) and Sam Walton (US) remained as oligarch entrepreneurs and built their business realm through vertical and horizontal expansions and practiced both top-down and bottom-up leadership styles. Entrepreneurial leadership focuses on the capabilities and competencies to lead others toward the organization's goal and manage resources strategically by utilizing both opportunity-exploring and benefit-seeking behaviors. Transformational leaders encourage organizational members to adapt to both planned and radical change management. Therefore, transformational leadership is viewed as a multifaceted meta-construct, which drives a positive impact on the attitudes, motivation, and performance of both internal and external stakeholders.

The transformational leadership insights in growing organizations encourage inclusivity in workplace and coevolve with the reverse accountability and control. The transformational leadership motivates collective actions on decisions at team workstations with commitment to stay innovative and competitive in the marketplace. Effective leadership also motivates continuous learning for employees and tunes the work culture of the organization with contemporary requirements. The community workplace provides the scope of organic thinking among the employees and stakeholders, which helps in developing inclusivity in business. Organic thinking is like brainstorming, which emerges out of interaction with peers and proactive debates in the community workplace. Organic thoughts are born out of thematic interactions within the society, organization, and teams when inflow of thoughts is supported by the mental space and freedom of expression. Organic thinking helps companies discover, define, and develop semantics, and deliver the concepts and applications on the problems, needs, and solutions (PNS) related to the stakeholders, customers, and society at large. Proactive learning, thematic interactions, and collective intelligence help community workplaces to serve as a vital organizational source for ideation, thought processing, innovation, commercialization, and profit-making.

Entrepreneurial Mindset, Decisions, and Strategies

Entrepreneurial thinking process demands a continuous flow of new ideas. The ideas for innovations are the precious currency of the new market economy but generating them has a mysterious process. Businesses that constantly innovate have systematized the production and testing of new ideas, and the system can be replicated by practically any organization. The best innovators use old ideas as the raw materials for new ideas. Most dynamic enterprises tend to move new ideas from one market to another and intend to build full-fledged consulting groups to refine the thought process and internal knowledge on entrepreneurial leadership by innovations. The most important issue in cultivating such thought process is to strike a balance between the organizational responsiveness to the innovating thinking and organizational work culture.[26] Entrepreneurial mindset involves the ability to rapidly sense, act, and mobilize even under uncertain conditions. Most entrepreneurs learn in a dual process way. This process suggests two-level interactive learning platforms based on the idea of the interaction by means of explicit and implicit learning through reinforcement. It accounts for many unexplained cognitive perceptions and phenomena based on casual and peer interactions. There is often an imbalance between the flow of ideas and implementing them to get solutions in a growing entrepreneurial firm. Entrepreneurs face a problem in fitting the ideas to resolve the complexes in innovation and growth, so most entrepreneurs jump immediately to focusing on crash solutions, devoting little time to analyze why the problem exists in the first place. This is one of the flaws in traditional thinking, which may lead to conclusions without any rationale. In the marketplace today, consistent thinking for continuous innovation becomes increasingly important for the simple reason that the challenges enterprises face are becoming more complex.[27]

Creative thinking in a company drives creative designing to cater to the consumer needs in a technologically feasible and strategically viable way. A good thinking process in a firm may be generated through collaboration between frontline employees and market players including distributors,

---

[26] Keidel, R. W. (2013). Strategy made simple: Think in threes. *Business Horizons*, 56 (1), 105–111.

[27] May, M. E. (2012). *Observe first, design second: Taming the traps of traditional thinking*. Working Paper, Rotman School of Management, April 1.

retailers, and consumers to reengineer the existing products and services or create new ones through innovation and technology. Entrepreneurial thinking should be based on close observation of the demand shifts, competitor's product portfolios, and changes in consumer preferences combined with brainstorming and rapid prototyping of innovative products.[28] The entrepreneurs are largely driven by a vision to create value for customers and earn profit through their applied entrepreneurial skills and customer-centric marketing actions. Entrepreneurship and marketing theories share some commonality as both disciplines focus on identifying opportunities and transforming resources into value-creation or co-creation for consumers. Successful entrepreneurs follow an effectuate route in entrepreneurship.[29] Entrepreneurs carry out thinking process and continuous efforts to improve customer value may be better off than what is prescribed in the traditional market theories. This attribute exhibits a better fit between external market conditions and the internal environment in which the market decisions are made. Influence from entrepreneurship allows understanding parts of modern market behavior better and analyzing the cognitive dimensions of entrepreneurs. The attributes of exploring opportunities and identifying the suitable one for doing business is also symmetrical process in both marketing and entrepreneurship. In principle, opportunities are identified through market analyses in traditional marketing theory. Within entrepreneurship, this is regarded as a much more complicated process and can be regarded as an important part of the value-creating process.[30] Entrepreneurial activities are an important part of today's business world and this should be reflected in how we teach and research marketing. The interface between entrepreneurship and marketing creates prolific business developments for marketing such as opportunity recognition processes,

---

[28] Brown, T. (2008). Design thinking *Harvard Business Review*, 86 (6), 84–92.

[29] Sarasvathy, S. (2001). Causation and effectuation: Toward a theoretical from economic inevitability to entrepreneurial contingency. *Academy of Management Review*, 26 (2), 243–263.

[30] Hills, G., Hansen, D., & Hultman, C. (2005). A value creation view of opportunity recognition processes. *International Journal of Entrepreneurship and Small Business*, 2 (4), 404–417.

decision-making and implementation, and strategic marketing.[31] Market entrepreneurship has developed strongly as a result of increasing global competition and is aimed at introducing novelty, innovation, or arbitrage into the production and exchange processes. Thus, the governments of developing countries stimulate productive entrepreneurship and make enterprises practical and operational through various public policies.

Firms desiring to continuously generating returns on investment and increasing margin of profit cannot rely on either strategy or entrepreneurship alone, but instead, must successfully engage in strategic entrepreneurship. However, profitable niches evolve, shift, and disappear rapidly in competitive market economy. Thus, some firms focus solely on entrepreneurial strategy, which might become an effective tool to sustain market competition in the long-run. Without an effective strategy to create competitive advantage in pursuing these entrepreneurial opportunities, a firm will soon experience imitation by competitors whose offerings will erode its profits. Strategic entrepreneurship begins with an appropriate mindset among executives and decisions that are then made within this mindset shape the firm-level actions on exploring and exploiting the opportunities. The balance of exploration and exploitation results in the key outcome of continuous innovation. One of the most pertinent challenges involved in pursuing strategic entrepreneurship is developing an appropriate mindset within the firm that can balance short- and long-term entrepreneurial objectives. A mindset refers to the cognitive frameworks through which new and existing knowledge is interpreted and used to inform decisions such as those regarding strategy and entrepreneurship.[32]

Most entrepreneurs believe they make decisions by using market analysis. To refine their decision-making skills, they must understand that real-world decisions are not always made through logical steps. Using the convergence of conventional wisdom with innovation and technological growth, entrepreneur should learn to define the problem, diagnose its causes, design possible solutions, choose strategic options, and finally implement the best choice. Entrepreneurs should focus on

---

[31] Hultman, C. M., & Hills, G. E. (2011). Influence from entrepreneurship in marketing theory. *Journal of Research in Marketing and Entrepreneurship*, 13 (2), 120–125.

[32] Webb, J. W., Ketchen Jr., D. J., & Ireland, R. D. (2010). Strategic entrepreneurship within family-controlled firms: Opportunities and challenges. *Journal of Family Business Strategy*, 1 (2), 67–77.

thinking first before choosing to interfere with a concurrent market situation and taking decision on complex issues. The decision-making process for entrepreneurs consists of three stages of thinking, visualizing, and applying. In-depth thinking is required when the innovation issue or market situation is clear, data are reliable, the context is structured, thoughts can be pinned down, and discipline can be applied. Entrepreneurs may visualize their ideas when many elements are combined into creative solutions. Commitment to those solutions is the key, and communication across boundaries is essential for carrying out innovation and technology projects. Applying ideas may work effectively when the situation is innovative and a few simple relationship rules are designed to carry out creativity in innovation and technology projects. Such an approach could help the firm move forward in the marketplace.[33]

---

[33] Mintzberg, H., & Westley, F. (2001). Decision making: It's not what you think. *Sloan Management Review*, 42 (3), 89–93.

PART II

The Transition

CHAPTER 4

Reverse Entrepreneurship

Reverse entrepreneurship is associated with reverse migration which stimulates investment in the local entrepreneurial activities with business potential. Often, long-standing and intensive engagement returned migrant communities in their countries of origin produces significant flows of capital, network relations, knowledge and technology, and political support. Researchers in the past have studied the significance of such communities for home countries in ambivalent terms. However, the 'classic' brain drain versus investment into the reverse entrepreneurship equation has come to be replaced by a much more differentiated and complex relationship between countries and their diasporas. Accordingly, this chapter discusses the role of reverse migration in stimulating investment in local enterprises and promoting reverse innovation through technology transfer. Upstream business modeling and creativity management to strengthen the entrepreneurial performance have also been discussed in this chapter.

Reverse Entrepreneurship

Globalization and advancements in information and communication technologies have bridged the spatial distances across the countries and set the business and life to real-time connectivity. Consequently, it has become

© The Author(s), under exclusive license to Springer Nature Switzerland AG 2024
Rebuilding Entrepreneurship at the Grassroots, Palgrave Studies of Entrepreneurship and Social Challenges in Developing Economies, https://doi.org/10.1007/978-3-031-43270-5_4

easier for entrepreneurs to assess demand, risks, and economic shocks occurring in any part of the world. Mobile communications and Internet have driven the butterfly effect in business, economy, environment, and other walks of life, which radiate the effects of small changes with larger differences across the globe. The butterfly effect significantly affects the global economy, entrepreneurship, and cross-border movement of people. The economic recession of 2007–2011 triggered in the western hemisphere has caused significant reverse migration of entrepreneurs and encouraged them to establish business ventures back at the grassroots. Thus, economic crises, recessions, or natural shocks hike unemployment rates and encourage entrepreneurs to explore alternatives in manufacturing, marketing, and services at native or different destinations. In reverse immigration, entrepreneurs migrate back to the homeland and explore alternate streams of revenue. Most entrepreneurs use both their learned and acquired skills to plan new enterprises or strengthen the existing ones to create better job opportunities and income. Similarly, the global business shutdown during COVID-19 pandemic had caused high reverse immigration by driving people back to their native destinations and contributing to the micro, small, and medium enterprises. In case of reverse exodus, governments of home countries adopt precautionary measures to protect employment opportunities of their natives providing entrepreneurial resources and administrative support.[1]

Broadly, reverse entrepreneurship can be defined as sub-urban or rural entrepreneurship initiated by either urban returnee or immigrant entrepreneur(s) with a focus to explore and exploit local opportunities. Reverse entrepreneurs are supported by the community in restructuring business through interconnecting various resources internally and externally. Such efforts lead to a series of changes toward new technological (or production, service), marketing, and organizational systems for sustainable livelihoods in rural communities. Consequently, reverse entrepreneurship is a multidimensional technological, economic, innovation-oriented activity supported by internal and external resources, and spread across spatial, economic, and social levels. Such entrepreneurial activities receive significant contribution from local communities and

---

[1] Ganguly, S. (2022). Reverse migration and exports at extensive margin: case of a small dependent economy. *Indian Economic Review*, 57 (2), 321–348.

external stakeholders to develop sustainable and quality livelihoods.[2] Reverse entrepreneurship, innovation, urban linkages, and rural development are linearly connected. Successful entrepreneurial rural–urban integration depends upon building a high value social capital with focus on both bonding and bridging low economic regions with high business destinations. Developing reverse entrepreneurship needs the right business strategy, adequate resources (financial and human resources), technology, dynamic business model, innovation-diffusion approaches, and market potential for innovative entrepreneurial products.

Rapidly increasing urbanization, shortage of workspace, and the rising costs of entrepreneurial activities also encourage reverse entrepreneurship. Besides these factors, continuous decline of the socio-cultural perspectives of ethnic entrepreneurship has been the reason for disintegration between rural–urban occupational harmony. The reverse entrepreneurship has focused today on manufacturing sustainable and organic products for urban elites and to the big-middle consumer segment to some extent. The artisanal food and beverage products, handicrafts, handloom textiles, and fashion accessories are manufactured in rural areas by the entrepreneurs migrated from urban destinations. Illustrating reverse entrepreneurship, these entrepreneurs have established microenterprises over the past in developing countries like Mexico and reconnected the business to urban markets. Ay Guey ethnic textile in Mexico has gained significant urban attention and is considered today an elite brand with high social value. Reverse entrepreneurship is a process of constructing the business for urban and global markets ergonomically by building mutual trust and cooperation between the rural enterprises and urban markets. Reverse entrepreneurs are engaged in restructuring the old enterprises, co-creating social enterprises, and developing new enterprises with innovative products and services, with high differentiation and competitiveness to sustain the urban competitive markets. These enterprises are largely benefitted by the collective intelligence, crowd behavior, and community values to stay innovative and competitive in the marketplace. Reverse entrepreneurship is also supported significantly by the community resources, public policies, and crowdfunding programs.

---

[2] Wu, B., Geng, B., Wang, Yi, McCabe, S., Liao, L., Zeng, L., & Deng, B. (2022). Reverse entrepreneurship and integration in poor areas of China: Case studies of tourism entrepreneurship in Ganzi Tibetan Region of Sichuan. *Journal of Rural Studies*, 96, 358–368.

Reverse entrepreneurship drives reverse innovation, which is pacing fast in the emerging markets giving a major competitive challenge to the companies intending to penetrate high technology-high-cost innovative products in the above marketplace. As the emerging markets are responding faster to the innovation and technology, the gap between premier and mass or bottom of the pyramid segments is narrowing down. As a result, the global dynamics of innovation are changing. No longer will innovations navigate the globe in the top-down consumer segments direction, in the emerging markets, they are also flowing in reverse. The reverse innovation guides the managers of the sponsor companies on how to make innovation in emerging markets happen and how such innovations can unlock opportunities in the global marketplace. Reverse innovation has become a think tank of innovative ideas in the emerging markets and is drifting them to flow uphill to markets in Europe and North America. Such trend has thrown immense challenges in the business community as it demands a company to overcome the institutionalized thinking that guides its actions toward managing innovative projects within the organization. Large companies roll over to local markets to identify the customer-centric innovations developed by the local enterprises and tend to evaluate the economics of their business projects. Delivering solutions of adequate quality at a competitive price is the primary challenge in developing innovations for emerging markets and catering to the customers therein.[3]

General Electric developed an Electrocardiograph (GE Mac 400) machine and a portable ultrasound machine for the Indian and Chinese markets as a reverse innovation product, which has been very successful in these markets. Similarly, Gillette had developed Guard razor for Indian market, which performed very well. Later, General Electric and Gillette introduced these products to consumers in the US and other developed markets.[4] However, products of social, frugal, and reverse innovations face the challenges of cost, time, and risk. Such problems have motivated micro, small, and medium companies to explore strategic alignment with

---

[3] Rajagopal (2016). *Innovative business projects: Breaking complexities, building performance (Vol. 2)-Financials, new insights, and project sustainability.* New York: Business Expert Press.

[4] Zhu, F., Zou, S., and Xu, H. (2017). Launching reverse-innovated product from emerging markets to MNC's home market: A theoretical framework for MNC's decisions. *International Business Review,* 26 (1), 156–163.

large companies or sponsors. Cost and marketability are the two factors that drive the strategy of reverse innovation. Large companies, thus, roll over to local markets to identify the customer-centric innovations developed by the local enterprises, and tend to evaluate the economics of their business projects. When a company with the capability of sponsoring the reverse innovation investigates a new product opportunity, it not only defines the problem to which an innovation serves as a solution, but also lists the requirements that are needed for commercializing the innovation.[5]

Reverse entrepreneurs make effort in pooling resources, validating the economic viability and technological feasibility of the selected trade, and using both the learned and acquired skills to begin a new venture. While working with the innovative projects back at the grassroots, entrepreneurial integration starts from social embeddedness, interconnectivity, and synchronization of T-5 factors (tasks, target, time, thrust, and trust) between the reverse entrepreneur and the community to understand local challenges and implement the new business model. It is one of the major challenges in this process to develop or enhance social capital (both bonding and bridging) for mobilizing and ensuring optimal use of critical resources. Reverse entrepreneurship can be explained in the following perspectives:

- Entrepreneurial integration to be constituted by establishing strong backward (community philosophy, PNS factors, industry attractiveness, and factors of production) and forward linkages (planning the business canvas)
- Mapping the relationship and operations flow on the business canvas holding nine major functional spaces comprising key activities, key resources, key partners, channels, segmentation, value proposition, customer relations, cost structure, and revenue streams
- Entrepreneurial integration with critical tangible and intangible elements such as available resources, organizational design, experience-innovation blend, and leadership styles

---

[5] Rajagopal (2016). *Innovative business projects: Breaking complexities, building performance (Vol. 2)-Financials, new insights, and project sustainability.* New York: Business Expert Press.

- Ensuring smooth transition through the critical entrepreneurial pathways comprising business strategy, critical capitals, business models, innovation diffusion, and business operations process

Analyzing logically the entrepreneurial integration across trades, territories, and transitions as a process of innovation and business, it can be reinforced that developing reverse entrepreneurship is a collective effort of internal (employees) and external (customers and key partners) stakeholders in business modeling and implementation. In the wake of increasing technology disruption, most reverse enterprises are built on hybrid platforms by synchronizing online and offline business activities to optimize cost, time, and proximity to the stakeholders.[6] Therefore, entrepreneurial restructuring is a process of intertwining social and economic structures in relocating the entrepreneurial activities. Reverse enterprises today also lean on nurturing open innovations by engaging both internal and external stakeholders, and crowd at large in the ideation process. Frugal and utilitarian innovations have been enriched by the consumers, stakeholders, and corporate executives in concept and prototype development across geo-demographic segments. Sustainability-driven innovations are often skewed by social bias while evaluating the ideas within a narrow knowledge base. Social innovations today are generated through open innovation. Social organizations and companies engaged in corporate social responsibility projects rely on consumer preference and evaluative criteria to design innovations, which are supported by the crowdsourced ideas.

The concept of inclusive and reverse entrepreneurship is interrelated, the reverse entrepreneurial business can be explained also in context of the various ecosystems that affect the business orientation and functionality of firms. Consequently, business-, social-, crowd-, and behavioral-ecosystems significantly contribute to the attributes of business inclusiveness. These ecosystems are built on triple and quadruple bottom-lines as explained in the above Figure. Most companies that are currently engaged in building inclusiveness in business aim at earning profit with people, purpose, and sustainability (triple bottom-line), while some companies tend to complement the inclusive business approaches

---

[6] Li, Y., Jia, L., Wu, W., Yan, J., & Liu, Y. (2018). Urbanization for rural sustainability–Rethinking China's urbanization strategy. *Journal of Cleaner Production*, 178, 580–586.

with people, reverse accountability, organizational control (social), and transformational initiatives[7] (quadruple bottom-line). Reverse accountability in monitoring performance in people-led business firms supplements the leadership perspectives on inclusive business. Such governance system creates competitive advantage through higher customer value and contributes to business growth of the company and society.[8] The frequent shift in business models has attracted considerable scholarly attention and managerial efforts toward increasing a firm's competitive advantages.[9] Continuous transition of business models of the firms in emerging markets has significantly moved the locus of value creation and value capture to the changing business ecosystems. Accordingly, the stakeholders (e.g., customers, competitors, suppliers, social organizations, and other institutions) and the key partners play an important role in determining (co-creating), implementing (coevolution), and monitoring (reverse accountability) the performance of businesses. Firms strengthen the relationships among all stakeholders associated with the business organizations as they increasingly rely on stakeholders within the business ecosystem to co-create and capture value by redesigning inclusive and crowd-based business models.[10] Various attributes and causes and effects of reverse entrepreneurship are exhibited in Fig. 4.1.

Entrepreneurs move from a foreign destination to home ground with high skills and business potential as illustrated in Fig. 4.1. Entrepreneurs need to explore the home ground to set-up a new enterprise in a new marketplace by adapting to the use of available factors of production comprising land, labor, capital, technology, and human skills. Besides the manufacturing infrastructure, proximity to markets in urban and semi-urban demographics, accessibility, logistics, and existing backward and forward linkages also help in reverse entrepreneurial decisions. One of

---

[7] Rajagopal (2022). *Evolving with inclusive business in emerging markets: Managing the new bottom-line.* New York: Business Expert Press.

[8] Bocken, N. M. P., Short, S. W., Rana, P., & Evans, S. (2014). A literature and practice review to develop sustainable business model archetypes. *Journal of Cleaner Production,* 65 (1), 42–56.

[9] Yi, Y., Chen, Y., & Li, D. (2022). Stakeholder ties, organizational learning, and business model innovation: A business ecosystem perspective. *Technovation,* 114. (in press) https://doi.org/10.1016/j.technovation.2021.102445.

[10] Wei, Z., Song, X., & Wang, D. (2017). Manufacturing flexibility, business model design, and firm performance. *International Journal of Production and Economics,* 193 (1), 87–97.

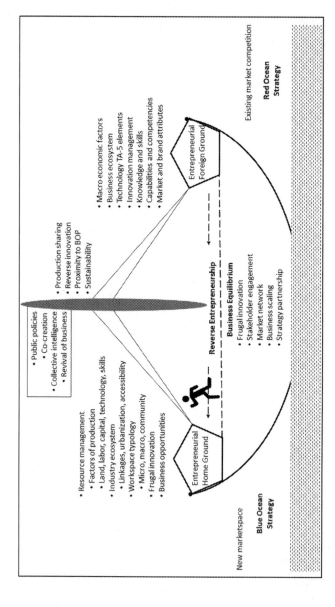

Fig. 4.1 Reverse entrepreneurship and business perspectives (*Source* Author)

the preferred strategies followed by the entrepreneurial firms to develop business in the home market is implementing frugal innovation at low cost, short time, and with less risk. Innovative products with acceptable utilitarian values are preferred by the consumers in the big-middle segment while the products with focus on ethnic fashion trigger the demand in the upstream markets, which contributes to the hedonic values of consumers. Most business opportunities remain latent in the home market, which calls for a consistent and goal-oriented exploration. Often public policies in developing countries encourage returning entrepreneurs to invest in promising business sectors in the short- and long-term. Make in India program launched by the Government of India has attracted many foreign entrepreneurs to invest in preferred business ventures and gain the benefit of foreign direct investment policy of the country. Entrepreneurs usually gain rich experience at work in foreign destinations because of macro-economic factors favorable to the business ecosystem that supports innovation, manufacturing, and marketing activities. These factors significantly contribute to the knowledge and skills, capabilities and competencies, and business operations. The major advantage that returning entrepreneurs gain while transferring the technology to the home markets is on TA-5 factors as stated below:

- Technology appreciation
- Technology acceptability
- Technology affordability
- Technology adaptability, and
- Technology augmentation

Reverse entrepreneurship at the home ground also provides cost-effective opportunities in many entrepreneurial ventures to implement production sharing, reverse innovation (local innovation and global marketing), and complying with the sustainability goals. The bottom-line of reverse entrepreneurship is to establish business equilibrium between the local production and enhanced market opportunities by focusing on frugal innovation, stakeholder engagement, business scaling, market networking, and developing strategic partnership.

Reverse entrepreneurship occurs as a consequence of spatial restructuring (production realignment, reforms in living and ecological spaces), politico-economic restructuring, (employment, shifts in political ideology, changes in economic policies), and social restructuring (such as farmers' organization and community restructuring). Among many factors of successful entrepreneurial restructuring, human and social capital are vital to align with the geo-demographic and economic transitions.[11] Public policies and corporate alignment are needed to be relocated and new enterprises to provide support on human capital, external markets, and knowledge for continuous learning and innovation. Entrepreneurial restructuring is interwoven with innovative trades, engaged in manufacturing and marketing a new product, services, or creating a new market.[12] While innovation platforms are important to engage external stakeholders in rural entrepreneurship, the question of how reverse entrepreneurs can initiate a process of platform building and ensure societal and government support in operationalizing the business and sharing benefits from the platform is raised. Thus, social embeddedness perspective provides valuable insight in catering to the reverse entrepreneurship activities. The socioeconomic integration in entrepreneurial activities is important to demonstrate the entrepreneurial process, performance and its impact.[13] Entrepreneurship initiatives need to be encouraged in developing countries with a new vision to meet the underlying challenges, opportunities, and livelihood strategies taken by reverse entrepreneurs. Entrepreneurial integration in participating multiple trades is to be viewed from the point of the adaptation to learned and acquired skills and build mutual trust with local and external partners to share visions, common interests, and action plans. Besides the structural support in nurturing reverse entrepreneurship, it is important to guide the entrepreneurs to develop appropriate business model for achieving competitive performance in the markets above the existing niche. This goal puts forward a new challenge of managing innovation diffusion, marketing, and adaptation to generate consumer consciousness.

[11] Long, H., Tu, S., Ge, D., Li, T., & Liu, Y. (2016). The allocation and management of critical resources in rural China under restructuring: Problems and prospects. *Journal of Rural Studies*, 47, 392–412.

[12] Wortman Jr., M.S. (1990). Rural entrepreneurship research: An integration into the entrepreneurship field. *Agribusiness*, 64, 329–344.

[13] Wu, B., Geng, B., Wang, Yi, McCabe, S., Liao, L., Zeng, L., & Deng, B. (2022). Reverse entrepreneurship and integration in poor areas of China: Case studies of tourism entrepreneurship in Ganzi Tibetan Region of Sichuan. *Journal of Rural Studies*, 96, 358–368.

Depending upon the availability of external initiative, resources, and managerial knowhow, reverse entrepreneurship contributes significantly to mobilizing and coordinating various resources including financial, physical, human, and social while exploring opportunities, both internally and externally. To support sustainable livelihoods the reverse entrepreneurship brings together the external connections, corporate alliances, and institutional grants that provide a useful business canvas with co-created strategies on new technology, production, and services to mark desired outcomes. Reverse entrepreneurship, often developed within the tourism industry, is considered as a positive, restoring family opportunity within rural communities, which significantly serves the sustainable livelihoods in the low-income areas. Such business efforts have attracted increasing attention as they bring new investments, entrepreneurial talents, experience, market knowledge, and capitals for enhancing the overall income.[14] Creating social and sustainable innovation, therefore, should be aimed at delivering the frugal and long-term solutions and building a strong business case for social marketing. Innovation is critical to social and economic growth as most companies tend to develop local business models to explore marketing opportunities. Consequently, large companies have shown interest in sponsoring and acquiring technology-led start-up enterprises and making them more competitive in the regional marketplace. Social entrepreneurs use traditional techniques to go to market and scale-up quickly with limited resources against large companies that emulate market strategies not only to innovate quickly, but also to commercialize innovation rapidly across the market layers. Therefore, the behavior of large companies deters the local innovation and its growth initiatives.

Changing practices of entrepreneurship can be adjusted to successfully transform social and business needs and upgrade industrial structure to support the reverse transmission of traditional enterprise to increase employment opportunities and solve the problems of employment.[15] Political and social pressure is built on companies to design and deliver social responsibility contextual to social needs, development, and

---

[14] Koyana, S., & Mason, R.B. (2017). Rural entrepreneurship and transformation: The role of learnerships. *International Journal of Entrepreneurial Behavior & Research*, 23 (5), 734–751.

[15] Xu, S., & Jiang, J. (2021). Entrepreneurial vitality, innovation ability and urban economic development efficiency—Empirical study based on the data of 283 prefecture level cities. *Journal of Shanxi University of Finance and Economics*, 43, 1–13.

consumption patterns. Sustainable innovation is usually grown in generic ways instead of adapting to the tested corporate strategies. Consumers today are sensitive to the innovation and technology that offer sustainable competitive differentiation and deliver competitive stakeholder value. Most companies follow a boom-bust cycle in managing their innovation for improving business performance in the competitive marketplace. As companies rethink their priorities analyzing the market demand, they try to deliver innovation-led products and bring competitive differentiation against the existing and potential threats. Sustainable innovation requires a new approach to manage innovation initiatives, and companies need to build capabilities on improving the innovation processes. A network of innovation intermediaries including independent innovators and start-up companies could visualize new opportunities from the market insights and technologies to provide solutions to several companies. Such ideas might never occur to companies while working on their own.[16]

INVESTMENTS IN LOCAL ENTERPRISES

Most entrepreneurs have conventional knowledge on finance, corporate structures, and governance, thereby requiring investors to educate them and fill the gaps. Consequently, among many critical factors business knowledge and appreciation of social capital networks, exploring the capital resources, understanding of entrepreneurial governance, stakeholder rights, commercialization of innovation, ability to manage intellectual property, and adapting appropriate business models to local conditions are critical to make the enterprises functional at the local level. In addition, adding managerial and technical value to young enterprises is one of the major challenges. Clear understanding of PESTEL[17] factors, challenges thereof, and implications of regulatory norms are atop the general conditions of enterprise management.[18] Fragmentation of globalization effects reveals that businesses are highly regionalized and have penetrated the bottom of the pyramid to win the market holistically. Most

---

[16] Wolpert, J. D. (2002). Breaking out of the innovation box. *Harvard Business Review*, 80 (8), 77–84.

[17] PESTEL factors consists of political, economic, social, technological, environmental, and legal norms and their implications.

[18] Kambil, A., Long, V. W., & Kwan, C. (2006). Seven disciplines for venturing in China. *MIT Sloan Management Review*, 47 (2), 85–89.

successful companies employ home base strategies creating localized portfolios, developing hubs to access local distribution and implement territorial operational approaches, developing hybrid marketing and services platform, and developing and reinforcing local business mandate.[19]

Companies functioning with localized innovative business models succeed in developing multi-stakeholder values, engagements, and operational alignments. Reaching out to local geo-demographic segments is a consistent philosophy among business organizations. However, their operational boundaries change across companies, stakeholders, and socioeconomic values. Companies employ different business model initiatives from *for-profit* and *non-profit* organizations by developing alignments among various players at normative, instrumental, and strategic dimensions in order to achieve social and economic value creation. However, during the implementation of sustainable business models, companies face complexity for alignment of value, diverging interests, investment risks, profitability, and corporate responsibilities. Multi-stakeholder engagement in implementing niche-based business plans enhances envisioned and perceived values in large companies. Most customer-centric firms are engaged in radical forms of reorganizing the business model to create perennial values, while conventional business models focus on satisfying customer needs and maximizing their returns. Local business models integrate multiple dimensions of economic, social, and environmental value, and adapt to customer-centric strategies.[20]

The sources of innovation have become dispersed as the market is turning increasingly demanding and the users have formed their niche. Accordingly, innovation has shifted from technology to business models and is more focused on marketing than the social needs. Many innovations are emerging in the market that are simplified or are scaling down on improving the existing products or services and positioning them as innovations. However, managers may align their business strategies with competitive advantages of markets and manage innovation in emerging economies to diffuse and commercialize (De Meyer, 2011). Traditional belief that positioning innovation of products and services makes a company competitive is a myth in the present state of global marketing.

---

[19] Ghemawat, P. (2005). Regional strategies for global leadership. *Harvard Business Review*, 83 (12), 98–108.

[20] Bocken, N., Rana, P., & Short, S. W. (2015). Value mapping for sustainable business thinking. *Journal of Industrial and Production Engineering*, 32 (1), 67–81.

Thus, firms continually reinvent in large and small ways in reference to shifts in market demand and changes in the economy and develop competitive marketing strategies in reference to shifts in the product and market behavior, knowledge of innovative products, and innovation positions. Though the firms may develop efficiency with regard to the above strategic positions of product/market, knowledge, and innovation independently, they are still risk-averse with the innovation (McDonough et al., 2008).

Innovations based on the existing needs of consumers are grown on a stronger commercial base than those developed with futuristic vision. Companies that engage in the latter type of innovation need to create demand among consumers and inculcate use value, which is a difficult proposition. Conventionally, innovations that are co-created involving consumers and stakeholders have strong foundation and are easily taken ahead to next generations. Innovations are improved to the design-to-market strategy by lowering the cost (frugal innovations) for gaining competitive advantage. Companies positioning innovations in the competitive marketplace also focus on continuous improvement of first-generation innovation and consider social perspectives to promote them in the market. Therefore, innovative products are extensively debated on social media and interpersonal forums. These innovations become market leaders generally in their third generation or ahead, as they focus on ambidextrous markets comprising premier and mass-consumer segments. The design thinking emerges as an active strategy in advanced generations of innovations. Design thinking is a process of problem solving through creative ideation. Design thinking in innovation is widely followed as co-creation for continuous improvement.

Micro, small, and medium enterprises need to align their businesses with the global growth and ride over the pressures exerted by scaling the business, meeting the changing demand and consumer preferences persistently, and looking for easy financers to the innovation projects. However, the greatly expanded role for governments, public policies, and financial regulation in the MSME segment might help in making these firms tensile against the market competition. Local firms must factor these developments into their strategies and carry out successful negotiation with matured strategic vision, and retool their approach to strategy for each entrepreneurial component as listed below:

- New product development

- Market focus to frugal innovations
- Redesigning organizational and supply chain structures
- Talent hunt and human resources management, and
- Management of entrepreneurial reputation and identity

In view of the above challenges MSMEs need to work harder to adapt to global–local differences and pay more attention to the markets in the developing countries. Investment in the communication, branding, innovation, technology, and marketing would leverage their business as launch pads for formidable new competitors.[21]

Value creation is a derivation of conscious cognition, actions in subconscious mind, unconscious perceptions, and materialistic reasoning. The cognitive ergonomics of customers (emotions, perceptions, and memories and storyboards), knowledge, beliefs, and trust, and the abilities of information analysis constitute the conscious cognition, which embeds customer value perceptions. Companies following the design-to-value philosophy tend to put customers first in building and implementing competitive marketing strategies comprising push (resource-based marketing approach with all elements of marketing-mix) and pull (psychodynamics and non-zero-sum game) approaches. Customer value-centric companies usually engage in knowing (exploring value perceptions), doing (implementing pro-customer strategies), and being (enjoying the state of win–win by serving the customers), which enables them to achieve performance with purpose. Companies tend to capitalize on social learning experiences and analyze psychosocial dynamics of communities to deliver value to customers. Most customer-centric companies aim at providing desired value and lifestyle, self-actualization, and comparative self-esteem in the value creation process. Patterns of consumerism are changing in the society, as there are shifts in the customer demography in the markets. The explosion of mass customer segments, urbanization, and increase in the size of the population of aging customers have contributed significantly to the shifts in customer preferences and overall consumption behavior. Co-creation and co-designing approaches of customer-centric companies like IKEA have established the

---

[21] Ghemawat, P. (2010). Finding your strategy in the new landscape. *Harvard Business Review*, 88 (3), 54–60.

business philosophy of connecting help firms in developing an emotion-based relationship with customers as the key to leveraging loyalty and advocacy behavior.[22]

A good customer value dashboard helps firms not only in increasing sales and marketing professionals, but also in developing design-to-society and design-to-value business modeling[23]. Creating customer value has, therefore, become the contemporary benchmark to measure market performance of a company and building design-to-value-based businesses. The customer value propositions resonate in marketing models to lead the business by putting the customer first. Such marketing philosophy has enabled large companies like PepsiCo to conceptualize and implement the business strategy of performance with purpose. Co-created customer values help companies focus on customer-centric product offerings to gain competitive leverage. Upon understanding the perceptions, emotions, and values of customers, companies make smarter choices about allocation of resources in customer services, advertisement and communications, and implementation of marketing-mix driven strategies. The co-created and co-evolved customer value constructs can deliver optimal benefits to customers by upholding their perceptions, choices, and self-esteem. Large companies with strategies focused on customers develop value dashboard to monitor customer touchpoints, which helps in co-creating customer value proposition.

Developing Local Markets

Successful consumer-led products in the competitive marketplace always try to gain a distinct place among competing firms and focus on acquiring new customers and retaining the existing ones. Repeat buying behavior of customers is largely determined by the values acquired on the product. The awareness, attributes, trial, availability, and repeat (AATAR) buying factors influence the customers toward making re-buying decisions in reference to the marketing strategies of the firm. The perception on repeat buying is affected by the level of satisfaction derived from

---

[22] Rajagopal (2021). *Sustainable businesses in developing economies—Socio-economic and governance perspectives*. New York: Palgrave Macmillan.

[23] Villanueva, J. (2013). Reading the signs of your customer value. *IESE-Insight Magazine*, 17 (2), 24–29.

the buying experience of customers.[24] Among growing competition in retailing consumer products, innovative point-of-sales promotions offered by supermarkets are aimed at boosting sales and augmenting the store brand value. Purchase acceleration and product trial are found to be the two most influential variables of retail point-of-sales promotions. Analysis of five essential qualities of customer value judgment in terms of *interest, subjectivity, exclusivity, thoughtfulness, and internality* need to be carried out in order to make the firm customer-centric and its strategies touching bottom of the pyramid.[25] Dynamic complexity in business may arise in oligopolistic market systems with high risk in investment, brand development, and generative customer loyalty. It may be observed that the switching behavior of consumers occurs when distribution of a company is weak in the market. In many cases companies are not able to carry out controlled experiments on implementing business strategies due to cost-related and ethical reasons. Hence, dynamic complexity not only slows down the learning loop, but also reduces the learning gained on each cycle. Developing right business strategies in a right market situation is a growing challenge among the systems thinkers and business strategists. Delays in developing appropriate strategies create instability in market dynamic systems and add negative feedback loops in the market, which reduces the sustainability of the company in the competitive marketplace.

The complexities in the internal fit consist of possible problems a company may face while developing and implementing the strategic and tactical approaches in introducing the differentiations. Besides administrative complexities, most companies face the problem of inability to build strong competitive intelligence for collecting the market information and sharing knowledge within the company. Such internal difficulties would drive the companies less competitive in the market in driving the co-creation of differentiated products, seeking consumer cooperation, and understanding the market behavior. Every company expects to enjoy temporary monopoly on the differentiation of products and services for a while until the disruptive or competitive products appear in the marketplace. The complexities in implementing tactical differentiation might arise for a short term but cause long-term effects for companies to

---

[24] Rajagopal (2019). *Contemporary marketing strategy: Analyzing consumer behavior to drive managerial decision making*. Cham, Switzerland: Springer.

[25] Dobson, J. (2007). Aesthetics as a foundation for business activity. *Journal of Business Ethics*, 72 (1), 41–46.

manage their business in the competitive marketplace. Often, the tactical complexities are observed when companies enter price wars, competitive promotions and go-to-market (GTM) strategies involving salesforce and consumers toward selling and buying of differentiated products. Another complexity observed by the companies is when the competitive congruence grows in the marketplace. This situation may occur when competitors follow the identical strategies for introducing their innovative differentiations in products and services to grid the consumer decisions.

The external fit consists of marketplace- and consumer-complexities that are highly uncontrollable and unpredictable. The inconsistent behavior of distribution channels and operational difficulties are highly uncontrollable marketplace factors that trigger complexity in managing the competitive differentiations of the companies. The response of the consumers toward the strategies of firms on creating awareness, illustrating AATAR of competitively differentiated products are also often intercepted by the competitors. Such situations in the marketplace could cause complexities in positioning the products in the market. Price fidelity is another major concern for most companies to uphold marketing in mass and bottom of the pyramid consumer segments. It has been a common practice among the retailing firms to appoint mystery shoppers who collect information on pricing from rival companies to help breaking the price fidelity of consumers with the competing companies. Mystery shoppers are often paid employees of retail companies or of local business intelligence organizations. Aggressive or deceptive advertisement and communication strategies for launching and marketing differentiated products create marketplace complexities, as such strategies might affect awareness, comprehension, conviction (purchase intention), and action (buying) among consumers in reference to competitor's call and peer review.

One of the major complexities arising during the process of product differentiation is deciding over the mass production and commercialization of the differentiated products to optimize both revenues and market share. Most firms begin with low scale and find it difficult to get into the economies of scale if the new product turns attractive in the markets. The fact is companies have strong incentives to be overly innovative in new product development, but making competitive decision in view of the anticipated consumer's and competitor's behavior often rolls back the corporate decisions in the market. However, continual launches of new products and line extensions add complexity throughout a market operation of a company; and as the costs of managing that complexity multiply, profits tend to shrink. To maximize profit potential, a company needs to identify its innovation pivot, the point at which an additional offering either increases or pulls back the profit of the company to enable the right decision on differentiation. The usual solutions to complexity remain unsolved because companies often treat the problem on the market platform rather than at its source where consumer value, product-line requirements, and latent demand in the market exist.[26]

Large organizations are complex by nature and face new business challenges such as globalization, innovative technologies, and regulations over the period. Market uncertainties and competitive threats add layer upon layer of complexity to the corporate structure and management. The technology marketing grid has several factors that pose conflicts and challenges to the innovation and technology development firms during different levels of process. The complexity grid comprises twelve commonly observed points of conflicts, which have independent effects of each point as well as in a matrix form. The conflict points in the grid include ideation, resources management, process management, capabilities and competencies, technology marketing, growth, and next generation innovation and technology issues, involvement, organizational policies, operational efficiency, competitive decision, business environment, and organizational culture, all of which nurture the innovation and technology development projects in the firm. The complexity grid ideation process and the extent of involvement of employees, consumers, and market players stage cognitive and organizational conflicts and challenges. However, management of resources and organizational policies raise various challenges during different phases of innovation and technology development. Similarly, the process and operational efficiency commonly drive various issues of concern in reference to capabilities and competencies and work culture of the organization. Firms face many conflicts during the innovation process on marketing of the technology-led products and the existing business environment. Moving the innovation and technology to next generation is not an easy step-up as firms often get snared in the unwise competitive decisions to push the innovation and technology-led products in the marketplace.

---

[26] Gottfredson, M. and Aspinall, K. (2005), Innovation versus Complexity: What is too much of a good thing? *Harvard Business Review*, 83 (11), 62–71.

Marketing strategies are derived by the firms in the context of business models co-created and coevolved with the customers and investors in crowd-based business environment. Such collaborative business models provide competitive leverage to the micro, small, and medium firms built on collective intelligence. The marketing-mix embeds 11Ps comprising basic elements (product, price, place, and promotion), extended elements (packaging, pace, people, promotion, and psychodynamics), and corporate elements (posture and performance). Products in the contemporary marketplace are consumer-driven and developed as a solution to the consumer needs. The intangible factor of perceived use value and tangible preference of consumers determining the value for money of products governs the decision-making process for products, among consumers. Consumer-centric companies like Apple, IKEA, Procter and Gamble, and General Electric consider that design and marketing strategies, both are important tools in creating product preference, perceived use value, and deeper emotional value for the consumers. Product differentiation is another major challenge for consumer-centric companies to stay ahead of marketplace competition. Most companies believe that successful product differentiation allows the consumer brands to enter mass-market segment in the emerging markets. Product lifecycle determines the longevity of the product in the market, its perceived use value, and the associated value for money. Consumer thus prefers to measure the quality-price relationship in products considering the longevity and competitive advantages. Pricing is one of the most complex decisions facing any company. Along with a lack of academic interest (especially among marketing academics) in the field of pricing, this complexity has contributed to the dominance of simplified, cost-based formulas when levying prices. Price is considered as the principal driver for determining profitability in a company. Price is also a cognitive determinant of consumer behavior that affects their buying behavior. Price is a sensitive tool for fixing profitability in the consumer-centric companies. Every fluctuation in pricing leaves a significant impact on both revenues and profitability of the company. Therefore, ineffective planning in pricing affects the profitability of products and services in a company. Accordingly, consumers assign different degrees of emphasis regarding price to determine their purchase decisions.[27] The increase in market competition has provided increasing choices of

---

[27] Kohli, C., & Suri, R. (2011). The price is right? Guidelines for pricing to enhance profitability. *Business Horizons*, 54 (6), 563–573.

products and services altering the consumption patterns frequently. Such marketplace situation has developed a consumer philosophy of touch, feel, and pick, which makes the consumers product loyal instead of brand loyal with instantaneous switching behavior. The emergence of e-commerce has prompted consumer-centric companies toward adapting to 'direct-to-customer' (DTC) distribution strategy. This strategy has been successful over the years as it helps companies in minimizing the cost, time, and risk (CTR) effects in managing distribution. The promotional strategies are evaluated by the companies in reference to its impact on volume of sales, market share, and their contribution to the profit specific to the products and services. The promotional strategies of consumer-centric companies consume a large and growing part of marketing budgets of companies worldwide.[28]

Packaging and marketing affect the business performance of production-led, sales-led, and marketing-led companies. Ergonomics of packaging today plays a significant role in establishing the product attractiveness, developing consumer preferences, defining the market, and determining price and the brand values. Etymologically, 'pace' indicates consistent and continuous speed in moving things. In the context of business, pace illustrates the marketing strategies for going ahead of competitors. Most companies in the competitive marketplace struggle to gain the first-mover advantage, increase the market share, and augment profit. People in the marketing mix constitute front-liners in markets, who manage sales of products and services. Selling is an art largely associated with the behavioral skills of the sale personnel of a sales organization. In a competitive marketplace, selling is performed using scientific methods of product presentation, advertising, and various approaches drawn to take the customer into confidence. Performance in the marketing mix is considered as a hybrid element. This element is evolved through various factors comprising all basic elements of marketing mix, innovation and continuous improvement, organizational culture, employee engagement, and consumer involvement in co-creating products to enhance consumer value. Grapevine effect has emerged as an outgrowth of psychodynamics, which has evolved as collective intelligence, and is a critical element in creating tangible interactions among consumers in a competitive marketplace. The grapevine effect is contributed by the social media through

---

[28] Rajagopal (2015). *Butterfly effect in competitive markets: Driving small change for larger differences*. Basingstoke, UK: Palgrave Macmillan.

word-of-mouth that stretches throughout the market irrespective of the various measures taken by the firms to build their brand and competitive posture. Grapevine develops psychodynamics among consumers by sharing various consumer experiences. Posture and proliferation of the firm constitute key corporate elements in the marketing-mix. Posture of the company and its path of business proliferation by diversifying the business operations to new markets and expanding the product portfolios constitute the design elements in the marketing-mix of a company. Corporate image develops the posture of a company within the industry and among the consumers in the marketplace. Among various facets of institutional growth, a social purpose, long-term focus, emotional engagement, partnering with the public, innovation, and team leadership would help in constructing building blocks of a more sustainable corporate reputation of a company (Kanter, 2011). Proliferation of business activities is commonly grown around product and market diversifications, and exploring new consumer segments for existing and future products developed using the advanced technologies. Diversification strategies respond to the desire for growth when current products/markets have reached maturity and stability by spreading the risks of fluctuations in earnings. The diversification strategies would also be required for business security when the company may fear backward integration from one of its major customers.

There are many intangible elements that make major contribution to the marketing strategies. Most consumers show initial resistance because of low trust, relative risk, low value for money, and low knowledge on 4As elements consisting of awareness, availability, adaptability, and affordability prospects. The 4Cs consist of consumer relations, convenience, cost to customers, and consumer conflicts in the marketing of products and services. Successful consumer products companies develop satisfactory relations with consumers during the process of prospecting consumers and providing post-sales services to build consumer confidence. As marketing technology is increasing rapidly, the expectation of consumers with a company is also growing-up. The marketing performance of companies is also affected by the 4Vs comprising value perceptions of consumers, peer validity, venue and shopping experience, and vogue exhibited in the market. The sharing of consumer experiences on social media provides validation to the consumer perceptions and expectations on products and services. In addition, the 4Es elaborate in the marketing-mix are associated with sharing consumer experiences on the social media and digital space, and developing perceptions led by emotions on brands. These elements allow the companies to develop strategies for exploring and expanding business in new geo-demographic segments and exploiting the markets by catering the demand to the fullest possible.

The start-up enterprises managing innovation need for the relatively smaller geo-demographic segments and at bottom of the pyramid may throw immense challenges for commercializing the innovations in the international markets. However, it requires a company to follow the institutionalized thinking that guides its actions in the global marketplace. The reverse innovations that are adopted by the sponsor companies need to make design adjustments, and fabricate for the mass consumers in the global markets in a radically simpler and cheaper way to serve the customer with high-perceived value. Companies can develop new products in emerging markets by using a radical change from below (generic innovation design) combined with smart leadership from top (up-market strategy). The small start-up enterprises may set audacious goals to match with the new organizational structure of sponsors, and adopt new design and commercialization methods. However, the start-up enterprises may also nurture the reverse innovation provided they could arrange adequate resources to up-scale the innovation by shifting the gravity of business beyond emerging markets[29]. Companies working with crowd-based business models usually develop products by following time-tested ideas of the crowd, which had overcome the constraints, and leveraged the benefits over the niche markets in developing economies. Such firms tend to develop and transform the crowd-based innovations by matching market segments to existing products, lowering price by keeping essential features, redesigning technical specification of generic products, upholding stakeholders' value, and scaling-up for penetrating into the low-income markets that could have mass appeal.

---

[29] Govindarajan, V. (2012). A reverse innovation playbook. *Harvard Business Review*, 90 (4), 120–124.

CHAPTER 5

Crowd-Based Entrepreneurship

The crowd-based enterprise tends to *solve, explore, understand,* and *listen* to people on a whole new functionality of firms through the technology platforms to acquire and analyze collective (crowdsourced) opinions on a greater scale. Indeed, the increasing use of information markets, wikis, crowdsourcing, the *wisdom of crowd* concepts, social networks, collaborative software, and other Web-based tools constitute a paradigm shift for companies in making customer-centric decisions.[1] Consequently, this chapter discusses crowdsourcing, open innovation, new product management, niche marketing, and decision-making perspectives of entrepreneurship. The attributes of crowd-based business models include integration of contributors from outside the traditional boundaries of a firm, data mining through digital peer-to-peer platforms, and the transfer of value-creating activities to a crowd. This chapter discusses the evolution of crowd-based business modeling and its prospects with firms operating in emerging markets in the context of crowd-engagement in businesses.[2]

---

[1] Bonabeau, E. (2008). Decisions 2.0: The power of collective intelligence. *MIT Sloan Management Review*, 50 (2), 45–52.

[2] Rajagopal. (2021). *Crowd-based business models—Using collective intelligence for market competitiveness*. Cham, Switzerland: Springer.

© The Author(s), under exclusive license to Springer Nature Switzerland AG 2024
Rebuilding Entrepreneurship at the Grassroots, Palgrave Studies of Entrepreneurship and Social Challenges in Developing Economies,
https://doi.org/10.1007/978-3-031-43270-5_5

CROWDSOURCING

Crowdsourcing can be described as an act of a company or institution that intends to invite opinions from an undefined and general mass at large to view their perceptions and experiences on the given call. Previous studies have discussed the act of crowdsourcing in conjunction with open innovation and idea competitions. The open innovation paradigm assumes that firms should use external sources to learn the embedded problems, needs, and expected solutions (PNS) on a given perspective to drive creativity and increase its market competitiveness.[3] Crowdsourcing integrates internal (employees and leaders) and external (customers and investors) stakeholders of the firm through interactive dialogues, knowledge hubs, and shared experiences towards building a promising endeavor. Advances in networked marketing have driven consumer innovation and creativity in firms as a collective intelligence, which supports firms to tap the wisdom of consumer crowds to innovate, commercialize, and compete in the markets.[4] Online marketing research has long recognized the opportunities of web-centered data-gathering methods. With increasing access to personal and digital information today, companies rely more on collective intelligence built through crowdsourcing than nurturing ideas inside the company. Consequently, innovations are not confined to a single path to reach out a market. Crowdsourcing has emerged as a dynamic people's approach over the isolated and individualistic ideation in exploring innovation, social values, and public–private business alliances. Previous research on innovation management suggests that contribution of ideas drawn in isolation is often overvalued anticipating the customer preferences, which jeopardizes the commercialization of innovation. The crowdsourced ideas hold customer preferences at the grassroots and are contributed consciously. Such tendency is positively correlated with the attributes of consumer-centric and social innovations. Business modeling practices are trending open-market with the emergence of social media and crowdsourcing. The mobile applications of information and communication technology today have driven the society

---

[3] Stieger, D., Matzler, K., Chatterjee, S., & Ladstaetter-Fussenegger, F. (2012). Democratizing strategy: How crowdsourcing can be used for strategy dialogues. *California Management Review*, 54 (4), 44–68.

[4] Kozinets, R. (2002). The field behind the screen: Using netnography for marketing research in online communities. *Journal of Marketing Research*, 39 (1), 61–72.

to stay dynamic, connected, and responsive. Consequently, the social learning has been widely supported by the collective intelligence motivating active users and firms to move toward open innovations. Social interactions on digital platforms and diffusion of ideas on public platforms have helped firms to restructure their conventional business strategies by transforming them as crowd-based businesses. Such transition has enabled start-up and unicorn organizations to harness the collective views and creativity of external stakeholders. By enhancing digital proximity to the people, companies through crowdsourcing processes can develop interface with a large but unknown population to create value. Such value generation can be defined as crowd-driven profit and, depending on the platform model, share revenue with the crowd.[5]

With the advancement of human interface on social media, the trend of developing frugal innovations within organization has been reverted to open platforms, which allows the voice of customers to be analyzed. The views of customers and stakeholders on developing new products have enhanced the scope of collective growth of firms in the niche market as compared to the conventional abilities of reaching the goals through in-company efforts. Teams confined to the corporate limits are also likely to overvalue the ideas they come up with, without exploring the market from the customers' perspectives. The social identity of business makes a significant contribution in customer-centric growth of firms today. Consequently, crowdsourcing has emerged as a promising tool in developing business models.[6] Crowdsourcing is an ideation process of sharing individual ideas, emotions, and experiences on business perspectives ranging from business diplomacy to corporate strategies, and social marketing to customer value creation. It is an informal pool of information, which circulates in the society and spreads across the social media channels and conventional word-of-mouth forums. The open innovation platforms and customer-centric innovations in a firm widely encourage crowdsourcing as a value-based tool to co-create community- and value-based business models. The crowdsourced information also guides manufacturing and business operations through the experiences of stakeholders, peers,

---

[5] Kohler, T. (2015). Crowdsourcing-based business models: How to create and capture value. *California Management Review*, 57 (4), 63–84.

[6] Sting, F. J., Fuchs, C., Schlickel, M., & Alexy, O. (2019). *How to overcome the bias we have toward our own ideas.* Harvard Business Review Digital Article. Cambridge, MA: Harvard Business School Press.

gatekeepers, and consumers. Inspirational stimuli such as analogies are the prominent mechanism used to support designers.[7] Collective intelligence also helps in the monitoring and evaluations of implementation and performance of crowd-based business models in companies. Collective intelligence also induces design-by-analogies and design-by-experience concepts, which helps in developing crowd-based business models.[8]

Crowdsourcing has been practiced as relatively new tool to generate ideas and communications, and develop bottom-up business models by the regional and multinational companies. Most multinational companies such as McDonald's, LEGO, Samsung, and Starbucks have successfully founded their growth on the crowdsourced information. Such practice has evolved the ways to analyze needs, attitudes, and behavior of the consumer using the collective intelligence tools and techniques. McDonald's invited ideas from customers to know their preferences on burgers. Upon analyzing the collective contents, the company has been successful in marketing its products by ensuring customer value. The franchise exercised by the customers in suggested competitive and local value-based innovations helps firms to develop new products catering to the customer tastes. Such efforts had been a great contribution of crowd. Starbucks, an American coffee brewing company, has a strong presence on multiple social networks, and it regularly encourages consumers to submit, view, and discuss the submitted ideas along with employees from various Starbucks departments. The company has a dedicated website, which includes a leader board to track the user-generated contents. Similarly, LEGO, a creative toy company allows users to design new products, and simultaneously test the demand for the new product. According to the company practice, any user can submit a design, on which other users are able to vote for. The idea with popular votes is accepted and moved to production. The creator receives 1% royalty of the net revenue on the shared

---

[7] Goucher-Lambert, K., & Cagan, J. (2019). Crowdsourcing inspiration: Using crowd generated inspirational stimuli to support designer ideation. *Design Studies*, 61 (1), 1–29.

[8] Moreno, D. P., Hernández, A. A., Yang, M. C., Otto, K. N., Hölttä-Otto, K., & Linsey, J. S. (2014). Fundamental studies in design-by-analogy: A focus on domain-knowledge experts and applications to transactional design problems. *Design Studies*, 35 (3), 232–272.

design idea.[9] Business models based on crowdsourcing have been experienced by customer-centric companies like IKEA, LEGO, and Starbucks as a powerful tool to demonstrate market competitiveness, but hard to replicate by the competitors at the same time because of their inherent community dynamics. However, implementing and managing crowd-based business models in firms is challenging as it requires critical data filters to be used to eliminate biasness and check the correctness of information. Thus, creating a thriving business built exclusively on collective intelligence is a difficult proposition. However, firms can rest the goal for crowdsourcing platform on several key indicators like data based on PNS factors, competition, semantics of ideas, similarity in innovations, willingness to pay, adaptability of the product, and capability of crowd to engage in value creation.

Crowdsourcing evolved over time with continuing research impetus, which has been a guiding source for start-up enterprises and the firms using open innovation to stay customer-centric and increase market competitiveness. Previous research on crowd-based business models suggests that firms should carefully analyze the consumer voting on the ideas submitted on open innovation platforms as it is often skewed by both personal and social bias. It has been observed that tendency of crowd to like and vote for ideas or concepts on social media platforms is often not driven by appropriate cognition or reasoning. Liking or positive voting largely emerges as a social consensus wave as a follower to previous posts or votes. Firms should validate reliability of the crowdsourced data while evaluating the ideas as the right answer may come from tapping a small number of the right people. It is important to categorize the expert opinions rather than pooling the randomized information contributed by the crowd. As crowdsourcing has evolved to contribute to the knowledge pool, innovations today are growing more customer-centric than before. Kickstarter and start-up firms are increasingly using open innovation platforms with internal stakeholders and key partners as compared to the customers due to low responses and embedded biases. To brainstorm new kinds of avalanche protection gear, Mammoth, the Swiss outdoor clothing and equipment company, had adapted to open innovation approach. It had planned to collect the crowdsourced data through an agency by convening an online group of mountaineers who have

---

[9] Rajagopal. (2021). *Crowd-based business models—Using collective intelligence for market competitiveness*. Cham, Switzerland: Springer.

design or engineering experience. The right responses came from tapping a small number of the right people rather than from polling a crowd of random idea generators.[10] Crowdsourcing-based business models have various intervening elements and dependent factors as discussed below[11]:

- Firms, which tend to grow customer-centric lean on building their business on the collective intelligence through processes and resources contributed by the external stakeholders.
- Open innovations transform a product only as a commercial entity but also evolve on an interactive platform for future generations.
- Inputs of crowd behavior appear significantly a greater set of resources available to the firm, which allows it to share ideas and technologies with customers, employees, and key business partners.
- Crowdsourcing platforms leverage technology to E-3 dimensions in business comprising explore, exploit and experience social networks.
- Peer-to-peer technologies, user-generated content, and mobile connectivity drive firms to invite users to participate in value-creation activities.
- The use of internet and rise of Internet of Things provide high degree of openness in business, enhance proximity, and rebuild connectivity with the communities to augment richness of information.
- Crowdsourcing and collective intelligence have stimulated many new participatory methods of value creation and social consumption.
- The collective and cord-based business models transfer value-creating activities to a crowd by engaging communities in co-creating value.

Crowd contribution serves as a significant resource for firms in finding new ideas and solutions to the problems of existing products and services. Collective intelligence drawn from user-generated contents offers potential payoffs to the contributions, which are valuable to the community and firm and have strategic effect on the market performance of the firms.

---

[10] Reto, H., Aryobsei, S., & Andreas, H. (2017). Rethinking crowdsourcing. *Harvard Business Review*, 95 (6), 19–22.

[11] E.g., Kohler, T. (2015). Crowdsourcing-based business models: How to create and capture value. *California Management Review*, 57 (4), 63–84.

However, a major challenge associated with the crowdsourcing of ideas and solutions is that the crowd participation is an open concept and is not governed by employment or contractual laws that might stipulate code of ethical conduct, digital rights of intellectual property, and rights ownership of communication. Consequently, in managing crowdsourcing activities, firms use consumer opinion frequently in developing strategies and business models, and incorporate plans for obtaining permission from rights owners to use their crowdsourced content. Success of a crowdsourcing campaign depends on the organization's ability to attract, acquire, and analyze (A-3 process) the crowd information. Nonetheless, retaining the knowledgeable and skilled crowd, and indicating the need for a persistent and mutually beneficial arrangement between the crowd community and the organization appears to be a major challenge among both small and large firms.[12]

Crowdsourcing adds value to the willingness of a firm to reaffirm democratic business approach and exercise its I-3 rights to ideation, innovation, and implementation with the key stakeholders. However, business design based on collective intelligence is delicate and may succumb to BAD factors comprising biases, adversities, and disruptions. There is always a compartment in business models that holds the possible negative and unintended consequences of crowdsourcing when stakeholders are empowered to speak their unjust thoughts, criticize organizational initiatives with no solid reasons, and direct personal initiatives overriding the business interest of the firms. The concepts of crowd-think and crowd-control are new to business firms, which empower crowdsourcing endeavors and collective bargaining on design-to-society, design-to-value, and design-to-market strategy cube concepts. By building the crowd connectivity and its strategic roles, managers can harness the power of crowds effectively to achieve business goals with limited negative consequences.[13] However, despite the planned efforts, firms may fall into the common mistakes in crowdsourcing, which may include the unclear focus in ideation and acquisition of collective intelligence, lack of agility in

---

[12] Franke, N., Keinz, P., & Klausberger, K. (2013). "Does this sound like a fair deal?": Antecedents and consequences of fairness expectations in the individual's decision to participate in firm innovation. *Organization Science*, 24 (5), 1495–1516.

[13] Wilson, M., Robson, K., & Botha, E. (2017). Crowdsourcing in a time of empowered stakeholders: Lessons from crowdsourcing campaigns. *Business Horizons*, 60 (2), 247–253.

core interactions, vertical integration with least strategy orchestration, too much social waste (tangible and intangible), and driving narrow network effects. Crowdsourced collective intelligence helps entrepreneurs in the business decision process from various managerial perspectives as illustrated in Fig. 5.1.

Crowd power has emerged as an effective tool to drive open innovations, suggest customer-centric market planning, and develop consumption landscapes across potential consumer segments as exhibited in Fig. 5.1. Collective intelligence is extensively used by the firms in developing new ideas for innovative products and business processes. Crowd behavior and collective intelligence derived through social media objectively converge market, consumption, and relationship matrices to support entrepreneurial business. Collective leadership and reverse accountability (stakeholder control) govern the crowd information flow and validate informational inputs. Collective intelligence has proved as a concurrent repository of consumer perceptions, emotions, and behavioral attributes, which helps enterprises to explore PNS factors. Crowd power is used effectively by the customer-centric multinational firms in managing information of social media and microblogs to understand the underlying market dynamics. Therefore, crowd behavior can be perceived as wisdom of crowds engrossed with customer emotions and experiences. The crowd power also guides entrepreneurs in building alignments with business partners and community.

Crowdsourcing has been philosophically defined as a new trend using the wisdom of crowds on the Internet, primarily for ideation initiatives and resolving problems of products and services within the consumer community. It converges cognitive and social factors comprising perceptions, semantics, social sharing, and interactive discussions. Managing crowdsourcing information needs huge information technology-based infrastructure and human resources. Since the mid-twentieth century, several crowdsourcing platforms emerged on various social media domains to facilitate virtual interface of network members. The landscape of crowdsourcing platforms is widely dispersed, but most tasks are controlled by the sponsors or domain owners. Finding out the tasks that closely match contributors' personal preferences and capabilities is difficult.[14]

---

[14] Li, Y. M., Hsieh, C. Y., Lin, L. F., & Wei, C. H. (2021). A social mechanism for task-oriented crowdsourcing recommendations. *Decision Support Systems*, 141, Art 113449 https://doi.org/10.1016/j.dss.2020.113449.

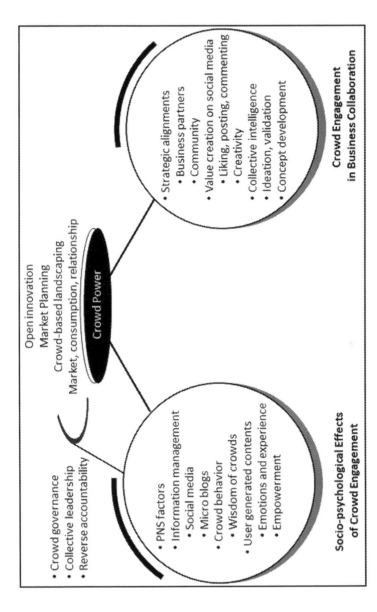

Fig. 5.1 Crowd power and its contributions to business (*Source* Author)

Broadly, there are two domains in crowdsourcing, which include crowd contributions and organizational processing. Of these, the nature of crowd contribution in business is important, which connects to the business objects and leads to the right customer solutions. Therefore, one of the most desired contributions of collective intelligence should be delivered to explore the PNS factors and put forth the right value propositions to a firm. Another domain relates to the aggregation of knowledge and its diffusion toward creating value and leading to the best solution. These two collective intelligence domains lead to various types of information-sharing activities[15] comprising crowd voting (aggregated), determining priorities (objective and subjective), microtasking and perceptual mapping (community-driven), idea generation (economic viability and technological feasibility), and solution crowdsourcing (perceived use value and business scaling).

Crowd creativity provides rich and applied manifestation of ideas, working strategies (draft), and user-generated contents to solve problems. However, such solutions largely remain untested, and stand on hypothetical grounds, which poses risks in developing and implementing prima *facie* public strategies due to social and legal risks associated with the I-3 elements comprising impulsive *ideation*, situation *interpretations*, and infringement of *intellectual property*. Consequently, companies relying on the crowd-based business modeling need to explore possibility of digital rights management to stand clear on the intellectual property issues while prospecting the crowdsourcing of solutions. The crowd-based information needs to be validated against the risks of using intellectual property and strategic-fit on the business performance perspectives. Crowd commonly delivers raw information, which mitigates the risks associated with soliciting solutions on any uncommon or less occurring problem associated with the products and services. The unrefined crowd information is commonly proactive, premature, possessive, and persuasive, which needs to be judged within the social and business ecosystems.[16] A small US-based crowdsourcing platform illustrates the entrepreneurial

---

[15] Wilson, M., Robson, K., & Botha, E. (2017). Crowdsourcing in a time of empowered stakeholders: Lessons from crowdsourcing campaigns. *Business Horizons*, 60 (2), 247–253.

[16] De Beer, J., McCarthy, I. P., Soliman, A., & Treen, E. (2017). Click here to agree: Managing intellectual property when crowdsourcing solutions. *Business Horizons*, 60 (2), 207–217.

challenges in a new industry to manage a virtual firm. The firm has chosen to focus initially on selling labor services to the American real estate market, which has successfully built a network of active partners and recurring clients.[17]

With advancements in the information technology, crowdsourcing has emerged as a prominent community interface built around the S-3 elements comprising philosophy comprising sharing, simulation, and semblance. Sharing the experiences of existing customers and the needs of potential consumers along with the simulated utilization of products and services met enormous opportunity in the crowdsourcing process. Semblance is an attribute of crowdsourcing wherein information has a commonality in many aspects as it grows in a snowballing pattern. Consequently, despite the aggressive and heterogeneous perception among the crowd participants, homogeneity in information also prevails in crowdsourcing. However, large companies tend to control the information intricacy and density, crowd behavior simulation,[18] emotion contagion, and collision avoidance as predefined filters to refine the collective information.[19] Emotional contagion is an observed behavioral change in one individual, which leads to reflexive production of the identical behavior by other individuals in proximity, with the likely outcome of converging emotionally.[20] Therefore, in crowdsourced information there exists a significant, repetitive behavior and biasness.

The collective information repository serves as a source of open knowledge to the company, and at the same time, as a part of social movement to provide voice to customers to reach out companies. This is an *outside-in* inflow of information, which helps companies in understanding the consumer perceptions, the trend of referrals, and styles of customer advocacy on products and services. Nonetheless, collective intelligence has open information feeds that require companies to employ robust information filters for quality output. Most customer-centric companies have

---

[17] Carmel, E. (2012). *Lifebushido: The challenge of the crowdsourcing labor markets.* Cambridge, MA: Harvard Business School Publishing.

[18] Narain, R., Golas, A., Curtis, S., & Lin, M. C. (2009). Aggregate dynamics for dense crowd simulation. *ACM Transactions on Graphics*, 28 (5), 1–8.

[19] Ta, X. H., Gaudou, B., Longin, D., & Ho, T. V. (2017). Emotional contagion model for group evacuation simulation. *Informatica* (Slovenia), 41 (2), 169–182.

[20] Panksepp, J. B., & Lahvis, G. P. (2011). Rodent empathy and affective neuroscience. *Neuroscience and Biobehavioural Reviews*, 35, 1864–1875.

developed their social media page on Facebook to make customers stay abreast with the new products and share opinions on the existing products and services. Some companies like Microsoft, Apple, and Amazon have also promoted customer communities wherein the customers interact to share their experiences and resolve problems. Discussions on the companies' Facebook and customer communities are monitored periodically and streamlined by the designated employees and community leaders. Companies set the following crowdsourcing principles:

- Induct stimulant topics in business and society to attract crowd communication,
- Develop information-screening processing and build information repositories to acquire and store information, and
- Analyze crowd communication systematically to use crowd inputs as the guide to business modeling and managing organizational performance.

Crowdsourced information enables companies to learn about customer perceptions and emotions through shared experience and values, co-create products and services, and coevolve with customers against competitors. In addition, text mining has also emerged as a tool to do research on user-generated contents across the Web and derive necessary output on key terms. Text mining has become a popular qualitative research tool to extract meaningful data available in text form. Text mining sources range from academic literature to social networking sites, posts and comments about the news, voice of the customer, speech-to-text data, and more tangible, digitally published documents.[21] Crowdsourcing practices are popular for co-creating product designs, problem solving, and developing crowd-based business models. The *wisdom of crowds* refers to the phenomenon that the average view of a group of individuals on a given perspective can be similar or close to the acceptable response. It requires a large group diversity of opinions, but the collective error, the difference between the average opinion and the true value, remains small.[22]

---

[21] Jung, H., & Lee, B. G. (2020). Research trends in text mining: Semantic network and main path analysis of selected journals. *Expert Systems with Applications*, 162, 1–12.

[22] Hertwig, R. (2012). Tapping into the wisdom of the crowd-with confidence. *Science*, 336, 303–304.

Crowdsourcing stimulates perceptual semantics among customers, stakeholders, and participants of social networks. Semantics exhibits connectivity of thoughts, perceptions, and values among customers on any given object or situation, or within an existing business ecosystem. Cognitive semantics is the continuity of the thought process that occurs in human mind. The cognitive semantics emerges as a process of thoughts and communication that connects to a core thought or mental state addressing the specific ecosystem.[23] Customers tend to develop compositions of contextual meaning and senses of given words, phrases, situations, concepts, or acquired information that affects the processing of complex thoughts, perceptions, and emotions. However, research on embodied cognition demonstrates that perceptual semantics is a synchronization of thoughts on lexical meanings and perceptual experience. The semantic thoughts are extensions of a principal thought leading to contextual interpretations and decisions. Therefore, perception-based information such as key terms in communication, advertisements, social media messages, and corporate announcements need to be meticulously drafted and posted.[24]

OPEN INNOVATION

Start-ups today not only serve as independent firms, but also strongly support large firms in carrying out open innovation initiatives. The differentiators, innovativeness, speed, and agility in managing innovation projects make them attractive business partners. Start-up firms are energetic in collaborating on new technologies and reinventing existing business models with the support of angel investors. The concept of open innovation emphasizes that knowledge on new ideas, products, use values, and innovation is widely spread in the world, and it is not possible for the companies to explore this wealth to their fullest capacity. However, business ideas, concepts, and innovation processes are licensed from other companies. In addition, internal inventions not being used in a firm's business are also taken outside the company to get them licensed and sell them to client organizations to earn royalty. Most companies that intend to use open-market innovation apply tools such as licensing, joint

---

[23] Brandt, P. A. (2005). Mental spaces and cognitive semantics: A critical comment. *Journal of Pragmatics*, 37 (10), 1578–1594.

[24] Rajagopal. (2021). *The design cube: Converging markets, society, and customer values to grow competitive in business*. New York: Business Expert Press.

ventures, and strategic alliances to bring the benefits of free trade to the flow of new ideas.[25] Design thinking has grown as a necessity in firms to make them competitive and has been widely popularized as one of the most effective approaches to complex conventional methods. Design thinking has significantly transformed as collective approaches to like crowdsourcing to drive open innovation. However, the prescriptive models of design thinking today are globally more challenging than before to establish stakeholder value, market competitiveness, and profitability. Open innovations tend to lower the development costs of innovation by the greater use of external technology in carrying out the research and development activities. This saves time as well as money, and the firm no longer restricts itself to the markets it serves directly. Open Innovation is an emerging model in which companies invite innovation ideas from crowdsourcing and use external ideas, screen them from the point of view of economic viability and technological feasibility of adopting the new ideas. Simultaneously companies also encourage employees to share ideas within the company or industry group and determine the internal and external paths to market. Crowdsourcing has become a new normal for many customer-centric businesses, which narrows down the distance between companies and customers. Empowering the crowd comprising customers, stakeholders, and potential investors has shown encouraging results in improving business practices of companies and strengthened their competitive position.

Goodbaby International Holdings Ltd[26] is a leading Chinese firm, which is engaged in manufacturing juvenile products for essential use. Amidst the brand umbrella, this firm dominates in designing and manufacturing strollers for childcare. The founder of this firm was a schoolteacher, who could register a single stroller patent in 1989. The group has since grown rapidly, and now designs and manufactures variety of similar products for extended use like car seats, cribs, bicycles, apparel, and personal care products, winning international recognition. The Group serves today millions of families through collaborative design, research and development, manufacture, marketing and sales of children and juvenile products. This is largely an open innovation company with

---

[25] Rajagopal. (2014). *Architecting enterprise: Managing innovation, technology, and global competitiveness*. Basingstoke, UK: Palgrave Macmillan.

[26] For details on the firm see https://www.gbinternational.com.hk/en-en/company/overview (Retrieved on September 15, 2023).

over seven thousand employees worldwide and has over twelve thousand patents with eight brands sold across four hundred self-management retail stores at international destination. This open innovation firm is recognized as a role model entity for intellectual property by the Chinese government. The firm has pioneered an inside-out open innovation strategy that allowed it to offer products under its own brands to domestic and international customers under their brands. This firm empowers crowds, business partners, customers, and employees to thrive in an environment of entrepreneurial spirit, innovation, passion, respect, and trust to co-create products.[27]

Open innovation is based on co-created platforms of architectures and systems by the various market players including consumers, distributors, retailers, and technology experts who set the innovation requirements and develop an appropriate business model. Building innovation capability in a company requires to employ the experimentation process for continuous improvement (Kaizen) by conducting experiments and assessing their results to improve the business performance within the company and in collaboration with the partnering firms. Kaizen is the practice of continuous improvement, which was originally introduced to the global marketplace by Japanese companies. Today Kaizen is recognized worldwide as an important pillar of an organization's long-term competitive strategy. Kaizen also supports the open innovation business models, and most companies use it as a tool for sourcing innovation ideas. Companies commercialize the open ideas selectively by deploying pathways to bring the innovation to the market while internal ideas are processed through channels outside of their current businesses in order to generate value for the stakeholders as well as to build competitive differentiation of the company.[28]

Collective intelligence and open innovation have become symbiotic today. Among others, social media platforms such as Facebook and Twitter are increasingly being used as the tools for external stakeholder engagement. The enhanced proximity and richness offered by these

---

[27] Chesbrough, H. W., & Zhu, A. (2021). *Goodbaby: How a Chinese underdog became a world leader through open innovation*. Berkley, CA: Haas School of Business, University of California.

[28] Rajagopal. (2016). *Innovative business projects: Breaking complexities, building performance (Vol. 1)—Fundamentals and project environment*. New York: Business Expert Press.

platforms facilitate extensive interactions and are a powerful knowledge source. Online communities let open innovation firms draw insights from the diverse knowledge pool through the social media platforms to promote open innovation with creativity and quality of contributions. A major challenge in the open innovation is to synchronize the information inflow from different backgrounds, expertise, sensitivity, and technology (BEST) with different areas of the industry, skills, and experience that make impact on open innovation. Open innovations are highly benefitted from the media-rich modalities for transfer of information including text, pictures, and videos, and a wide range of thematic topics characterized by the high image sensitivity. Growing information and communication technologies provide firms with a powerful means of knowledge exchange and generation of ideas that can be applied to open innovation. Public and commercial creativity are synchronized through network interactions across a crowd segment with the diffusion of diverse knowledge and skills. Consequently, engagement with external stakeholders helps firms tap edge of E-3 factors which in turn boosts creativity and innovativeness in the firm to explore and exploit opportunities at different stages of the innovation funnel.[29]

Crowdsourcing has emerged as an effective tool for open innovation, which aims to boost idea generation in innovation processes. The underlying rationale of crowdsourcing is that the collective intelligence of a large number of contributors outside the firm's boundaries increases the likelihood of achieving high-quality ideas with exceptional business potential. Collective intelligence generates a plethora of new ideas, which need to be classified and differentiated to match with planned or on-going research. Accordingly, companies develop action plan to carry out open innovations by adopting the crowdsourced ideas. Various social media channels contribute to the dissemination of new ideas and serve as a pool of collective intelligence. However, the review of previous literature suggests that the overall effect of crowdsourcing on business modeling has not been thoroughly investigated. This book fills this gap by integrating the customer ideation in developing business models to achieve performance with purpose. Drawing on the resource-based view, the book argues how crowdsourced information can become a valuable resource for

---

[29] Mount, M., & Martinez, M. G. (2014). Social media: A tool for open innovation. *California Management Review*, 56 (4), 124–143.

the firm to extract value from it, build value chain, deliver to stakeholders, and stay competitive in the marketplace.[30]

Open innovation has emerged in the technology-led paradigm shift contributes by the crowd-based ideation process. IKEA, a creative home furnishing company, is an example of open innovation company which relies on both internal and external ideation process to advance their innovation process or to access new markets. Inbound, outbound, and coupled sources of information are associated with the open innovation domain. The inbound dimension includes practices that aim at internalizing external resources to innovate, whereas the outbound approaches toward information acquisition aim at outsourcing the company's internal resources to open new markets with new products developed through the collective intelligence (Radziwon & Bogers, 2019). Open innovation model is built around the external (crowd-based) and internal (in-company) ideas targeting both predetermined and alternate markets. Such innovations are congruent with the customer needs and preferred solutions at affordable prices. The concept of open innovation emphasizes that knowledge on new ideas, products, use values, and innovation is widespread in the world, and it is not possible for the companies to explore this wealth to their fullest capacity. However, business ideas, concepts, and innovation processes are licensed from other companies. In addition, internal inventions not being used in a firm's business are also taken outside the company to get them licensed and earn royalty by selling them to client organizations. Most companies that intend to use open-market innovation apply tools such as licensing, joint ventures, and strategic alliances to bring the benefits of free trade to the flow of new ideas. The French multinational insurance firm, AXA, has relied on open innovations to develop customer-centric strategies and created 'AXA Labs', as innovation outposts based in Shanghai and San Francisco. These outposts enabled company to explore crowd-led ideation innovation and identify talented entrepreneurs, emerging trends, and new customer needs. The AXA Labs teams explore innovations in their respective regions to develop partnership alliances with the potential start-ups or adapt to the best-performing models tested in the industry by other

---

[30] Cappa, F., Oriani, R., Pinelli, M., & Massis, A. D. (2019). When does crowdsourcing benefit firm stock market performance? *Research Policy*, 48 (9). https://doi.org/10.1016/j.respol.2019.103825.

companies. The Labs work closely with start-up enterprises at every stage, to develop and accelerate disruptive business models.[31]

The open innovations tend to lower the development costs of innovation by the greater use of external technology in carrying out the research and development activities. This saves time as well as money, and the firm no longer restricts itself to the markets it serves directly. Open Innovation is an emerging model in which companies invite innovation ideas from crowdsourcing and use external ideas, and screen them from the point of view of economic viability and technological feasibility of adopting the new ideas. Simultaneously, companies also encourage employees to share ideas within the company or industry group and determine the internal and external paths to market. Open innovation is based on co-created platforms of architectures and systems by various market players including consumers, distributors, retailers, and technology experts who set the innovation requirements and develop an appropriate business model.[32] Creativity in innovation projects should be based on analyzing consumer preferences, scope of open innovation, and carrying out 'experience innovation' involving consumers and stakeholders of the company. Customer-centric companies develop innovation project designs that could generate high consumer use value, competitive differentiation, long and sustainable product lifecycle, and charter of serviceability of innovative products.

Collective intelligence and open innovation have encouraged new ideas and solutions through social media and community interactions, which has made firms experience the longitudinal and latitudinal outreach in the consumer markets. Such ideation process is driven by the analysis of PNS factors in the community. By adapting to the design-to-society and design-to-values business foundations collective intelligence and open innovation approaches deliver design-to-market ideas and products. Accordingly, stakeholder and employee engagement help firms to analyze collective inputs and develop innovative products and services to provide consumer convenience, satisfaction, and enhance the business performance of firms. The main challenge faced in managing open

---

[31] Rajagopal. (2021). *Crowd-based business models—Using collective intelligence for market competitiveness.* Cham, Switzerland: Springer.

[32] Rajagopal. (2016). *Innovative business projects: Breaking complexities, building performance (Vol. 1)—Fundamentals and project environment.* New York: Business Expert Press.

innovation is measuring economic viability and technological feasibility accurately to enable the firms to take up innovation projects alongside the growing technology and develop convergence with the business model. Commonly, open innovations are low-priced and gain first-mover advantage in the market, however, these products operate in a predetermined niche to survive the competition. Most companies focus on employing new technologies to serve customers with value, which not only delivers competitive advantage over the existing products in the market, but can also create high-perceived value. For example, Nintendo with the Wii; and Swatch with its fashionable and affordable watches provide the rationale of value-based innovation that is congruent with the customer expectation and the product design.[33] Customers evaluate the open innovation products in the context of 6As comprising awareness (on product and market), attributes (competitive features), applicability (PNS matrix, utilitarian values), availability (routes to market and shopping convenience), affordability (price), and adaptability (experience and perceived use value). To launch successful open innovation breakthroughs, most firms analyze the innovation-to-market ratio within a financial year to determine the market share and profit contribution of innovative products. Such analysis helps companies predict the rate of success of breakthrough innovations and expected perceived customer values. Accordingly, firms develop alliances and plan to grow in diverse markets by determining the degree of standardization and customization in the open innovation products.[34]

Crowd-based business models emerge out of the collective intelligence generated through crowdsourcing. As crowdsourcing evolves, new research finds a pitfall companies should be alert of: Consumer voting on the ideas submitted on open innovation platforms is often skewed by social bias, or people's tendency to like and vote for ideas whose progenitors have liked and voted for their own. Collective intelligence-led business models rely more on consumer preference and social criteria while evaluating the ideas that are generated through open innovation. Successful crowdsourcing ventures require more than an online platform and some kind of brand connection. Without an understanding of participant motivations and behaviors, casual attempts to leverage the

---

[33] Verganti, R. (2011). Designing breakthrough products. *Harvard Business Review*, 89 (10), 114–120.

[34] Fleming, L. (2007). Breakthroughs and the long tail of innovation. *MIT Sloan Management Review*, 49 (1), 69–74.

wisdom of the crowd may backfire and lead to unintended results. Prominent examples of crowdsourcing failures are myriad.[35] Consider General Motors, which provided users with web tools to make their own ads for the Chevrolet Tahoe, resulting in several viral videos that lampooned the company's products and the American automotive industry's gas guzzlers more generally. In the fast-moving consumer goods industry, Mountain Dew successfully crowdsourced part of its product development through the *Dewmocracy* contest series, but a similar project asking fans to name the brand's new apple-flavored drink brought on a slew of ironic suggestions, including *Diabeetus*.[36]

Crowdsourcing knowledge and building collective intelligence repositories have also been beneficial to overcome the troubled times that had driven the economy and business down. Many countries had experienced the crowd contribution to revive businesses in the post-economic recession (2007–2011) and during the COVID-19 pandemic (2020–2022). As firms struggled to adapt to the fallout of such crisis, many turned to open innovation, a collaborative approach that strengthens all companies involved in exploring creative and differentiated solutions. Open innovation is a kind of public collaboration, which focuses on creating value, exploring stakeholder PNS factors, developing a productive working relationship with new partners and pursue through open innovation to deliver differentiated benefits. Mercedes-Benz's Startup Autobahn[37] is an open corporate accelerator (CA) built on an open innovation platform that enabled the firm to identify various start-ups, execute over 150 pilot projects, and implement 17 innovative solutions between 2016 and 2021. Most automobile firms tend to respond to the emerging demand on electrification and connectivity, while many new competitors are staging products up-front in the market to meet the advanced new expectations of the customers. Experience of Mercedes-Benz demonstrates the ways to leverage the open corporate accelerator model by integrating start-ups effectively into the corporate research and development processes

---

[35] Rajagopal. (2021). *Crowd-based business models—Using collective intelligence for market competitiveness.* Cham, Switzerland: Springer.

[36] Fedorenko, I., Berthon, P., & Rabinovich, T. (2017). Crowded identity: Managing crowdsourcing initiatives to maximize value for participants through identity creation. *Business Horizons*, 60 (2), 155–165.

[37] Dahlander, L., & Wallin, M. (2020). Why now is the time for open innovation. In *Harvard business review digital article*. Cambridge, MA: Harvard Business School Press.

and accelerating their innovation efforts. Unlike a conventional corporate accelerator, an open CA welcomes multi-sponsor companies and can attract a wider range of start-ups operating with the high maturity level.

Start-up ecosystem has been radically changing in the recent past (2011 onwards) identifying multiple opportunities to receive financial and managerial support for growth. Therefore, the accelerator programs play an important role as they embed the promise to start-ups toward managing their portfolios through crowdsourcing, crowdfunding, and exploring corporate alliances. The engagement of these firms in open innovation, rapid ideation and process iteration cycles, and fundraising campaigns supports this consortium accelerator business model and drives it competitively. CA approach harnesses the network effects of open innovation and platforms by inviting the participation of multiple sponsors, start-ups, and other stakeholders rather than establishing exclusive sponsor-start-up relationships.[38]

New Product Development

Product design is often considered as a process for creating functional differentiation through added features, superior performance, and so forth. However, with the emergence of more design-oriented companies, product design is increasingly being seen as an important strategic tool in creating preference and deeper emotional value for the consumer. Hence, managers should learn how different design elements can be used strategically to create two very different outcome chains from a consumer's perspective. It is observed that certain design elements are more likely to create functional product differentiation and transactional consumer outcomes, while other design strategies tap a more emotional form of value creation. The emotional focus in value creation is more likely to create desired and powerful outcomes such as loyalty, joy of use, and even passion. Given current business trends toward relationship-based customer management, this emphasis on emotional value creation through product design is particularly relevant.[39] The

---

[38] Moschner, S. A., Fink, A. A., Kurpjuweit, S., Wagner, S. M., & Herstatt, C. (2019). Toward a better understanding of corporate accelerator models. *Business Horizons*, 62 (5), 637–647.

[39] Noble, C. H., & Kumar, M. (2008). Using product design strategically to create deeper consumer connections. *Business Horizons*, 51 (5), 441–450.

well-built-in product designs benefit both company and consumer by simplifying decision-making, enhancing customer satisfaction, reducing risk, and driving profitable purchases. On the contrary, ill-conceived product designs can leave consumer's money on the table, fuel consumer backlashes, put users at risk and trigger lawsuits costing companies huge amounts. It has been observed that despite such high stakes in product designing, manufacturing companies slip the quality control process in setting built-in or default product designs. Setting default designs in products require companies to balance a complex array of interests, including customers' wishes and the company's desire to maximize profits while minimizing risk. At a basic level, built-in designs can serve as manufacturer recommendations, and more often consumers may not be happy with what they get. Most companies also strive to set default product designs in ways that align with customers' preferences.[40] In developing collaborative product designs, managers should consider the following perspectives:

- Being an involved consumer of their own and competitor's goods and services
- Transfer of knowledge
- Documenting experiences to retain personal knowledge
- Relativity of needs in reference to average consumers
- Obtaining information through mutual cooperation
- Critically observe and live with consumers
- Critical observation rather than casual viewing
- Investing time
- Realistic and precise conclusions
- Talk to consumers and get needs information
- Structured, in-depth, one-on-one, situational interviews
- Engineering trade-offs during product development
- Technical design information
- Exploring tacit and product-related needs of consumers.

Co-creation process is considered as a socio-organizational process. In collaborative new product development, there are many actors who are

---

[40] Goldstein, D. G., Johnson, E. J., Herrmann, A., & Heitmann, M. (2008). Nudge your customers toward better choices. *Harvard Business Review*, 86 (12), 99–105.

involved in the process. An actor executes three main activities during this social process.

Idea generation in the process of new product development is a major exercise. This technique calls for listing of all major attributes of the existing product and the needed attributes in order to improve the same product. The forced relationship of the new product with the existing accessories also needs to be studied e.g., developing a new television set may be related with the consumer need of clock, multi-channel viewing on one screen, microphone attachment and a built-in video game. Such forced relationship must be identified by the company before launching the product. The morphological analysis calls for identifying the structural dimensions of a problem and examining the relationships among them. The need identification can be done by interacting with the potential and existing customers in a focus group meet. The industrial marketers can identify new product ideas by working in association with the lead users of the product. Brainstorming has a major role in the idea-generation process. Contemporary methods for ranking the relative merits of ideas generated by brainstorming sessions rely on comparing average scores across members of the group. The average is a measure of the overall merit assigned to an idea but does not measure unanimity or the concentration of opinion across members of the group with respect to the idea under consideration. The standard deviation of responses is the accepted measure of group consensus but is rarely used in brainstorming possibly because the ranking of ideas is a more complex cognitive procedure.

The ideation process in more advanced way encompasses the following perspectives:

- 3Rs: Record, Recall and Reconstruct
- Return on ideas to match with returns on investment in reference to time and organizational resources
- Brainstorming
- Define the problem as a question
- Select an idea link word or phrase from the list of people, places, or products
- Record a list of ideas associated with the selected idea link
- Choose the link connection and brainstorm the ideas about its potential relationship to the problem defined as question
- Repeat the above step till the time runs out
- Brain-writing

- Distribute blank paper to the participants
- Write the problem as a question
- Review the divergent thinking
- Record three ideas and then exchange with other participants
- Draw the worksheet of ideas and list the best ideas in the lot
- Repeat these steps for 4–5 rounds until the time runs out.

Companies often begin their search for new ideas either by encouraging brainstorming, outside-the-box thinking or by conducting quantitative analysis of existing market and financial data, and customer opinions. These approaches may produce acceptable ideas at best. The problem with the first method is that few people are very good at unstructured and abstract brainstorming while the second approach may cause fabricated databases usually compiled to offer biased information and customers can rarely reveal if they need or want a product they've never seen.

Product ideas have to be turned into concept, and product concept can be turned later into the brand concept. The concept testing calls for testing of these competing concepts with an appropriate group of target consumers. The concepts can be presented physically or symbolically. The consumers' responses may be summarized, and the strength of the concept may be judged. The need-gap and product-gap levels may be checked and modified thereafter. The concept testing and product development methodology applies to any product or service. The business analysis includes the estimating sales as it would be of one-time purchase, frequently purchasing product or at regular interval purchase product. The estimates should also be made in relation to the tendency of first purchase, replacement purchase, or repeat sales. Besides, the company should also assess the marketing costs and the profits from commercialization of this product.

Testing new products in markets is a scientific process. Successful test marketing leads to proper uses and poses serious limitations. It provides a measure of sales performance and the opportunity to identify and correct any weaknesses in the product or in the marketing plan. It is, however, expensive and arduous. Managers need to weigh the cost and risk of product failure against the profit and probability of success, the difference in scale of investment between a test and a national launch, the likelihood of being copied and pre-empted by the competition, and the costs in money and reputation of a product failure. Product development at this stage involves designing the prototypes on the lines of the derived concept that has passed through technical tests. The consumer testing of the product may be taken up in two forms—laboratory testing and home testing.

Stage-gate model is a conceptual and operational roadmap for moving a new product project from idea to launch. This model divides the effort into distinct stages separated by management decision gates. Cross-functional teams must successfully complete a prescribed set of related cross-functional tasks in each stage prior to obtaining management approval to proceed to the next stage of product development. Stage-gate processes have a great deal of appeal to management, because, basically, they restrict investment in the next stage until management is comfortable with the outcome of the current stage. The gate can be effective in controlling product quality and development expense. Stages-and-gates in the model function as sequential phases and may run into some overlapping activities, especially when they cross the decision points. The stage grate processes may not lead toward completing tasks in earlier phases to keep them off the critical path, but they foster a mindset in which the work proceeds sequentially step by step. A newer alternative to stage-gate process is the bounding box approach, which is essentially a management by exceptions technique, in which certain critical parameters of the project such as profit margin, project budget, product performance level, and launch date are negotiated as the bounding box. Firms need to conduct regular checks so that the process managers remain within bounds. The criteria used in the gate review involve aspects such as:

- Strategic fit
- Market attractiveness
- Competitive advantage
- Patent/legal issues
- Technical feasibility
- Regulatory aspect of health, safety and environment
- Supply and market entrance
- Financial attractiveness.

The stage-gate process begins with the identification and documentation of a new idea in improving business. Tasks associated with the development of the product are then divided into a sequence of logical steps called *stages*, each of which is preceded by a *gate* where the attractiveness of the project is assessed. During each stage, a cross-functional project team carries out tasks that result in the completion of the defined deliverables including those related to technical (manufacturing, R&D, quality, regulatory) and business (sales, marketing, business development) functions. The advantages of using the stage-gate process are as follows:

- Improved customer satisfaction
- Shorter time to market
- Improved new product success rates
- Improved new product launches
- Earlier detection of failures
- Increased innovation and productivity
- Less recycling and rework.

Competitive technology-oriented decisions are the strategic business initiatives that involve significant resources and managerial skills. New technology-led products fail because the market tests are not elaborative to forecast their commercial success accurately. Firms need to develop systems thinking and the stage-gate process that capitalizes on the power of the wisdom of market players by allowing managers to interact in organized markets governed by well-defined rules. The consumer-centric technologies motivate users to analyze information and explore customer values. The stage-gate process demonstrates the power of the decision manger to perform strategically in the competitive markets.

Niche Marketing Strategy

Multinational and large domestic firms offer standardized and mass-produced products that are adapted to the preferences of various geo-demographic segments. Such product portfolios cater to large super-market chains, which serve mass-consumer segments. The local competitors also tend to manufacture their products to adapt to the needs of the niche markets emphasizing the importance of destination brands, their identity, and contextual geo-demographic attributes to enhance product quality. The strategy of companies to create and manage niche markets is typically characterized by demand-led manufacturing, branding, and marketing to develop long-term customer relationships.[41] Niche markets focus on small, profitable, and homogeneous market segments, which are also redefined as minimum viable market segments. Niche marketing strategy has outgrown as one of the popular conventional marketing designs. Niches or minimum viable segments in traditional market settings focus on a narrow share of the total market pie and operate on lower costs as compared to the large companies. The niche markets operate within unique preferences, and cater to the needs of a narrow, well-defined group of buyers, better than the potential rivals. However, niche markets, over time, tends to face oligopolistic market competition, where each competitor operates in a niche of similar or identical product portfolios, causing further fragmentation of geo-demographic segments. Such business scenario, over a longer period, drives market entropy which can be explained as a degenerating market phenomenon. Market entropy causes unregulated market competition, narrowing market segment, thin market shares among competitors, operational chaos, and asymmetric consumer defection across brands.[42]

Niche strategies provide a classic instance of such situations. No market is entirely homogeneous. There are always groups of customers that differ in terms of their needs. The possibility of the occurrence of niches, which individual competitors may occupy, always exists. Niches are unlikely to be complete, separate, and well-defined. There is always some overlap. However, if such niches are rather subtly defined, they may not always be obvious to all the players. Therefore, niche players may appear to compete. But in practice, they do not do so, or at least not fully. The area of operation or the size of the market also determines the consumer responsiveness and the effectiveness of delivery of goods and services. Thus, a follower in the large market may be the leader in the small market or niche. Smaller firms normally avoid competing with the larger firms. However, it has been observed that there is an increasing interest of big companies to serve the small area of operation or niche by setting up small business units. The niche strategy is profitable for the firms with low shares of the total market. The main reason is that the niche strategy

---

[41] Hammervoll, T., Mora, P., & Toften, K. (2013). The financial crisis and the wine industry: The performance of niche firms versus mass-market firms. *Wine Economics and Policy*, 3 (2), 108–114.

[42] Rajagopal. (2020). *Market entropy: How to manage chaos and uncertainty for improving organizational performance*. New York: Business Expert Press.

provides total knowledge about the customer segment to the company to enable it to serve better through value addition. The niche marketing strategy provides *high margin* to the company, while the mass-marketing strategy may provide the advantage of *high volume* to the company. Companies operating in niche may consider the following strategies:

- Adequate size of the market
- Purchasing power of the segment to the tune of profitability
- Potential for growth
- Negligible interest to the competing companies
- Appropriate skills and resources to serve the niche in a superior fashion
- Well-knit defensive strategy to counter the competitors' attacks.

The most important challenge in the niche marketing is specialization. There are three major tasks to be attended by the companies looking for developing the niche marketing strategy by creating a niche, expanding the niche, and protecting the niche markets. However, the niches are always risk averse to the attacks of the competing companies. The market niche also helps in encouraging the foreign direct investment with specific focus on the products and services.[43] Niche market players adhere to cost-effective operations and carry out customization of their products and services to the possible extent within the geo-demographic segments. However, niche market players operate within a low-yield cycle and protect customer value. Various industries like consumer products and services, international technology, and business-to-business products are engaged in consortium manufacturing and creating marketing strategies to lower their cost of production and co-create products across destinations. The cooperative dairy industry in India, and business-to-business products industries in China are the good examples of consortium business strategies. Therefore, smaller firms, through consortium, pose challenge to the large firms by adapting multiple market disruption strategies like low prices, disruptive innovation, mass marketing, and building

---

[43] Rajagopal. (2016). *Sustainable growth in global markets: Strategic choices and managerial implications*. Basingstoke, UK: Palgrave Macmillan.

customer loyalty at the bottom of the pyramid segments.[44] Companies continuously engaged in handling innovative business projects should periodically measure the employee performance for the purpose of work force planning, and networking broader collaborative contributions with other innovation management enterprises.

As a large market fragments into niches, it boosts up local competition. These niche players are engaged in manufacturing and marketing lookalike products of large companies at relatively low prices with marginal differentiation in features and use values. Such niche companies lead to disruptive innovations and tend to cannibalize the market share of large companies through disruptive marketing strategies. Co-creating can also be considered as a disruptive strategy to some extent. Small companies with relatively older business, such as convenience stores, or group of companies in an industry, lead to streamlined market operations in extended market niches. Companies growing with diversified business operations in a niche also incubate new businesses in smaller niches. Some niches grow independently in the marketplace engaged in the frugal and reverse innovation activities. Radical niches sometimes emerge as social enterprises and co-create community products and services. Small segments of consumers develop homogenous needs. Therefore, niche segments provide companies the opportunity to develop ethnic and socially distinctive brands. Such brands tend to have low market share and serve smaller customer base because of their specialized nature.[45] Many buyers tend to have an alternate brand along with their preferred brand as a change-of-pace. The pace refers to the contextual attributes like time, vogue, and trends demonstrated in social buying behavior. This gives rise to potential large-share brands with derived loyalty, as a larger customer base reinforces its preferred choice. Therefore, a change-of-pace strategy captures only a limited share of the market, as consumers always look for an alternate brand to stay abreast with the vogue and social dynamics. Reinforcing brands in the niche market in such instances is relative to the competing brands.

---

[44] Rajagopal. (2016). *Sustainable growth in global markets: Strategic choices and managerial implications*. Basingstoke, UK: Palgrave Macmillan.

[45] Jarvis, W., & Goodman, S. (2005). Effective marketing of small brands: Niche positions, attribute loyalty and direct marketing. *Journal of Product & Brand Management*, 14 (5), 292–299.

CHAPTER 6

Alternate Business Modeling

Agility in business is a value-based project-driven flexible approach for functional strategies like manufacturing, innovation, finance, distribution, and marketing. A central and novel feature of the crowd-based social marketing strategy model for entrepreneurial firms is about the simultaneous targeting of an upstream decision maker and influential peripheral (upstream) audiences to triangulate and increase campaign effectiveness.[1] This chapter is woven around the elements of agility in marketing, brand taxonomy, and behavioral shifts driving the need for upstream marketing among niche enterprises. In addition, the increasing importance of branding and value creation, internationalization, and entrepreneurial clusters (such as export-oriented units) have been discussed to support the concept of upstream business alliances. The agile approach to upstream social marketing ensures consistent, persuasive messages specifically crafted for the selected target audiences and coordinated through precise channels to maximize impact.[2]

---

[1] Key, T. M., & Czaplewski, A. J. (2017). Upstream social marketing strategy: An integrated marketing communications approach. *Business Horizons*, 60 (3), 325–333.

[2] Papasolomou, I., Thrassou, A., Vrontis, D., & Sabova, M. (2014). Marketing public relations: A consumer-focused strategic perspective. *Journal of Customer Behaviour*, 13 (1), 5–24.

Agility in Marketing

Agility in business is a value-driven, project-oriented, and flexible process to develop and implement functional strategies like manufacturing, innovation, finance, distribution, and marketing. Agile attributes of an entrepreneurial strategy consist of re-aligning and re-deploying its resources to create value collectively to manage continuity in business against the uncertainty and disruption in the business operations. Agile marketing practices encourage enterprises, irrespective of their size, to build value protection approaches for attaining high market share and profit through integrating the internal and external stakeholder engagements within the business ecosystem.[3] The success of agile practices in business has been observed in developing and launching of value-generation campaigns. For example, a co-created marketing project with customers and stakeholders can be developed as webpage for the products or services, advertising campaign, and content creation that illustrates a collective and flexible output. These activities can be operationalized, reviewed, and aligned with the changing business requirements to ensure high performance of enterprises at various geo-demographic, competitive, and market levels.

Design thinking has been the principal tool for all types of innovations following the five stages of design process including empathy, defining, ideation, developing prototype, and testing the design before commercialization and delivery to the clients. The focus of design thinking has shifted from corporate domain to public domain with the advancement of information and communication technology, asocial media, and crowdsourcing approaches. Consequently, design thinking is practiced widespread by the large and medium-sized enterprises. Many successful design thinking projects have been documented and their value is shown in empirical studies. However, it has been experienced by the enterprises that the success of design thinking practices depends on the nature of the project and its ecosystem. Design fit with agile business approaches helps in solving problems by aligning lean start-ups, scientific methods, Six Sigma in processes improvement, critical thinking, and systems thinking. Digging into the basic capabilities combining both agile practices and

---

[3] Teece, D., Peteraf, M., & Leih, S. (2016). Dynamic capabilities and organizational agility: Risk, uncertainty, and strategy in the innovation economy. *California Management Review*, 58 (4), 13–35.

design thinking helps in better understanding the problems, needs, and expected solutions (PNS factors). Accordingly, firm can better fit the design thinking process in the agile strategies and develop alternative approaches. In rapidly growing digital transformation across industries, the ability to frame and reframe agile strategies is increasingly becoming critical. Faced with significant disruption, there remains a long-standing question, often implicit, as to how they thrive with agile approaches and stay customer-centric keeping the desired level of profit.

Among many core capabilities, some constitute design thinking and help firms in framing and solving problems. These core elements augmenting entrepreneurial capabilities are as listed below:

Observe and document: This is a human approach to understand PNS factors as against the computer-aided programs or self-reporting platforms. Observations are common to stakeholders, which can be linked with the experience and collective intelligence.

Frame and reframe: This is a dynamic process in conceptualization of agile designs through collective intelligence. Firms make alignment with the market trends and learn to manage decisions, conflicts, and choices (DCC) concerning business strategies.

Create and design: At this stage the conceptualized design is actively experimented with prototypes and consumer jury with multidisciplinary teams comprising designers, key partners, consumers, strategists, and legal experts. It is a process to understand crowd behavior, and analyze collective intelligence for making appropriate business decisions with agility.

Deliver and commercialize: This is a critical stage as besides manufacturing, delivering, and commercializing the jury-approved designs, firms also need to evaluate the potential of scaling. Reaching the economy of scale in agile business environment is highly challenging. This entrepreneurial capability can be developed as M-3 framework incorporating competitive strategies on manufacturing, marketing, and mobilizing products and services in geographic pockets. In addition, enterprises must also focus on E-3 elements that include experience, emotions, and expansions of business (both vertically and horizontally).

Managing these core capabilities requires aligning of the current business models and developing alternative ones. Most organizations struggle with framing and reframing their organizational decision-making capabilities within resource constrains. Consequently, organizations develop core rigidities and often stay ineffective in creating a dominant agile environment.[4]

Agile Marketing is broadly a work management methodology within the Scrum framework that requires teams to adapt to the collaborative work environment with focus on 5T elements comprising task, target, time, thrust, and trust. Agile marketing practices function with self-organizing skills for teams to carry out cross-functional activities in a repetitive pattern with continuous feedback. These activities are driven by the temporal marketing planning (short-, medium-, and long-term planning). Implementation of agile marketing strategies varies by T-7 factors comprising task, territory, target, thrust, time, transition, and trust for specific products and services. The organizational context, in which the T-7 elements are managed, determines the marketing management approach based on an array of practices over the traditional marketing. Commonly, agile marketing practices encourage team culture on common objectives centered around the customers' needs. In the agile marketing process, teams periodically evaluate the efficiency of the process and eliminate redundancy to align and optimize marketing operations accordingly. Accordingly, companies practicing agile marketing strategies can achieve higher customer engagement and value and an increased ability to adapt to market uncertainties, and change stimulate speed toward market demand.[5] Transformational leadership effectively drives the agile practices in an enterprise. Successful leaders engaged in implementing agile practices at all levels in the organization timely respond to changes in the business environment by exploring and exploiting opportunities. The uphill challenge in this process is to overcome the internal and external resistance in throwing out old models and developing new ways of doing business. Entrepreneurial leaders in collaboration with the crowd tend to make changes incorporating radical changes and embedding them into the manufacturing and business processes. The transition to agile practices moves through the daily interactions to the most complex strategy. Leaders demonstrate changes in enterprise with empathy and

---

[4] Beckman, S. L. (2020). To frame or reframe: Where might design thinking research go next? *California Management Review*, 62 (2), 144–162.

[5] Gera, G., Gera, B., & Mishra, A. (2019). Role of Agile marketing in the present era. *International Journal of Technical Research & Science*, 4 (5), 40–44.

agile behavior engaging internal and external stakeholders to create organization synergy to increase efficiency at the workplace. They share a compelling, competitive, and clear purpose of the organization with the employees, key partners, and customers and encourage them to explore and exploit new opportunities. They create a safe socio-psychological space for teams to discuss the challenges and meet them in an integrated manner working together with predefined accountability. Transformational leaders promote agility in business with a calculated risk-matrix considering the cost, advantages, and time factors. However, agility in business must be carried out in a phased-experimentation manner by encouraging cross-sectional collaborations to design and manufacture products, attract customers, market with competitiveness, and achieve results.[6]

Firms must develop abilities on market sensing, flexibility, speed, and responsiveness for an effective implementation of strategies with marketing agility, and to co-create and coevolve with customer-centric strategies and respond rapidly to the complexities by reconfiguring their marketing tactics in a changing environment.[7] Managers implementing the agile marketing strategies must respond quickly to the rapidly changing and challenging market situations. Agile marketing processes involves easy adjustments of plans and strategies for quickly responding to the emerging opportunities and challenges. Companies must implement flexible marketing strategies in view of the crowd behavior and social consciousness of customers while marketing in the interactive digital environment of the social media channels. Agile methodology is an alternative to Waterfall methodology, which is a rigid, top-down approach to project management followed by most marketers.

The agile marketing strategies focus on the following management perspectives to increase the process speed and quality of deliverables to create value:

- Flexibility to meet the market challenges.
- Social and interactive marketing campaigns of products and services.

---

[6] Harvey, E. O. (2018). *5 behaviors of leaders who embrace change*. HBR Digital Article, Cambridge, MA: Harvard Business School Publishing.

[7] Zhou, J., Mavondo, F. T., & Saunders, S. G. (2019). The relationship between marketing agility and financial performance under different levels of market turbulence. *Industrial Marketing Management*, 83, 31–41.

- Proactiveness to crowd opinions, collective intelligence, and changing social conventions.
- Numerous small experiments to explore new markets and increase consumer outreach in existing markets.
- Encouraging group community behavior within target markets.
- Driving co-creation, coevolution, and reverse accountability in managing customer-centric innovations.
- Engagement of stakeholders and transparency in marketing process.

The increasing uncertainty in business environment today contributes to highly volatile market conditions. Agile business approaches have, therefore, become more important than ever. Agile management practices may appear appropriate, but many firms struggle to effectively integrate them into their operations. To implement agile practices, it is necessary for the enterprises to identify collaboration networks and manage them effectively by engaging with the key partners. Such operational synchronization helps in bridging the gaps between planning, implementation, and operational tasks in the organization. Agile enterprises can build systems integrating planning and implementation tasks with bottom-up monitoring and evaluation approaches to grow holistically with internal and external stakeholders.[8] The ambience for agile marketing consists of the team-based operations with flexible decision to manage the changing consumer preferences within a predetermined period and stay proactive and responsive to the market. The specific attributes of agile marketing are inclusivity and reverse accountability (customer engagement and role in agile governance), which help companies to encourage agile teams to participate in co-creation of products, services, brands, and marketing strategies along with the customers and stakeholders. The co-creation will be meaningful for the companies if the problems, needs, and probable solutions are meticulously explored by the agile teams, customers, and stakeholders.

Community participation in managing agile practices is one of the prerequisites, which helps in developing open innovations. Firms can succeed in creating open innovations by developing communities that have both interest and willingness to participate in the process. The

---

[8] Crocker, A., Cross, R., & Gardner, H. K. (2018). How to make sure Agile Teams can work together. *Harvard Business Review*. https://hbr.org/2018/05/how-to-make-sure-agile-teams-can-work-together.

willingness of a community to innovate products and processes must demonstrate a clear sense of purpose, values, and rules of engagement. Volkswagen (VW), a German automaker nurtured a sense of purpose in the marketing team by asking its members to reflect on what being part of VW meant to them and reinforced their shared values by encouraging them to pursue innovation, responsibility, and value creation as three distinctive attributes of the brand. One of the intrinsic purposes of agile business practice is to guide the work dynamics of stakeholders and inculcate significant responsibility and autonomy into their rules of engagement. To implement agile practices successfully, companies must generate ideas through brainstorming, collective conceptualization, pilot testing, implementation, and alignment with gaps.[9]

Rapid Market Appraisal (RMA) and Participatory Market Appraisal (PMA) are the tactical approaches used by most companies to explore opportunities. Value-based decisions, instead of usual data-driven decision, can be made by companies with the help of RMA and PMA analysis. Crowd behavior and collective intelligence also facilitate agile marketing decisions, and the implementation of agile marketing approaches is managed in a project environment with effective monitoring and periodical evaluations. Effective agile campaigns based on the user-generated contents and collective intelligence can be launched by the companies with the help of the crowd-and stakeholder engagement in agile marketing. Controlling the scope creep with a flexible marketing philosophy is a big challenge faced by the companies in managing agile marketing projects. Finance and human resource management are the core areas in agile marketing. Marketing agility enables the firm to identify the latent needs in the market, and motivates managers to develop a marketing program at the grassroots in each geo-demographic arrangement. Firms can identify opportunities and threats in a business situation, and redesign the existing marketing program suitable to the current market needs by taking into confidence the stakeholders and key partners, and developing the marketing programs to enhance flexibility and speed of marketing operations. Firms must also build motivated and responsive corporate teams to engage stakeholders and key business partners in implementing agile marketing programs. Agile marketing practices have

---

[9] Hill, L. A., Brandeau, G., Truelove, E., & Lineback, K. (2014). Collective genius. *Harvard Business Review*, 92 (6), 94–102.

been proved to be successful for many firms in deriving high business performance and growth in a competitive market ecosystem.[10]

In many firms, building organizational capabilities and competencies, by observing the success and failure incidences and developing a critical path through strategic thinking, is considered as a learning task. Often these companies exhibit high optimism level in demonstrating the advances in agile strategy and adopt elaborated organizational matrices and face impairing between the planed strategies and realistic achievements. To keep a company strategically agile and to successfully coordinate its activities across divisions, the decision-making process should be redesigned with the social approach by eliminating the gaps with organizational relationship and workplace hierarchy. Firms must aim at building a matrix comprising corporate values, strategies, and priorities to negotiate the best business deals with high pay off.[11]

Agile strategies encourage collective decisions emerging out of community networks and collective intelligence. Open innovation has also become a part of agile approaches, designed to ensure the long-term viability of enterprises through adaptability. Broadly, open innovation is about the purposive management of PNS factors and utilization of crowd-based knowledge, which is contributed by the external partners for innovation. Open innovation strategies have become part of a portfolio of crowd information practices, which is used largely by the frugal innovation firms at the grassroots. Crowd-driven ideation and consultative information has become a viable alternative to agile practices and community innovation. Several recent studies have argued that open innovation has the potential to generate solutions to complex and chronic social and business problems. Agile practices have enabled the open innovations to undergo a public process and the small firms to manage and explore solutions to very diverse problems through continuous learning. The increasing uncertainty and the divergence of stakeholder perspectives associated with growing complex problems make the crowdsourcing,

---

[10] Khan, H. (2020). Is marketing agility important for emerging market firms in advanced markets? *International Business Review*, 29 (5), *in press* https://doi.org/10.1016/j.ibusrev.2020.101733.

[11] Bartlett, C. A., & Ghoshal, S. (1990). Matrix management: Not a structure, a frame of mind. *Harvard Business Review*, 68 (4), 138–145.

open innovation, and agile management approaches more appealing in the changing business situations today.[12]

Brand Architecture

Brands are successful because people prefer them over the unbranded products. In addition to the various soi-psychological factors brands give consumers the means whereby they can make choices and judgments. Based on these experiences, customers can then rely on chosen brands to guarantee standards of quality and service, which reduces the risk of failure in purchase. Today's world is characterized by complex technology, and this can be extremely confusing to the people who are not technology-minded. Brands can play an important role by providing simplicity and reassurance, and offering a quick, clear guide to a variety of competitive products. It may be stated that animism is another process that directly explains the specific ways in which the vitality of the brand can be realized.[13] Over time, personalities of the spokespersons are transmitted to the brand. Obviously, marketers have little control over this aspect, and indirectly, the brand personality is created by all the elements of the marketing-mix. The personality of a brand is created over time by all the constituents of marketing-mix.

Following agile business strategies, a firm can comfortably rely on co-branding strategy which is an important differentiation for the transition of brands. As a strategy, co-branding has been a successful approach across the business destination and firms of various sizes with business operations both in developed and developing countries. Several co-branding agreements have proliferated across various business contexts comprising advertisements, manufacturing and marketing of ethnic products, and developing retail services for introducing innovative consumer products. With the increasing use of brand extensions and brand leveraging, many new products are launched as cobrands, specifically fashion apparel (ethnic style and texture), sustainable textile (organic clothing based on naturally grown cotton), leather products, and many vegan fashion accessories. Moreover, rural–urban brand alliances are capitalizing

---

[12] Ooms, W., & Piepenbrink, R. (2021). Open innovation for wicked problems: Using proximity to overcome barriers. *California Management Review*, 63 (2), 62–100.

[13] Fournier Susan. (1998). Consumers and their brands: Developing relationship theory in consumer research. *Journal of Consumer Research*, 24 (March), 343–373.

on the emerging markets and establishing business leads in developed markets. Such brand transition is triggering reverse marketing effect in the global marketplace by entwining complementary upstream market features with downstream designs in different brands. Consequently, co-branding strategy is becoming a common practice in multinational brands expanding at the bottom of the pyramid market segment. Such brand transition tends to build market on the inherent equity of local–global brands in the rapidly changing market environment. During this transition phase, attributes of brand stretching from both rural to urban and local to global are kept unchanged, and a minor adjustment is done with the new product name as a transitional identity. This is a contemporary practice to integrate the brand attributes, values, and equities by harmonizing the design, value, and logotypes. This ensures all consumers and drives them to stay loyal to the brand and gradually learn to appreciate both the verbal and non-verbal language of the brand in the marketplace.[14]

Fabindia, India is an iconic ethnic garments and home furnishings company, which began its modest beginnings as an export house in 1960, marketing handloom fabrics to overseas customers. Over next sixteen years (by 1976) it started domestic manufacturing and operations in India, and over the following four decades, became synonymous with socially conscious company of quality handmade products procured from artisans and marketed to customers who have ethnic tastes. The business of the firm is blended with the twin objectives of making a profit and providing a sustainable livelihood for rural artisans. However, with the changing preferences of consumers and transitions across the generation of consumers like Baby boomers, Generation-X, and Generation-Z, the ethos of *Fabindia* was not associated with the transitory generations and consumers, which affected significantly their consumption behavior.[15] The firm had made dramatic growth of *Fabindia* from its inception through 2013, and is able to override the changing consumer's perception of the brand. There are various ways for brands to thrive the diminishing effects of market demand and consumer perceptions. To grow brands with their customers, it is important for the firms to mitigate

[14] Abratt, R., & Motlana, P. (2002). Managing co-branding strategies: Global brands into local markets. *Business Horizons*, 45 (5), 43–50.

[15] Chattopadhyay, A., Sabhaney, P., Chainani, S., & Wee, J. (2014). *Fabindia: Branding India's Artisanal crafts for mass retail*. Cambridge, MA: Harvard Business School Publishing.

cost, time, and risk factors, and revive relationships with the key partners to regain the market share.[16] Firms managing local brands and markets need to develop empathy and transparency, and use media with agility. Such brand strategy can help firms in tracking the behavioral trends of consumers to build scenarios. Besides the above strategies, firm can also adapt to new ways of co-creating strategies with consumers to enhance the brand promise and deliver desired value.

Companies with flagship brands follow an outside-in approach to manage brands in the competitive marketplace. Brands are built and communicated to create clear awareness among customers, and are supported by the required set of management skills. Toyota has built Lexus brand of luxury car meeting the expectation of technology perfection by managing the quality processes. Building customer-centric brand demands that managers balance business skills with brand quality and competitive advantages. The outside-in approach helps the companies nurture their reputation for high-quality brands to gain customer's trust and deliver company's promises. Companies with robust brand leadership attributes drive managers toward setting sustainable brand management strategies and designing the brands to serve the marketplace. Companies also engage brands to serve customers and meet their expectations. Most companies learn lessons from the performance of previous brands, and make efforts to build new brands by analyzing the feedback of customers and observations of the employees of the company and other market players. In the process of building strong brands, companies invest in brand management programs that attract potential customers, and sustain in the marketplace among competing brands. It is necessary to track the performance of brands over the long term.[17]

Consumer emotions are largely set through the verbal and non-verbal market communications extended by the companies. Advertisements play a critical role in stimulating the consumer emotions. Right from the late twentieth century, as the usage of computers has rapidly grown, the Internet has been the prime anchor of the marketing communications and stimulant of consumer emotions. The increased participation of people on the social network platforms has brought the emotions associated with

---

[16] Balis, J. (2020). *Brand marketing through the Coronavirus crisis*. HBR Digital Article, Cambridge, MA: Harvard Business School Press.

[17] Ulrich, D., & Smallwood, N. (2007). Building a leadership brand. *Harvard Business Review*, 85 (7/8), 92–100.

the products, services, and companies very close to the market players. Compared to offline media communications, social network platforms possess unique characteristics that affect the likelihood of generating emotions and reactions to the experience on the brand among fellow customers and employees of the firm. The online emotion is largely driven by the vividness of social networks, interactivity, challenge, interaction speed, machine memory, and allowable social interactions. Depending on how a social network platform performs on these dimensions, positive or negative emotions may result on the products, services, or the image of the company. For example, using machine memory to automatically generate purchase recommendations based on the prior consumption patterns may be perceived as pleasantly surprising, while a firm sending unsolicited emails based on a user's cookie trail may be annoying. Such feelings generated and shared by the consumers get attached to the brand and build its equity in the market. Thus, the challenge of the brand managers is to get consumers to associate positive emotions with a brand, and manage company sponsor's social network websites by understanding the consumer emotions and their ramifications.[18]

Social learning is a conscious effort to connect PNS factors between the society and individuals. It affects the behavioral transformation and alignment regarding the social, technological, and market interventions. Different global and local communities have different learning portfolios and approaches. The social leaning generates common value system and social intelligence to promote co-creation and the coevolution of business and society relationship; develops community brand; and disseminates new trends of ethnicity. Social learning is an outcome of collective intelligence generated from crowd-driven diffusion of knowledge based on the experiences (user-generated contents) within the community and corporate efforts. The digital social media channels have come into prominence since the early twenty-first century due to the growing support of video and photo interactive tools, and the advancement in the information technology has helped in the evolution of the learning platforms.

Brand knowledge, which consists of two dimensions: brand awareness and brand associations in consumer memory, is abstracted as an 'associative network memory model'. Familiarity with the brand, and favorable and strong brand associations in memory of the customer leads to positive

---

[18] Jones, M. Y., Spence, M. T., & Vallester, C. (2008). Creating emotions via B to C websites. *Business Horizons*, 51 (5), 419–428.

customer-based brand equity. The scope of measurement and management approaches used by an organization is determined by the culture. Brand strategy is formulated practically by the companies, with focus on the effectiveness of their brand efforts from a communications and financial perspective. They apply a strong measurement framework involving financial-based variables to measure the financial impact of brand efforts, and non-financial variables like customer perceptions and behaviors to measure the impact on customer actions and beliefs. The brand laddering implies development of a brand from attributes to benefits, and their repeated reinforcement in the consumer segments by highlighting their benefits to serve unique values. Firms disseminate the attributes and benefits of the brands to get them associated with the lifestyles of the consumers.[19]

Most consumer products companies drive their brands to penetrate the marketplace without developing enough awareness about them among consumers and market players. Companies deploy such brands through offensive tactics. It has been observed that such brand marketing tactics help companies to successfully launch new products, enter new markets, and gain share over existing products in the local markets. However, in managing every new brand launch intending to build its market share, the brand should defend its position against the competing brands. The basic types of defensive brand marketing strategies include positive, inertial, parity, and retarding. The first two types of brand marketing strategies tend to establish and communicate the attributes of brand superiority in reference to brand features and values relative to the existing brands; while the other two categories of brand marketing establish and communicate competitive advantages and strategic gains in the long term as compared to the rival brands in the marketplace. Companies meticulously choose strategies to support identity of brands, and products and services, to develop an appropriate communication plan. As the brands are established in the market and gain high brand equity and customers' value, they become vulnerable to the market competitors.

Although popular brands and unique capabilities help a company sustain competitive advantage, they cannot be built by imitation. Managers have been able to develop sustainable capabilities not by emulating others, but by using their organizational designs and processes

---

[19] Kumar, S. R., & Minj, E. (2012). *Himalaya face wash: Brand associations and lifestyles*. Harvard Business School Press, Cambridge, MA.

to identify, build on, and leverage their 'asymmetries'. Such asymmetries may occur even in the simplest organizations. Unfortunately, they are often concealed, of little apparent use, and unconnected to value creation. Thus, they require new making strategies and organizational approaches for their discovery, development, and application.[20] Social media has emerged as a collective intelligence repository to support managers in the golden age of branding, which has a hybrid effect today covering both virtual and physical platforms. Several channels of social media like Facebook, LinkedIn, and Instagram, YouTube, and Twitter have become the mainstream media to directly connect with customers all over the globe. Penetration of information and promotions on these channels is attracting huge audiences across geo-demographic clusters to their brands. Firms spend billions producing co-creative contents. Social media has significantly promoted crowd-cultures as the prolific cultural innovators to co-design products suitable to the concurrent consumer preferences and market competition. The impact of branded content and crowd-cultures have encouraged alternative approaches such as cultural branding in promoting a new ideology that diffuses from the crowd. Chipotle, a food chain of the USA, experimented cultural branding successfully linking the Mexican taste to the American consumers by focusing on the organic-farming subculture and blew up into a mainstream concern on social media.[21]

Frequent introduction of new brands also leads to instability in the brand management process as new brands are pushed through piggy-backing tensile brands to cater to temporary market demand, and companies make high investments to sustain such brands against the fluctuating market demand. These brands are categorized as 'agitating brands', which may also be recognized as boomer brands in a given time. To sustain with agitating brands, it is necessary for a company to make differentiation and add value to the brand. Such distinction is necessary in the brand architecture approach for overcoming any conflicts in defining the role and level of the brands. Categories of brands play significant role in the process of brand architecture for a firm in the following ways:

---

[20] Miller, D., Eisenstat, R. A., & Foote, N. (2002). Strategy from the inside out: Building capability-creating organizations. *California Management Review*, 44 (3), 37–54.

[21] Holt, D. B. (2016). Branding in the age of social media. *Harvard Business Review*, 94 (3), 40–50.

- Creating coherence and effectiveness.
- Allowing brands to stretch across the products and markets.
- Stimulating the purchase decisions by brand drivers.
- Targeting market niches and benefits positioning.

Building tensile brands has become a marketing priority for many firms. The presumption is that building a tensile brand yields a number of marketing advantages. Strength of such brands drives loyalty in various ways and creates differential responses by consumers to various marketing activities, which would help in building brand equity in the long term.

Companies face growing challenge in co-creating brand experience and maintaining long-term customer value by integrating customer-brand relationship, due to increased fragmentation of customer communities and media channels. Such engagement of brands with media has enabled customers to interact with brands on traditional and digital media channels. Positive interactions of customer with the brand enhance digital diffusion of user-generated and corporate brand content, whereas negative experiences are seen on the micro blogs of smaller communities within the niche. These interactions of customers with brands on social media may be by liking, sharing, or commenting on branded content. User-generated branded content is being increasingly used by the marketers to drive customer emotions on popular social media channels like Facebook, Twitter, Instagram, and LinkedIn. Interaction of customers and the crowd (gatekeepers, reviewers, critics and referrals, and the competition) with the user-generated brand content reveals the underlying customer preferences, emotions of the customers, and their brand association. Branding strategies can be developed accordingly by the brand owners and sponsors, and the users to improve the brand attitude, brand equity, brand loyalty, and purchase intention of customers.

Companies can improve customer-centric brand strategies by understanding brand association of customers and user experiences derived from temporal and spatial experiences. Brand experience is the feeling emerged on interacting with a brand psychophysically, while online customer experience is the feeling emerged on interacting with the retailer's website, crowd impulse, and augmented reality. User-generated experience is the feelings emerged on interacting with social media contents. Therefore, customer interaction with a brand is a significant tool to measure the brand value. It also helps in developing competitive branding strategies by reviewing the sensory, intellectual, affective, and behavioral facets of customer-brand relationship.[22]

Proximity, Relationship, and Optimism

The companywide customer relationship management includes functional-level strategies and front-end strategies toward building customer relationship. The functional-level strategies are associated with the blend of sales and services, innovation and technology, and product distribution in the context of 4C elements comprising customer value, cost to customer, convenience, and probable conflicts. Therefore, the functional level CRM perspectives execute customer-related tasks and technology orientation to provide real-time services to customers. The customer-facing front-end CRM strategies are focused on single-window approach to explore problems, needs, and solutions through the front contact channels including the social media. In addition, the front-end CRM strategies focus on disseminating customer experience in a reverse pyramid design by diffusing customer experience from macro to micro market segments. The effective distribution of customer intelligence within and outside the company encompasses customer communities, crowd platforms, and social networks. In this process, information coordination is the major challenge across companies by size.

The psychosocial factors also affect the customer relationship and initiatives of firms in staying pro-customer and pro-competition. The perceived attribute of relationship is largely originated from the stakeholders, which embeds anticipated services and benefits from the firm. However, in complying with the perceived attributes of customer relations, the firms meticulously evaluate the costs associated with the relationship programs. Consequently, the cost of loyalty programs and break-even points of investment in customer relations contribute to decision-making. Firms evaluate the cost–benefit ration of customer relationship programs and implement them in high-inflow customer destinations. The periodical assessments of psychosocial factors include measurement of the extent of satisfaction, incidence of loyalty, the rate of retention and defection, and the degree of customer dependence on the

---

[22] Waqas, M., Salleh, N. K. M., & Hamzah, Z. L. (2021). Branded content experience in social media: Conceptualization, scale development, and validation. *Journal of Interactive Marketing*, 56, 106–120.

product portfolios of firms. These periodical assessments benefit the firms in evaluating, redesigning, and implementing the customer relationship programs to generate customer value. In addition, the divergent factors of value streams are spread across the customer engagement (emotional association), role of influencer (transfer of knowledge and decision-making), and motivation through referrals (customer advocacy), all of which play significant role in implementing the customer relationship programs. Most customers conceive the benefits of customer relationship programs as a social drive and get motivated through the crowd behavior. Therefore, firms engage customers in developing relationship programs through 4D paradigm comprising designing, differentiating, disseminating, and delivering. The involvement of stakeholders helps the relationship programs in operating as a co-marketing alliance,[23] which has a triadic focus of corporate performance, customer engagement, and profit-making by developing brand loyalty and corporate image as core drivers for success.

The relationships between stakeholders and organizations largely depend on the stakeholders' needs and personal attitudes of managers, which constitute the corporate behavior demonstrating the social, economic, and financial health of the firms. The co-created and coevolved stakeholder relationship with the firms contributes toward mutual benefits in the long run. However, agile relationships between firms and stakeholders (customers and investors) raise individual optimism and the degree of risk in governance and leadership over time. Such behavior jeopardizes the inclusivity in business and fragments the role of stakeholder engagement in the governance of the firm. The innovative and risk-taking behavior of corporate executives and stakeholders affect the firm's actions toward investment in innovation and technology, value creation, and delivering social responsibilities.

Optimism has evolved as a social perspective in the firms of various sizes and performance. Geo-demographic differences determine the level of people's involvement and accountability in social growth of the firm, and help in projecting their future. The psychosocial behavior of most business-to-consumer and business-to-business firms drives coevolution process. These firms develop an energetic and task-focused approach,

---

[23] Farrelly, F., & Quester, P. (2005). Investigating large-scale sponsorship relationships as co-marketing alliances. *Business Horizons*, 48 (1), 55–62.

which is reinforced as corporate goals and connects with the socioeconomic leverages.[24] Making financial, marketing, and strategic decisions with corporate involvement is common in conventional practices. However, the current business philosophy focuses on stakeholder engagement (inclusivity) and social responsiveness and value creation (optimism) to stay competitive at the triple bottom-line comprising people (stakeholders), planet (sustainability in business), and profit (profit-with-purpose).

Organizational culture is one of the determining factors of corporate decision-making efforts and the subsequent corporate behavior, but inclusivity in business facilitates convergence of social values and business governance. The corporate philosophy of inclusivity in developing countries has a positive influence in motivating stakeholder investment and business governance. It has been pointed out by previous research studies, that organizational effectiveness in the customer-centric firms relies on three critical factors: belief, emotion, and trust. Operational involvement of stakeholders in a firm can be reinforced by personal beliefs, emotional attachment with the organization, and trustworthiness. Hence, consistency, clear communication, and a democratic philosophy among the social enterprises result from the inclusivity of stakeholders in business. The inclusivity in business requires strong relations between the personal attitude of managers, stakeholder engagement, and relative public–private investment in developing countries.[25] The major reasons of a diminishing organizational performance are low trust, inconsistent flow of decisions from top management, variability in operational standards, tolerance to incompetence or bad behavior, dishonest feedback and functionality, and downplaying the stakeholders' suggestions to improve business operations.[26]

The chronological evolution of interactive marketing can be observed in the changing directions of the journey from broadcasting marketing (radio, catalogue, and physical mails) to electronic interactive marketing

---

[24] Ikeda, N., Inoue, K., & Sugitani, S. (2021). Managerial optimism and corporate investment behavior. *Journal of Behavioral and Experimental Finance*, 30 (in press) https://doi.org/10.1016/j.jbef.2021.100492.

[25] Graham, J. R., Harvey, C. R., & Puri, M. (2013). Managerial attitudes and corporate actions. *Journal of Financial Economics*, 109, 103–121.

[26] Galford, R., & Drapeau, A. S. (2003). Enemies of trust. *Harvard Business Review*, 81 (2), 88–95.

(television and telemarketing), and virtual marketing (seamless smart television and smart mobile phones, social media, and online marketing). The course of interactive marketing is changing continuously with the advancement of information and communication technology. Global penetration of digital technologies, and the online diverse spread of social networks, blogs, and video platforms have revolutionized the engagement of firms with consumers.[27] Interactive marketing today empowers consumers to raise voices both for and against the firm's innovation, manufacturing, distribution, and marketing policies. The interactive marketing on digital platforms has given an enormous rise to e-commerce supported by visual and functional technologies like artificial intelligence, augmented reality, and virtual reality. Online interactions have expanded the customer outreach and refined the value perceptions and co-creation perspectives in managing disruptions in business and competitive leverage for growing firms. Firms embrace and listen to customer-community dialogues to understand their views and suggestions to improve the business strategies.[28]

The domains comprising communication-mix, meta-social behavior, relationship inflators, relationship drivers, social attributes, and public policies for setting the information dissemination norms play a significant role in connecting C3 factors that include corporate, consumer, and the crowd participation. The C3 information management practices are widely founded on the interactive communication mosaic, which has six information quadrants, each focusing on the following strategies:

- Assimilation of information.
- Efficiency in disseminating information.
- Managing surprises in communication (unthinkable).
- Validating acquired information.
- Structuring situational information.
- Diffusing generic user-based contents to build proximity between consumers and firms.

[27] Berezan, O., Krishen, A. S., Agarwal, S., & Kachroo, P. (2018). The pursuit of virtual happiness: Exploring the social media experience across generations. *Journal of Business Research*, 89, 455–461.

[28] Rajagopal. (2021). *Crowd-based business models—Using collective intelligence for market competitiveness*. New York: Palgrave Macmillan.

The communication-mix suggests that interactive communication can be effective if it is co-created through user-generated contents including both verbal and non-verbal contents to optimize the visual emotions. However, transparency in communication is a non-compromising attribute in both physical and digital diffusion of communication. The above discussed approaches can generate high psychodynamics (consumer-to-consumer interactions) in crowd-based and corporate communication. Effective communication increases the proximity of firms with consumers and other business partners to keep abreast of corporate policies, consumer needs, and market competition. Interactive communication and marketing strategies help in developing meta-social behavior, which converges crowd behavior, collective intelligence, and corporate values to openness. The socio-psychological factors of 4Es comprising emotions, experience, empathy, and ecstasy significantly affect the meta-social behavior. However, machine learning and robotic information management with artificial intelligence also encourages interactive marketing and social proximity.

Customer-centric firms practice interactive marketing using various customer-convenience tools like direct mail, catalogue retailing, telemarketing, social media channels, digital advertising and marketing, and mobile marketing. Firms operating congruent to the information and communication technology adapt to network technology to encourage crowd participation and collective intelligence to stimulate psychodynamics among consumers to review, react, and reaffirm the brands in the social media. A positive psychodynamics helps companies to lower the brand promotion costs and enhance the customer outreach across geo-demographic segments. Firms gain attention of consumers through new, green, digital, and consumer-friendly technologies. Interactions through social media beyond boundaries enable consumers to express their views, needs, probable risks, and the preferred solutions.[29] A pooled repository of such knowledge forms collective intelligence, which can be used by the firms effectively to develop customer-centric marketing strategies. Therefore, putting the people together to create collective intelligence through psychodynamics is central to proximity marketing.

---

[29] Gere, A., Harizi, A., Bellissimo, N., Moskowitz, H., & Kókai, Z. (2022). *Consumer-driven- and consumer-perceptible food innovation*. In Galanakis, C. M. (Ed). *Innovation Strategies in the Food Industry* (Second Edition). Cambridge, MA: Academic Press, 97–120.

EYE model of proximity marketing comprising empowerment, yearning, and emotions can be framed by the firms by encouraging the consumers' experience sharing in social media followed by analysis of their cognitive feelings, firms can architect, which comprises. Customer-centric companies can provide information literacy to enhance social proximity by accelerating vertical expansion within a specific market, and horizontal expansion across geo-demographic segments in new destinations. By measuring the input and output time of processing visual communications, information decomposition effects (number of views and extent of information entropy), and information effectiveness to proximity, firms can analyze the proximity metrics. Customer proximity, outreach, and value perceptions (POV) can be enhanced by empowering consumers to lead and manage interactive information forums on products, competition, corporate policies, and PNS factors. Localized forums such as LEGO forums and handicrafts forums in India can grow into regional and global forum, where local artisans interact with the institutional forum, and put forth their point of view to improve their design thinking concepts. Physical interactions are replaced by digital platforms through proximity technology, which generates sensory perceptions, like knowing, feeling, and being. Hybridity in information systems and social robotics have significantly contributed to indoctrinating the wisdom of nudge, feel, and analyze the crowd information or collective intelligence, which is pivotal in building proximity between people, society, and firm.[30] Firms can analyze social consciousness and sensitivity in the perceptions of people by their interactions in and across social domains and interest groups on an individual and social level.

Corporate behavior and relationship marketing are the intertwined determinants to be managed proactively to develop effective synergy in building customer value and achieving desired level of performance. Managing synergy depends on the kind of attributes of relationship marketing, which might develop proactive corporate behavior toward stakeholders and employees. The corporate behavior is affected by leadership, organizational design, culture, and workplace norms. Positive streamlining of these domains in an organization helps in convergence of employee engagement and customer orientation to co-create and coevolve sustainable stakeholder value. Consequently, companies invest

---

[30] Rajagopal (2024). *Proximity marketing: Converging community, consciousness, and consumption.* New York: Business Exprert Press (in press).

in customer relationship-marketing strategies expecting a high benefit–cost ratio, which tends to improve the quality of relationship, operational performance, and profitability in the long run.[31] Customer-centric firms periodically evaluate the customer voice, analyze the crowd behavior, and measure the quality indicators to develop proactive behavior. The relationship-marketing attributes also affect the corporate behavior, as the stakeholder perceptions and values drive the corporate behavior. Among many pro-customer characteristics, companies with inclusive business principles focus on co-creating innovation and relationship programs.

---

[31] Lo, F. Y., & Campos, N. (2018). Blending Internet-of-Things (IoT) solutions into relationship marketing strategies. *Technological Forecasting and Social Change*, 137, 10–18.

PART III

Thematic Fusion

CHAPTER 7

Synthesis: Managing Enterprises at the Grassroots

Entrepreneurship in developing countries has an economic motivation and it is taken up as a livelihood to enhance the quality of life and social values. Broadly, social value is dynamic, and customer-centric firms periodically monitor the perpetual changes in social values, culture, and ethnicity. The bottom-line of the entrepreneurship is social and stakeholder engagement to achieve expected outcomes. An effective, convergent business strategy, therefore, creates social and customer values by coevolving the business model and entrepreneurial brands in the society. The connecting thread between society and business consists in developing cognitive ergonomics among the stakeholders and stimulating co-creation of business design while co-creation allows enterprises to tap the skills and insights of stakeholders and develop new ways of building value chain. This chapter discusses the bottom-line of entrepreneurship, its transitional journey to contemporary business environment, and convergence among the market, society, and embedded values.

© The Author(s), under exclusive license to Springer Nature Switzerland AG 2024
Rebuilding Entrepreneurship at the Grassroots, Palgrave Studies of Entrepreneurship and Social Challenges in Developing Economies,
https://doi.org/10.1007/978-3-031-43270-5_7

The Bottom-line

Socio-cultural dimensions of entrepreneurship in some countries are more catalytic to poverty alleviation and local growth than others.[1] The increasing formal businesses in the private and publicly owned firms are largely built on external resources, and it is a difficult proposition to manage enterprises on borrowed resources in developing countries. The underdeveloped markets restrict the growth of these enterprises in developing countries. The growth of informal businesses such as family businesses, and micro and small enterprises in several developing countries including Argentina, Brazil, Chile, India, Malaysia, Mexico, Nicaragua, Pakistan, South Korea, South Africa, Taiwan, and Turkey have shown slow growth due to resources and market limitations.[2] Collective entrepreneurship has emerged as an effective strategy to alleviate extreme poverty. This concept is an outgrowth of inclusive entrepreneurship through which helping the poor integrates as a social process by managing multiple intertwined liabilities of both government and society. Entrepreneurial clusters have been regarded as the possible solution to reduce the incidence of poverty as they can provide the abjectly poor with access to resources, training, and market support. Collective entrepreneurship is a coordinated action to create economic value in the social commons, which holds the unique potential to transfer skills and expertise, hedge against the market risk, and provide support against adverse life circumstances.[3] However, it has been found that family and community support have a positive effect on micro and small entrepreneurship in rural India and Bangladesh, though the business partners' support is negatively associated with entrepreneurship. Therefore, developing countries have mixed growth of these enterprises. Thus, entrepreneurship in emerging markets considerably differs from that in the developed markets. Digital technologies offer unique entrepreneurial opportunities

---

[1] Antonacopoulou, E., & Fuller, T. (2020). Practising entrepreneuring as emplacement: The impact of sensation and anticipation in entrepreneurial action. *Entrepreneurship & Regional Development*, 32 (3–4), 257–280.

[2] Guillen, M. F. (2000). Business groups in emerging economies: A resource-based view. *Academy of Management Journal*, 43 (3), 362–380.

[3] Kimmitt, J., Muñoz, P., & Newbery, R. (2019). Poverty and the varieties of entrepreneurship in the pursuit of prosperity. *Journal of Business Venture*, 35 (4), 1–18.

to overcome the major challenges of poverty in both farm and non-farm enterprise sectors in emerging markets.[4]

Entrepreneurship in developing countries has an economic motivation, and it is taken up as a survival occupation. Both push and pull factors influence entrepreneurship in low-income demographics. The push factors include the need for earning and employment and continuing the family legacy of entrepreneurship, whereas pull factors include the market attractiveness, market for innovative products, potential market-share need for achievement, autonomy, and financial success. Individuals, who are pushed into entrepreneurship, are often labeled to be necessity-motivated, and those pulled into entrepreneurship are labeled to be opportunity-motivated.[5]

Organized entrepreneurship represents a natural pathway to alleviate poverty. It is arguably a social path to raise per capita income at minimum wages to assure social and personal benefits. Entrepreneurship helps in exploring the opportunity for economic advancement and improving the quality of life.[6] Thailand and The Philippines have a notably high level of entrepreneurial activity in all age groups and a significant proportion of the adult population engaged in entrepreneurial activity. Economies in the earlier stages of development are often more focused on getting basic requirements in place, while more economically advanced societies attract innovation and entrepreneurship factors like development of a formal venture finance sector and transfer of technology.[7] Entrepreneurial activity is influenced by the framework conditions of the environment in which it takes place, and it ultimately benefits this environment through social value and economic development. For example, entrepreneurs create jobs for themselves and others, which generates income for families within the community and improves their quality of life. They develop new products that improve people's lives, and advance the knowledge and

---

[4] Soluk, J., Kammerlander, N., & Darwin, S. (2021). Digital entrepreneurship in developing countries: The role of institutional voids. *Technological Forecasting and Social Change*, 170. https://doi.org/10.1016/j.techfore.2021.120876.

[5] Amorós, J. E., Cristi, O., & Naudé, W. (2021). Entrepreneurship and subjective well-being: Does the motivation to start-up a firm matter? *Journal of Business Research*, 217, 389–398.

[6] Morris, M. H., Santos, S. C., & Neumeyer, X. (2020). Entrepreneurship as a solution to poverty in developed economies. *Business Horizons*, 63 (3), 377–390.

[7] IDRC (2016). Asian Regional Entrepreneurship Report (2015–16), Kulalumpur.

competitiveness of their societies. Consequently, innovations at various entrepreneurial levels are driven by the socio-cultural factors. A regional innovation system helps in developing industrial clusters surrounded by various social organizations. Since innovations occur more frequently in the situation of geographical concentration and proximity, the regional entrepreneurship grows at an economy of scale within the fast-growing knowledge-based economy.[8]

Value is often measured either in economic or in social terms. The blended-value proposition emphasizes that true value, which is a blend of economic, social, and environmental components, is indivisible. After the success of networking practices of business activities with social media over decades, profit-seeking firms have laid explicit emphasis on the creation of social value. This business philosophy has grown in non-profit organizations as well. Social value is dynamic, and customer-centric companies continuously monitor the perpetual changes in social values, culture, and ethnicity. Consequently, companies have developed social corporate entrepreneurship, which intends to create social as well as financial value. The social business value is therefore defined as a function of corporate social initiatives to support business and the extent of social values absorbed in the society and the market. To drive the business deep into the social environment, companies adapt to the triadic philosophy of gaining social insights, ideation on blending business values in the society, and co-creating innovative socio-business strategies. The best practices reveal that these elements boost business results by driving business social and solving complex problems.

Social engagement is a socially responsive approach in managing tasks and socioeconomic practices with expected outcomes. Social engagement aligns with individual, community, civic, and institutional benefits including leverages from business and economy. While social scholarship focuses on the individual and community attributes as a state of engagement, the social perspective of engagement endorses collective impact on co-created businesses through a socially determined process. The design-to-society philosophy is, therefore, aligned with the social engagement theory and social presence maxim, which refers to the degree of presence perceived by the community participants in generating and disseminating

---

[8] Su, Y. S., & Chen, J. (2015). Introduction to regional innovation systems in East Asia. *Technological Forecasting and Social Change*, 100, 80–82.

communication. Social presence theory advocates that social media (physical and digital interactions) should align with psychological perception of involvement (presence), and transmit visual and verbal cues.

Sharing of stakeholder emotions and experience on brands contributes to the collective intelligence, which is used by the firms in developing customer-centric strategies. The inherent satisfaction of co-creation with crowd guides companies in developing customer-centric marketing strategies and leads to novel and superior value propositions. The case of LEGO is a very good example. The company has grown over the philosophy of low-cost alternative to creative wooden building blocks to technology-driven mechanical building blocks giant. The growth of the company relied on customer inputs and analysis of their personality and behavior in transforming its business. The company has built effective systems to engage and use the crowd-contents to review and update its product portfolios constantly.[9]

Customer-centric companies explore possibilities of seeking new ideas from the stakeholders and coevolve their business models over time in the competitive marketplace. Advances in digital technologies have given enormous boost to the outsourcing business activities on public domain comprising several independent contributors. Neuromarketing is the part of neuroscience research that focuses on contemplating the purchaser's conduct through the cerebrum's instinctual procedures and reactions. It is an emerging field that focuses on deriving the marketing implications by understanding the cognitive and emotional interactions in human behavior through neuroscientific methods. Large multinational companies are using the neuromarketing approach in developing customer-focused products, advertisements, and promotional strategies.[10] Social engagement is a socially responsive approach in managing tasks and socioeconomic practices with expected outcomes. Social engagement aligns with individual, community, civic, and institutional benefits including leverages from business and economy. While social scholarship focuses on the individual and community attributes as a state of engagement, the social perspective of engagement endorses collective impact on co-created businesses through a socially determined process. The

---

[9] Robertson, D., & Hjuler, P. (2009). Innovating a Turnaround at LEGO. *Harvard Business Review*, 87 (9), 20–21.

[10] Lim, W. M. (2018). Demystifying neuromarketing. *Journal of Business Research*, 91 (2), 205–220.

design-to-society philosophy is, therefore, aligned with the social engagement theory and the social presence maxim, which refers to the degree of presence perceived by the community participants in generating and disseminating communication. Social presence theory states that social media (physical and digital interactions) should align with psychological perception of involvement (presence) and transmit visual and verbal cues.

Evaluating human behavioral traits is getting complex today. Society, people, leaders of both social and business forums, and political personalities constitute the external ecosystem of the consumers which influences the personality and behavioral traits. The social phenotype (William's Syndrome) is related to the personality, social attention, and hypersociability of individuals, which manifests crowd-led influences, dynamic shifts, perceptual inconsistency, and social autism.[11] The social phenotype behavior of consumers triggers incongruency among corporate assumptions and predictions affecting the consumer personality. Such mismatch leads to the failure of predetermined customer-centric strategies. The social phenotype can be explained as the functional behavior of people which integrates with the neurological functions and alters neurobehavioral traits of people. Consequently, consumers and stakeholders tend to build their consumption behavior on sensitive social moves and neurophysiologically integrated endpoints. Social phenotypes are sensitive to consumption behavior, choices, and loyalty, which can be conceptualized as social intuitive behavior. Firms need to analyze such behavior through psychometric tools to understand consumer perceptions and develop customer-centric strategies.[12]

In a simplistic view, design-to-market can be explained through a 3-D model comprising discover, design, and deliver. Most companies have been successful in finding growth by acquiring new companies and tapping new markets to manage products, segments, and destinations. Coevolution is the fundamental concept to the design cube. Customers offer solutions in the form of products or services. Companies then deliver these tangibles, and customers just do not buy. Consumer-centered

---

[11] Thurman, A. J., & Fisher, M. H. (2015). The Williams Syndrome social phenotype: Disentangling the contributions of social interest and social difficulties. In Hodapp, R. M., & Fidler, D. J. (Eds), *International Review of Research in Developmental Disabilities*. Amsterdam: Academic Press, 191–227.

[12] Tylka, T. L. (2006). Development and psychometric evaluation of a measure of intuitive eating. *Journal of Consumer Psychology*, **53**, 226–240.

market design delivers value and gains lead in the competition. Most companies have exhibited best practices in many industries, particularly those characterized by utilitarian products that hold emotional appeal. The social investment and co-creation of values lead to improved performance with product innovation. Fashion accessories and core fashion products have short lifecycle, and are often affected by the creative disruption and changing social values and lifestyle. Using this highly developed and commendable area of science as context, one can see how consumer market suffers from the chaotic mindset.[13]

THE TRANSITION

In large organizations, design perspectives are becoming central to the process of business modeling and strategy implementation. Several approaches in business design have emerged over time as collective approaches in the organization involving decision-makers, employees, and stakeholders. Most organizations have realized today that staying in business as learning organizations helps them grow competitively and consistently in the marketplace. Such business maxim has been described as 'systems thinking' that leads to the design principle in business known as 'design thinking'. Companies pursue this concept as a response to the mounting complexities in business operations. Design thinking in business has been conceived as an essential tool for simplifying the business operation by interlinking organization, society, and stakeholders, and more comprehensively humanizing the business. The extended principles of design thinking in business converge with the market attributes (market players, ethics, and business growth), social responsiveness (marketing with purpose), and customers' (stakeholders') value propositions. Such integrated, interlinked, and interlocked business philosophy guides the new business architecture as the 'Design Cube'. A design-centric business grows by socially involving stakeholders, and evolves in the markets by inculcating high value among customers. The design cube advocates the cooperative philosophy as a win–win business model to manage the competitors and lead the market.

---

[13] Rajagopal. (2020). Barriers and benefits towards sustainability driven business models. In Hashmi, S., & Choudhury, I. A. (Eds). *Encyclopedia of renewable and sustainable materials.* Elsevier, 318–327.

The central argument to the theory of change management is that the companies operating in a competitive business environment consider consumer preferences, innovation, technology, and growth-related investments. Customer-centric companies, therefore, tend to build simpler products to help consumers choose the right product. In the design cube, companies that opt to stay customer-centric in business develop product design characterized by the emotional appeal of customers and mend the market competition in their favor to improve performance. The best practicing companies develop emotional connections with the stakeholders through value-based design. Consumers exhibit positive behavior for products and services that ensure social pricing. Social interactions often motivate a sustainable and social consumption of products. The interplay of consumers within the social (interpersonal) and digital (remote response) platforms also helps companies to go social and stay distinctive in the competitive marketplace. Consumers today are increasingly looking for brands that have a social purpose above functional benefit. As a result, most companies are taking social stands in highly visible ways. An effective, convergent business strategy creates social and customer values by coevolving the brand in the society. The connecting thread between society and business consists in developing cognitive ergonomics among the stakeholders and stimulating co-creation of business design. It is argued in the book that the socio-business convergence can be better understood through continuous learning for entrepreneurial growth.

Leading businesses today have adapted to customer-centric business model, which is an outgrowth of crowdsourcing and understanding customer perceptions, emotions. Working with such business models encourages customer engagements with brands. Such strategy supports business agility, and customer-centric management processes that need to be designed implemented in need-based planning.[14] The crowd's value to the firm is represented as the concept of *crowd capital*, which embeds customer perceptions and emotions. The crowd capital has been defined as the organizational resources acquired through crowdsourcing in the form of collective intelligence.[15] Most companies have experimented

---

[14] Worley, C. G., Williams, T., & Lawler, E. (2016). Creating management processes built for change. *MIT Sloan Management Review*, 58 (1), 77–82.

[15] Prpić, J., Shukla, P. P., Kietzmann, J. H., & McCarthy, I. P. (2015). How to work a crowd: Developing crowd capital through crowdsourcing. *Business Horizons*, 58 (1), 77–85.

radical shifts in business strategies over the conventional wisdom to gain sustainable competitive advantage. Some of these strategies are people-centric and crowd-based, which have encouraged customer engagement in today's heterogeneous and hypercompetitive global business environment. Consequently, empowering people in various geo-demographic segments (communities, entrepreneurs, women, and leaders) gained dynamic capabilities such as sensing local opportunities, enacting global complementarities, and appropriating business with local values. Nestlé (Latin America), Unilever (India), and IKEA (Europe) are good examples of the companies engaged in people-based business. These companies can operate successfully across emerging and established markets. The strategic agility, therefore, is a meta-capability of companies that enables them to create customer- and stakeholder values and deploy dynamic competitive strategies in a balance over time.[16] Co-creation allows companies to continually tap the skills and insights of stakeholders and develop new ways of building value chain. Crowdsourcing platforms (physical and digital forums) are largely interactive for exploring new experiences and connections. The crowd-based collective intelligence process grows organically over time in the organization as a system.[17]

The analysis of collective intelligence not only opens a new range of business opportunities for companies, but also helps in exploring reverse innovations (evolved in niche or remote destinations) that have the potential for commercialization. Commercializing a reverse innovation is a disruptive leap to hit a commercially established product in the target market. Reverse innovations demand to develop organizational insights into how a new product could drive an impact in emerging markets.[18] The customer engagement in the emerging firms today is instrumental to value-based business modeling and exploring customer-centric business opportunities. Consequently, customers, stakeholders, and leaders hold the power to respond to major market shifts and let firms grow with

---

[16] Fourne, S. P. L., Jansen, J. J. P., & Mom T. J. M. (2014). Strategic agility in MNEs: Managing tensions to capture opportunities across emerging and established markets. *California Management Review*, 56 (3), 13–38.

[17] Gouillart, F., & Billings, D. (2013). Community-powered problem solving. *Harvard Business Review*, 91(4), 70–77.

[18] Rajagopal (2016), *Innovative business projects: Breaking complexities, building performance (vol.2)-financials, new insights, and project sustainability.* New York: Business Expert Press.

the collective intelligence and necessary social interventions.[19] Therefore, the cutting-edge of marketing strategies across the geo-demographic segments is widely influenced by the individual and group behavior, collective intelligence, and neuro-centric emotions. People (crowd) tend to disseminate persuasive messages which aim to alter the attitude of consumers and overall consumption behavior. Besides many operational elements, agility in business is primarily linked to the social and economic postulates of the consumer behavior. The change of mind among consumers is induced by self- and social concepts that govern the business strategies, technologies, and end-user values to leverage market competition. In addition to customer satisfaction, majority of business operating models are mainly driven by corporate values by *putting the people first* and agility to adopt the revised norms quickly.[20]

Sustainable Entrepreneurship

Contemporary marketing has evolved alongside the sustainability perspectives as a dynamic science and spanned across temporal and spatial dimensions involving society, public administration, and market players. In the process, global sustainable commitment and consumers' welfare form the foundations of markets. The production and consumption patterns are associated with a wide range of sustainability issues throughout the lifecycle of both domains. The conventional industry practices in developing economies result into various social and ecological problems. Industries that pioneer sustainability consciousness in the society integrate strategies to manage the ecosystem through their business models. The integrated business models with sustainability commitment can be explained in terms of their value proposition, and value creation and delivery though effective corporate social responsibility. These perspectives need to be discussed in terms of cleaner production and consumption, and managing constituents of sustainable ecosystems through global–local

---

[19] Christensen, C. M., & Overdorf, M. (2000). Meeting the challenge of disruptive change. *Harvard Business Review*, 78 (2), 65–76.

[20] Nath, U. K., Jagadev, A. K., & Pattnaik, P. K. (2021). Agile transformation for better business values using orchestration model. *Materials today: Proceedings* (in press). https://doi.org/10.1016/j.matpr.2021.02.177.

business models. Though the literature proposes several conceptual solutions, there is a need to rethink on modular designs and product-service systems within global–local business dynamics.[21]

Another significant development in the recent past is about the application of circular economy, which supports the global sustainability move and induces shifts in consumption patterns. The circular economy (CE) is modelled as an industry, which encourages recycling of wastes for producing industrial products, and adheres to the global sustainability commitments. However, conventional industrial system tends to collapse as the consumption level increases due to the scarcity of ecosystem-based resources. The circular economy has been implemented in industries such as steel, paper, polymers, and products such as mobile phones. In the various industrial sectors, the CE has shown positive impact on the resources management.[22] Therefore, holistic assessment of systemic influences of the circular economy is necessary from a global sustainability point of view and guides companies to develop sustainable business modeling. CE comprises of end-of-life (decline stage) management of a product, so that the product after its completion of functional life could regain commercial value and could be brought back into the supply chain process by various means rather than considered as a waste.[23]

Sustainability concerns, pro-environment knowledge, and the social dynamics of markets drive the consumption behavior of green products among consumers. As the management of green products is based on intangible factors, trust plays a central role in building cognitive ergonomics among the consumers. In addition, consumer knowledge and social consciousness build the foundation of green consumer behavior. Some previous studies reveal that the global sustainability drive has influenced consumers to change their behavior and purchase decisions through

---

[21] Bridgens, B., Hobson, K., Lilley, D., Lee, J., Scott, J. L., & Wilson, G. T. (2017). Closing the loop on e-waste: a multidisciplinary perspective. *Journal of Industrial Ecology*, 39 (1), 1–13.

[22] Hanumante, N. C., Shastri, Y., and Hoadley, A. (2019). Assessment of circular economy for global sustainability using an integrated model. *Resources, Conservation and Recycling*, 151, Art. 104,460.

[23] Govindan, K., & Soleimani, H. (2017). A review of reverse logistics and closed-loop supply chains: a Journal of Cleaner Production focus. *Journal of Cleaner Production*, 142, 371–384.

the consumption of eco-friendly alternatives.[24] The green consumption behavior has emerged over time in food consumption and transport sustainability, and toward renewable energy usage. Public policies and social consciousness have also contributed significantly in transforming the consumption behavior at macro level. Therefore, many consumers are interested in modifying their consumption behavior with less impact on natural resources, particularly fossil fuels,[25] as the social dynamics are also contributing to the development of green energy. Consumers in the energy market today are committed with environmental protection through green electricity.[26]

Sustainable business widely depends on environmentally friendly logistics and inventory management with low carbon emissions. The refrigerated transportation and inventory are more susceptible to environmental pollution than other ways of distribution sources. Freight transportation firms are facing the mounting challenges of fuel consumption, and need to reduce the significant environmental imbalances that accrue from transport vehicles.[27] However, most small and medium enterprises are observing a major fix between lowering the logistics and inventory cost and stay price competitive in the market. The operations of freight transport industry in developing economies is highly competitive due to increased production and consumption coupled with government pressures to achieve sustainability. Therefore, eco-innovation has become the principal concern among the business corporations not only toward following the sustainable parameters to satisfy stakeholders' values such as

---

[24] Paco, A., & Rapose, M. (2009). Green segmentation: An application to the Portuguese consumer market. *Market: Intelligence and Planning*, 27 (3), 364–379.

[25] Chen, M. F. (2016). Extending the theory of planned behavior model to explain people's energy savings and carbon reduction behavioral intentions to mitigate climate change in Taiwanemoral obligation matters. *Journal of Cleaner Production*, 112, 1746–1753.

[26] Strupeit, L., & Palm, A. (2016). Overcoming barriers to renewable energy diffusion: business models for customer-sited solar photovoltaics in Japan, Germany and the United States. *Journal of Cleaner Production*, 123, 124–136.

[27] Bektas, T., Ehmke, J. F., Psaraftis, H. N., & Puchinger, J. (2019). The role or operational research in green freight transportation. *European Journal of Operations Research*, 274 (3), 807–823.

reducing negative environmental externalities, but also toward reaching governments' green requirements and consumer demands.[28]

In context of the above discussion, most developing nations have promulgated comprehensive public policies to streamline corporate governance on implementation of sustainability-driven business model in all industries. Public policies are focusing on macro-economic disruption due to sustainability issues in developing economies.[29] Therefore, large companies are developing alliances with local governments on public–private partnerships (PPP) in implementing sustainability norms and enhancing social value. The PPP initiatives in various geo-demographic sectors have generated social awareness among people and inculcated the environmentally conscious consumption in the society. Environmentally conscious consumption is one of the key concerns in the modern society, and it is increasingly affecting the urban consumers. However, consumers often overstate their willingness to purchase environmentally conscious products; the global purchasing of these products is relatively low. Most research studies on environmentally conscious consumption suggest that the purchase intention is driven by intrinsic factors such as demographics comprising income, education and social status, consumer cognition, and personality attributes.[30] In addition, external factors and social influences also affect the environmental consumption behavior of an individual.

Previous studies on social entrepreneurship have focused on the personality and background of the social entrepreneur and the entrepreneurial performance. The social entrepreneurs have unique characteristics including knowledge, cognitive capacities, and altruistic values. Social innovation is an interactive bottom-up collective learning process implemented through social enterprises. As a boundary-spanning activity across the public and private sectors, the interactive learning process and associated capability building for social innovation serve as a catalyst for wider social reform. Social innovations help value creation in emerging

---

[28] Garcia-Graner, E. M., Piedra, M. L., & Galdeano, G. E. (2018). Eco-innovation measurement: A review of firm performance indicators. *Journal of Cleaner Production*, 191, 304–317.

[29] Béal, V. (2015). Selective public policies: sustainability and neoliberal urban restructuring. *Environment and Urbanization*, 27 (1), 303–316.

[30] Tsarenko, Y., Ferraro, C., Sands, S., & McLeod, C. (2013). Environmentally conscious consumption: The role of retailers and peers as external influences. *Journal of Retailing and Consumer Services*, 20 (3), 302–310.

economies involving stakeholders and firms in the broader projects.[31] Social entrepreneurship has high value proposition and is intended to drive societal transformations. Such entrepreneurs address social issues and problems and empower transformational progress throughout the system. The dominant factor for the rise of social entrepreneurship is the societal pressure on green recovery and sustainability governance.[32]

In view of the above arguments the sustainable business ecosystems can be developed with customer-centric and value-based business modelling. Contributions of circular economy and production systems, green consumption behavior, cleaner energy perspectives would motivate sustainable entrepreneurship with low-cost technology-driven management with the support of public policies in developing countries. In addition, effective public policy, strong leader-member exchanges and collective business governance can boost significantly the conscious consumption, innovation and technology, and social entrepreneurship.

THE CONVERGENCE: MARKET, SOCIETY, AND VALUES

The manifold growth of interactive virtual communities has led to the social attention and hyper-sociability of individuals, which inculcates social phenotype personality traits. The social networks encourage sharing of consumers experiences over temporal and spatial dimensions that drive an integrated effect on geo-demographic consumer behavior. The social phenotype effects drive neuro-physical changes among consumers, stimulating preferences for the products, sensory impulses (*touch, feel, and pick*), and need for peer or social validation on their buying decisions. Consumers on social media channels are influenced by the socially affective language, peer narrations or perspective, including attributive emotions or motivations to communication, using intensifiers (really, very,

---

[31] Rao-Nicholson, R., Vorley, T., & Khan, Z. (2017). Social innovation in emerging economies: A national systems of innovation-based approach. *Technological Forecasting and Social Change*, 121, 228–237.

[32] Gandhi, T., & Raina, R. (2018). Social entrepreneurship: the need, relevance, facets and constraints. *Journal of Global Entrepreneurship Research*, 8, Art. 9, 1–13 https://doi.org/10.1186/s40497-018-0094-6.

so) and sound effects, direct quotes, character speech, and verbal anchors for 'hooking' the listener's attention.[33]

Despite the importance of female entrepreneurship and growth in the number of female-owned enterprises worldwide, entrepreneurship remains a male-dominated endeavor. Therefore, understanding and exploring the scenario of women entrepreneurship is more important to examine the gender gap in entrepreneurship across nations.[34] The entrepreneurial marketing strategies of entrepreneurs in the emerging markets evolve from social and ethnic entrepreneurial cultures encompassing niche- or regional-marketing strategies. These enterprises largely use bricolage practice in developing marketing strategies. Bricolage is an approach to create new marketing strategies from diverse ecosystems spurring out from the mainstream competitive strategy.[35] The business models of small micro and small enterprises are knitted around triadic interrelated dimensions comprising market-driven changes in manufacturing and operational strategies, bootstrapping new portfolios, and effective risk management to drive positive effect on organizational performance.[36]

Some management thinkers including C. K. Prahalad, Gary Hamel, Gerald Zaltman, Vijay Govidarajan, and Henry Mintzberg advocate that society is an integrated part of business, and companies should understand the social values embedded in the business. Therefore, most multinational companies like Nestle, Apple, and IBM develop their business models as 'design-to-society' to not only create social value to their business, but also to gain customer confidence as a principal tool to pave the path in the dense market competition today. Explaining this concept, the book discusses the reasons of success behind the companies in specific industries such as telecommunication (mobile phones),

---

[33] Jarvinen, A., Korenberg, J. R., & Bellugi, U. (2013). The social phenotype of Williams syndrome. *Current Opinion in Neurobiology*, 23 (3), 414–422.

[34] Thébaud, S. (2015). Business as plan B institutional foundations of gender inequality in entrepreneurship across 24 industrialized countries. *Administrative Science Quarterly*, 60 (4), pp. 671–711.

[35] Yang, M. (2018), International entrepreneurial marketing strategies of MNCs: bricolage as practiced by marketing managers, *International Business Review*, 27 (5), 1045–1056.

[36] Eggers, F., Neimand, T., Kraus, S., & Breier, M. (2020). Developing a scale for entrepreneurial marketing: revealing its inner frame and prediction of performance. *Journal of Business Research*, 113, 72–82.

diet and health products (organic food), and transport (hybrid passenger automobiles), architecting community marketplaces and developing social marketing strategies. The emerging concepts of 'marketing with purpose' and coevolution of business designs are dealt as the core themes to illustrate 'design-to-society' concepts that are being practiced sporadically by large companies.

Social values are founded in the customer cognition process which stimulates customers on knowing about the brands, doing with the prescribed brand purpose, and attaining perceived value and satisfaction being a conscious customer. The factors of knowing, doing, and being form the core of design-to-society approach. Understanding the attributes, personality, corporate image, and prescribed values of brands, customers tend to increasingly evaluate the social and consumption purpose of the brands to have a social purpose beyond mere functional benefits. As a result, companies are taking social stands to build business models on social welfare and development philosophies. The design-to-society programs benefit both society and the brand strategically to establish brand competitiveness and social push to the brand. However, investing in design-to-society programs to inculcate social values in brand without appropriate design-to-market approaches might reduce the expected growth, profits, and business expansion of companies. The design-to-society approaches provide the companies the scope for competing in market with a social purpose by exhibiting the most ambitious social aspirations brands with the desired spatial and temporal growth touchpoints.

The Quadruple Bottom-line in Business

The bottom-line in business is shifting rapidly since the mid-twentieth century with the advancement of information technology and changing business philosophy.[37] The bottom-line of business has moved over time from aggressive manufacturing to market competition, to supply-led business models, and to customer-centric business focus. With the extensive usage of social media by the firms and people, companies have learned to follow a new pace in business led by the voice of

---

[37] Guillet de Monthoux, P. (2015). Art, philosophy, and business: Turns to speculative realism in European management scholarship. *European Management Journal*, 33 (3), 161–167.

crowd and collective intelligence.[38] Consequently, the bottom-line of the business today is shifted to a functional combination of People, Accountability, Control, and Transformation (PACT), which has constituted the quadruple bottom-line in business. PACT has induced people (crowd comprising potential consumers, technocrats, creative business thinkers, stakeholders, potential investors, market operations players, and existing customers) to actively participate in the business processes. People tend to suggest transforming the existing businesses to profitable ventures through co-creation and coevolution. The involvement of people has stimulated firms to design and implement agile business models based on the following measures[39]:

- 4As Attributes (consumer preference-based product designs and complementarity to other products), availability (360° availability through multi-channel marketing), affordability (value for money), and adaptability (enhancing perceived use value of customers)
- 4Cs Cost to customer-tangible and intangible, convenience, communication (transparency and user-generated contents)
- 4Vs Validity (developing business strategies based on peer reviews, influence, and social self-concept), venue (attractive channels, visual merchandizing, web-layouts), value (creating customer value through channels), and vogue (adhering business to the fashion and consumption trends as perceived through collective intelligence), and
- 4Es Expansion (planning business expansion based on the geo-demographic needs), exploring (co-creating new ideas for products and services, coevolving business in new markets), emotions (customer engagement in business and embedding emotions in business to acquire and retain customers), and experience (continuous learning to improve business strategies by analyzing customer experiences)

[38] Dong, W. X. (2016). Crowd intelligence: Analyzing online product reviews for preference measurement. *Information & Management*, 53, 169–182.

[39] Rajagopal (2019), *Contemporary Marketing strategy: Analyzing consumer behavior to drive managerial decision making*. New York: Palgrave Macmillan.

People's involvement in business has proved effective in social institutions which attained commercial significance over time. For example, *Gramin Bank* (Rural bank) in Bangladesh has emerged as a social institution, which is built by the people as a self-help group and attained the status of a national commercial bank over time. Similarly, dairy farmers cooperatives in the state of Gujarat in India have evolved in the mid-twentieth century as people's organization for mutual benefits and grown as a largest commercial organization with the corporate brand AMUL (Anand Milk Union Limited). In these organizations, the stakeholders (members of the institution) have exercised social control and reverse accountability to manage the business with commitment. In view of the above and several such example, it is evident that the PACT philosophy is embedded in the customer-centric and social business organizations. This book discusses the attributes of PACT philosophy in business and critically examines its role in enhancing the business performance from the crowd perspective.[40]

Philosophically, the crowd dynamics can be explained as collective intelligence, which reveals that no one knows everything while everyone knows something.[41] Contemporary marketing has evolved alongside the customer-centric perspectives as a cognitive science and has spanned across advanced marketing-mix comprising twenty-seven elements.[42] Therefore, customer value has become central to business modeling. Most companies develop marketing strategies (a principal constituent of business model) on assumptions of customer values, which might be a misfit while implementing a business model. Collective intelligence provides the real perceptions of customers and the rationale for new products and services.[43]

---

[40] Prpić, J., Shukla, P. P., Kietzmann, J. H., & McCarthy, I. P. (2015). How to work a crowd: Developing crowd capital through crowdsourcing. *Business Horizons*, 58 (1), 77–85.

[41] Lévy, P. (1997). *Collective intelligence: Mankind's emerging world in cyberspace.* New York: Plenum Trade.

[42] The advanced marketing-mix consists of 11 Ps as core elements and 16 Ps as peripheral elements. The 11 Ps include product, price, place, promotion, packaging, pace, people, performance, psychodynamics, posture, and proliferations. The peripheral elements have been discussed in the text referred to this footnote. The attributes of advanced marketing-mix are discussed comprehensively in the following footnote (Rajagopal, 2019).

[43] Rajagopal. (2019). *Contemporary marketing strategy: Analyzing consumer behavior to drive managerial decision making*, Chapter 5. New York: Palgrave Macmillan, 121–149.

Behavioral Analysis

Consumerism is evolved in a society, and businesses are built within the society. Convergence of such relationship between the society and business constructs the consumer behavior. Consequently, collectivism influences the consumerism and consumer groups (including individuals), which tend to share consumer experiences on innovations, products, values, and the market developments to generate awareness among the society. The collective opinions influence purchasers and the society for meeting their needs. Knowledge of consumers' conditions, factors, and behavioral reasons ensure competitiveness in businesses.[44] Companies tend to get closer to the customers by engaging them in co-creating new products and carrying out incremental innovations, improving packaging, developing attractive promotions, and competitive business strategies. Firms aim at attracting emotional customers so that the bonds with the firms grow deeper. Over time, firms can share emotional experiences with potential customers and motivate their engagement.[45] Consumer behavior is a set of socio-psychological indicators that cultivate a cognitive process in the human beings. It refers to the range of personality attributes exhibited by people, which are influenced by societal values, culture, attitudes, emotions, values, ethics, power, relationships, and persuasion. Behavior in humans is grown as a learned, acquired, or shared process over the spatial and temporal factors. Consumer-centric companies periodically map behavioral patterns of consumers by understanding major perceptional and attitudinal patterns and interpret them to develop appropriate marketing strategies. However, consumer behavior is sensitive to the social dominance, self-esteem and self-actualization, hedonic values, and vogue in the marketplace.[46]

Companies often undermine the behavioral changes in consumers and suffer from market setbacks. The neurobehavioral dimensions affect the consumer perceptions and consumption patterns. The cognitive processing styles, motivational interests and concerns, prioritization of

---

[44] Sirgy, M. J. (2018). Self-congruity theory in consumer behavior: A little history. *Journal of Global Scholars of Marketing Science*, 28 (2), 197–207.

[45] Das, G., Agarwal, J., Malhotra, N.K., and Varshneya, G. (2019). Does brand experience translate into brand commitment? A mediated-moderation model of brand passion and perceived brand ethicality. *Journal of Business Research*, 95, 479–490.

[46] Carter, T. J., & Gilovich, T. (2010). The relative relativity of experiential and material purchases. *Journal of Personality and Social Psychology*, 98 (1), 146–159.

personal values, and neurological structures and physiological functions of consumers broadly determine their cognitive process in developing perception on the products and services.[47] Exploring the recent scientific developments in the neurobehavioral areas, this book argues that stimulus–response is a psycho-physiological process, and it meticulously affects the neuromarketing strategies. Consequently, the marketing strategies developed on the neurobehavioral foundations develop emotional appeals in marketing.[48] In the decade of 2020s, several groundbreaking studies linking neuroscience and consumer behavior have demonstrated their potential to create value for marketers. However, most studies relied on measuring the physiological and neural signals to gain insight into customers' motivations, preferences, and decisions as a neuromarketing goal in the marketing research.[49] This book discusses beyond the basics of neuromarketing and argues that neurobehavioral impact on business makes grater appeal to managers engaged in exploring the agile consumer-centric business strategies. Managers today struggle hard to uncover factors driving customers' attitudes and behavior to develop customer-centric strategies and take a competitive lead. Unfortunately, the conventional wisdom to attract customers has largely unchanged since their introduction. Consequently, there is growing interest in brain-based approaches that motivate managers to directly probe customers' underlying thoughts, feelings, and intentions.[50] This book focuses on converging the neural effects on consumer behavior and their implications in infusing agility in marketing approaches.

[47] Jost, J. (2017). The marketplace of ideology: "Elective affinities" in political psychology and their implications for consumer behavior. *Journal of Consumer Psychology*, 27 (4), 502–520.

[48] Hannah, S. T., & Waldman, D. A. (2015). Neuroscience of moral cognition and conation in organizations. In Waldman, D. A., & Balthazard, P. A. (Ed.) *Organizational neuroscience* (Monographs in Leadership and Management, Volume 7), London: Emerald Group Publishing Limited, 233–255.

[49] Harrell, E. (2019). *Neuromarketing: What you need to know*. Harvard Business Review Digital Article. Boston: Harvard Business School Publication.

[50] Hsu, M. (2017). Neuromarketing: Inside the Mind of the Consumer. *California Management Review*, 59 (4), 5–22.

Profiling Innovations

The development of social enterprises, fugal innovation start-up enterprises, and sustainability driven small and medium enterprises is an outgrowth of social engagement, empowerment, and public participation embodying crowdsourced and crowdfunded entrepreneurial activities. Consequently, crowdfunding plays a vital role in promoting innovation and entrepreneurship with low cost, and encourages operations in the niche market.[51] The combination of social innovation and digitalization has encouraged crowdfunding to promote social and sustainable entrepreneurship, which drives new relationships between citizens, enterprises, and business organizations. The concept of urban entrepreneurship based on the attributes of sustainability and circular economy has gained increasing attention in the production and marketing segments. Successful innovation leads to customer involvement and profits, which can be achieved through co-creation by aligning consumers and market players in the innovation process. Some multinational companies have invested in sustainability projects by taking advantage of social media to diffuse new ideas and stimulating co-creation of innovative products and services. For example, the role of co-creation has become central to sustainability management in the social initiatives of the twenty-first century. Energy market transition, which is enabled by new affordable energy technologies and digitalization, opens novel opportunities for developing innovative energy solutions through collective intelligence and public–private co-creations.[52]

Upon understanding the perceptions, emotions, and values of customers, companies make smarter choices about allocation of resources in customer services, advertisement and communications, and implementation of marketing-mix driven strategies. The co-created and co-evolved customer value constructs can deliver optimal benefits to customers by upholding their perceptions, choices, and self-esteem. Large companies with strategies focus on customers and develop value dashboards to monitor customer touchpoints, which helps in co-creating customer value proposition. A good customer value dashboard helps firms not only

---

[51] Caré, S., Trotta, A., Caré, R., & Rizzelo, A. (2018). Crowdfunding for development of smart cities. *Business Horizons*, 61 (4), 501–509.

[52] Rajagopal (2021). *Crowd-Based business models—Using collective intelligence for market competitiveness*. New York: Palgrave Macmillan.

in increasing sales and marketing professionals, but also in developing design-to-society and design-to-value business modeling.[53] The process of co-innovation is stretching the ideation process through extensive use of digital platforms and stakeholder involvement. Co-innovation is an ecosystem-wide activity that involves multiple stakeholders who collaborate toward a shared social goal and explore niche strategies to commercialize eco-innovations. However, in active societies like Chinese sociological and business culture, the co-innovators simultaneously compete with one another across geo-demographic segments to market their innovative products and services.[54]

With the advancement of information technology, the digitalization of business operations has significantly supported the platform economy, which has shown a huge shift in expanding outreach to end-users and creating value among consumers. Digitization in marketing has induced rapid shift in the consumer behavior through open access to brand communication, consumer experiences, and socio-psychological cognition toward building their preferences and values. However, many multinationals are encouraging 'value chain localization' strategies which still focus on only the premier segment of consumers.[55] Social media, digitalization of business, attractive purchase offers, and the rapidly changing fashion trends have become the major motivational sources for the consumers toward perceiving new consumption and value paradigms. The existing neuroscience applications can be applied to consumer cognition including social awareness, judgments, reasoning, and effects of moral emotions on moral reasoning, and ethical ideology.[56] Digitalization has changed the relationship among conventional word-of-mouth, traditional information dissemination, and sharing of experiences within the community. Consequently, with the advancement of information technology,

---

[53] Villanueva, J. (2013). Reading the Signs of Your Customer Value. *IESE-Insight Magazine*, 17 (2), 24–29.

[54] Kotilainen, K., Saari, U.A., Mäkinen, S. J., & Ringle, C. M. (2019). Exploring the microfoundations of end-user interests toward co-creating renewable energy technology innovations. *Journal of Cleaner Production*, 229, 203–212.

[55] Prahalad, C. K., & Ramaswamy, V. (2000). Co-opting customer competence. *Harvard Business Review*, 78 (1), 79–87.

[56] Hannah, S. T., & Waldman, D. A. (2015). Neuroscience of Moral Cognition and Conation in Organizations. In Waldman, D. A., & Balthazard. P. A. (Ed.) *Organizational Neuroscience* (Monographs in Leadership and Management, Volume 7), London: Emerald Group Publishing Limited, 233–255.

social media channels have made a significant dent in the stakeholder relationship. The collective intelligence and social behavior have significantly supported the relationship between stakeholders. The effective network of customers and service providers is supported by the Internet of Things, big data analysis, and relational fusion technologies, which empowers stakeholders to learn the operations processes within the organization and participate in the decision-making.[57]

Digital Media and Markets

Various social media channels contribute to disseminating new ideas and serve as a pool of collective intelligence. However, the review of previous literature suggests that the overall effect of crowdsourcing on business modelling has not been thoroughly investigated. This book fills this gap by integrating the customer ideation in developing behavioral business models to achieve *performance with purpose*. Drawing on the resource-based view, the book argues how crowdsourced information can be an important resource for the firm to develop value chain, deliver it to stakeholders, and stay competitive in the marketplace.[58] Socialization of business is a process where people build trust through interpersonal interaction, learn market trends, co-create products and services, and inculcate value-based organizational culture. The collective intelligence has evolved over time through the experiential interactions on social media channels. Socialization of businesses encourages people from different segments, socio-cultural backgrounds, and ethnicity to co-create innovative business ideas. The socialization process of business helps firms to grow agile and customer-centric.[59]

With the advancement of technology- and convenience-led marketing, elderly consumers are feeling out of place in the market today as they are unable to cope with the technology-driven marketing approaches, applications, and self-service platforms. Consequently, *reverse socialization* is

---

[57] Wang, Y., & Yu, C. (2017). Social interaction-based consumer decision-making model in social commerce: The role of word of mouth and observational learning. *International Journal of Information Management*, 37 (3),179–189.

[58] Rajagopal (2021). *Crowd-Based business models—Using collective intelligence for market competitiveness*. New York: Palgrave Macmillan (in press).

[59] Fayard, A. L., Weeks, J., & Khan, M. (2021). *Designing the hybrid office*. Harvard Business Review Digital Article, Boston: Harvard Business School Publication.

gearing-up in the families as elderly consumers are being influenced by the young consumers. Reverse socialization is a process, which allows adolescents' influence on their parents' knowledge, skills, and attitudes related to consumption. Such behavior is driven by emotions, changing perceptions on products and services, and restructured cognitive ergonomics.[60] There is a growing need for the firms to adapt to the agility in business in the context of reverse sociology, socio-neurological behavior, and social self-concept. Individual's cognition on social consumption and relative changes contributes to the social self-concept, which determines the buying decisions and the relative degree of influence.[61] Research studies converging behavioral and neural mechanisms in social media use and self-concept indicate that the cognitive weights between self-judgements and derived-peer-judgements are often narrow and highly correlated. Social media enables to get frequent crowd-based feedback as compared to interpersonal interactions and conventional meetings with peers. Consequently, the social media drives peer emotions in socialization of business among young consumers.[62]

The impact of perfect alignment of entrepreneurship with innovation and technology would not only improve business performance but also develop economic synergy in meeting the chronic and recurring social challenges. Among many such mounting pressures related to poverty, gender inequality, sustainability and climate change, income disparity, social healthcare, community housing and homelessness, and the drive to cleaner food and water supplies development of a systematic process-based entrepreneurship is often challenging. The inclusive entrepreneurial strategies to meet the above social challenges through transformational leadership in the developing economies is a collective move in developing countries through synchronization of the P3 factors comprising people, politics, and public policies. Digitalization, hybridity in enterprises, cost- and profit-based performance, design-to-society and design-to-value strategies, value co-creation, public policies,

---

[60] Gentina, E., & Muratore, I. (2012). Environmentalism at home: The process of ecological resocialization by teenagers. *Journal of Consumer Behaviour*, 11 (2), 162–169.

[61] Singh, P., Sahadev, S., Oates, C. J., & Alevizou, P. (2020). Pro-environmental behavior in families: A reverse socialization perspective. *Journal of Business Research*, 115, 110–121.

[62] Valkenburg, P. M. (2017). Understanding self-effects in social media. *Human Communication Research*, 43, 477–490.

private sector contributions, entrepreneurial finance management, and people's participation in driving the entrepreneurial growth are central to the development of a competitive entrepreneurship. The success and failure of enterprises at the grassroots need to be analyzed logically and rationally to augment learning in entrepreneurship and help in resolving the social challenges. The geographic spread of the discussion includes case illustrations from south-east Asia, Africa, and Latin America.

THEMATIC CONVERGENCE

The thematic convergences address multi-layered topics between the broad domains of entrepreneurship and social challenges through various contemporary strategies with focus on changing business dynamics. Social challenges in generating continuous income, employment, sustainability, and infrastructure have been growing complex with economic transitions and technology growth. Historically, entrepreneurs face a lack of desire to grow amidst social challenges, which causes decision conflicts for artisans. However, the increasing demand for artisan-made goods and services in emerging markets implies that artisans face a seemingly challenging dilemma toward upholding artisanal values and resist growth or embrace it.[63] The interrelationship between the topical discussion across chapters is illustrated in Fig. 7.1, which reveals that entrepreneurship, social challenges, marketing strategies, and entrepreneurial behavior are aligned linearly.

Figure 7.1 illustrates the entrepreneurial base with the concept of promoting entrepreneurship as a key driver to meet the social challenges in farm and non-farm sectors, housing, community health, education, and sustainability. The future perspectives have been conceptualized in this chapter in view of the conventional entrepreneurial practices and discuss the possibilities of scaling entrepreneurship to upstream markets. The entrepreneurial base operationally complements the entrepreneurial ecosystem embedding the social systems and family businesses, which argues that establishing the backward and forward entrepreneurial linkages with effective public policies would play significant role in improving

---

[63] Solomon, S. J., & Mathias, B. D. (2020). The artisans' dilemma: Artisan entrepreneurship and the challenge of firm growth. *Journal of Business Venturing*, 35 (5), in Press. https://doi.org/10.1016/j.jbusvent.2020.106044.

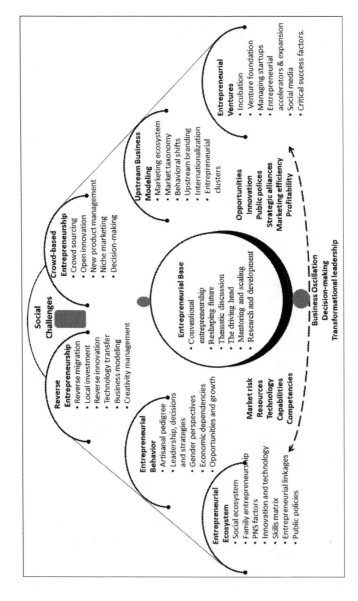

Fig. 7.1 Synchronizing entrepreneurship with business and societal ecosystems (*Source* Author)

innovation, technology, and skills among entrepreneurial activities. Developing new entrepreneurial ventures can, therefore, proactively contribute to the society and economy holistically in reshaping both the future and existing social challenges. Accordingly, the future perspectives of incubating innovation and technology start-ups through entrepreneurial accelerators can be nurtured systematically at the grassroots. Such economic, behavioral, social, and political convergence would help to drive a prolific shift in entrepreneurship by taking a long leap from the conventional practices through efficient mentoring, skills development, and social dynamics. The emerging domains of crowdsourcing and crowdfunding also play a dominant role to nurture entrepreneurship in future and grow along with the changing perspectives of innovation, technology, and market competition in an up-front digital revolution.

The entrepreneurial behavior and crowd-based entrepreneurship respectively are turning symbiotic today. However, the artisanal pedigree has shown immense impact on entrepreneurial trade and skills over the generational transcend. Such transition entrepreneurial philosophy is affected by the leadership, crowd effects and the boom of open innovations. These factors are also contextual to the gender and economic dependencies, which significantly affect decision-making and entrepreneurial propensity to explore new opportunities by enhancing the proximity to regional markets. In addition, the reverse entrepreneurship and upstream business modeling have also shown a growing trend in conjunction with reverse migration (from far-home destinations to the home destination) with the intention to invest in local enterprises and develop upstream market branding, internationalization, and behavioral shifts in business.

Methodologically conceptual frameworks on entrepreneurial growth, contributions, hybrid social entrepreneurship models, and empirical evidence on the collective entrepreneurial practices should be drawn to address the social challenges. Poverty alleviation is facilitated by connecting innovators, entrepreneurs, and investors. Harnessing innovative potential of individual and communities provides an entrepreneurial approach to poverty alleviation.[64] There is a need for the effective convergence of strategies related to technology, innovation, and poverty

---

[64] Dey, A., Gupta, A. K., & Singh, G. (2019). Innovation, investment and enterprise: Climate resilient entrepreneurial pathways for overcoming poverty. *Agricultural Systems*, 172, 83–90.

alleviation to influence the entrepreneurial performance. The social enterprises contribute in resolving the social problems (e.g., vulnerable value segments, innovation, investment, and risk-taking attitude) and their social networks (e.g., more frequent social interactions with community and friends), thereby promoting entrepreneurial motivation to serve the community.[65]

An upstream social marketing strategy for niche enterprises can be founded effectively on integrated marketing communications (IMC). The engagement of IMC approaches includes target audience research and determination, channel selection and integration, strategic message creation, and measurement and control. A central and novel feature of the IMC-based social marketing strategy model for entrepreneurial firms is about the simultaneous targeting of an upstream decision maker and influential peripheral (upstream) audiences to triangulate and increase campaign effectiveness.[66] The core elements in market-oriented entrepreneurship today constitute marketing ecosystem, market taxonomy, and behavioral shifts, which drive the need for upstream marketing for the niche enterprises. In addition, the increasing importance of branding and value creation, internationalization, and entrepreneurial clusters (such as export-oriented units) bridge prolific upstream business alliances for local enterprises. The IMC approach to upstream social marketing ensures consistent, persuasive messages specifically crafted for the selected target audiences and coordinated through precise channels to maximize impact.[67]

---

[65] Levine, R. & Rubinstein, Y. (2017). Smart and illicit: who becomes an entrepreneur, and do they earn more? *Quarterly Journal of Economics*, 132 (2), 963–1018.

[66] Key, T. M., & Czaplewski, A. J. (2017). Upstream social marketing strategy: An integrated marketing communications approach. *Business Horizons*, 60 (3), 325–333.

[67] Papasolomou, I., Thrassou, A., Vrontis, D., & Sabova, M. (2014). Marketing public relations: A consumer-focused strategic perspective. *Journal of Customer Behaviour*, 13 (1), 5–24.

Index

A
abilities, 57, 107, 119, 151
agile business, 60, 81, 82, 148, 149, 152, 153, 155, 187
agile marketing, 62, 148, 150–153
alternate business modeling, 147
artisanal pedigree, 67, 72, 197

B
behavioral analysis, 189
brand architecture, 155, 160
brand knowledge, 158
business planning, 33
business scaling, 28, 101
business strategy cube, 7

C
capabilities, 11–13, 15, 16, 23–27, 48, 52, 62, 72, 80, 85, 101, 104, 111, 124, 148–150, 154, 159, 179
change management, 5, 8, 68, 78, 85, 178
channels, 10, 13, 26–28, 30, 32, 40, 83, 97, 110, 119, 131, 132, 147, 151, 158, 160–162, 166, 184, 187, 193, 198
circular economy (CE), 38, 62, 76, 181, 184, 191
co-creation, 4, 10, 26, 27, 37, 56, 60, 61, 82, 87, 106, 107, 109, 138, 152, 158, 165, 171, 175, 177–179, 187, 191, 194
collective intelligence (CI), 7, 19, 33, 38, 39, 41, 43, 44, 48, 50, 52, 54, 56, 57, 59–61, 74, 83, 85, 95, 112, 113, 118–124, 126, 127, 131–136, 149, 152–154, 158, 160, 166, 167, 175, 178–180, 187, 188, 191, 193
collectivism, 50, 69, 189
competencies, 11, 14, 16, 23, 24, 26, 33, 48, 52, 71, 72, 76, 77, 85, 101, 111, 154

consumer philosophy, 30, 113
creativity, 19, 20, 23, 67, 74, 79, 80, 89, 93, 118, 119, 126, 132, 134
crowd-based business model, 33, 53, 59, 62, 82, 99, 115, 117, 120, 121, 126, 128, 135, 193
crowd-based entrepreneurship, 197
crowd behavior, 44, 50, 74, 83, 95, 122, 124, 127, 149, 151, 153, 163, 166, 168
crowd capital, 178, 188
crowd cognition, 50
crowdsourcing, 10, 20, 48, 53, 55, 57–59, 117–124, 126–130, 132–137, 148, 178, 179, 188, 193, 197
CTR factors, 8, 19, 31, 52, 157
customer-centric, 55, 61, 62, 96, 97, 105, 107–109, 117, 119, 121, 122, 124, 127, 130, 133, 134, 149, 151, 152, 157, 161, 164, 166–168, 171, 174–176, 178, 179, 184, 186, 188, 190

D

design thinking, 10, 38, 52, 54, 74, 87, 106, 130, 148, 149, 167, 177
design-to-market, 7, 33, 43, 61, 63, 68, 106, 123, 134, 176, 186
design-to-society, 7, 33, 43, 81, 82, 108, 123, 134, 185, 186, 192, 194
design-to-value, 7, 33, 43, 81, 82, 107, 108, 123, 192, 194
developing local markets, 108
digital media, 83, 161
digitization, 14, 50, 60, 192

E

emerging markets, 12, 13, 29, 35, 38, 46, 55, 58, 64, 65, 69, 96, 99, 112, 115, 117, 154, 156, 172, 173, 179, 185, 195
engagement, 4, 10, 11, 18, 22, 32, 47, 55, 60–62, 74, 78, 80, 81, 83, 93, 101, 105, 113, 114, 131, 132, 134, 137, 148, 150, 152, 153, 161, 163–165, 167, 171, 174, 175, 178, 179, 187, 189, 198
entrepreneurial ecosystem, 38, 39, 41, 72, 195
entrepreneurial mind-set, 86
entrepreneurial transition, 3
exploring markets, 33, 50
EYE model, 167

F

Fabindia, 156
family business, 3–6, 8, 10, 67–72, 74–78, 172, 195
family ownership, 68–70
frugal innovation, 7, 15, 20, 33, 46, 47, 57–59, 65, 101, 106, 107, 119

G

global market, 20, 26, 29, 35, 64, 65, 95, 115
governance, 18, 34, 43, 49, 52, 70, 72, 79, 81, 83, 85, 99, 104, 152, 163, 164, 183, 184

H

human element, 67, 83

I

ideation, 33, 48, 50, 53, 54, 57, 59, 85, 98, 106, 111, 118–120, 123, 124, 126, 132–134, 137, 139, 148, 154, 174, 192, 193
IKEA, 107, 112, 121, 133, 179
industry alliance, 10
integrated marketing communication (IMC), 61, 147, 198

K

knowledge, 4, 10, 18, 19, 23, 32, 34, 35, 38, 39, 41, 43, 44, 46–50, 53, 55, 65, 72, 81, 86, 88, 93, 98, 101–104, 106, 107, 109, 114, 120, 121, 126, 127, 129, 132, 133, 136, 144, 154, 158, 163, 166, 173, 181, 183, 189, 194
knowledge, skills, and abilities (KSA), 23, 24

L

leader-member exchange (LMX), 53, 72, 83, 184
leadership, 3, 5, 10, 18, 23, 26, 37, 38, 41, 52, 53, 67, 70–72, 74, 75, 78–83, 85, 86, 97, 99, 114, 115, 124, 157, 163, 167, 197
LEGO, 120, 121, 167, 175
local enterprises, 14, 33, 59, 96, 97, 197, 198
    investment in, 93, 104

M

market competition, 15, 28, 30, 32, 35, 36, 50, 60, 63, 68, 81, 88, 106, 112, 143, 160, 166, 178, 180, 185, 186, 197
Marketing 4.0, 14

marketing-mix, 10, 11, 28–32, 52, 62, 107, 108, 113, 114, 155, 188, 191
micro, small, and medium enterprises (MSME), 13, 14, 16, 18, 19, 23, 24, 27, 28, 33, 50, 52, 55, 62–65, 79–83, 94, 106, 107
multiple ecosystems, 41

N

new product development, 4, 52, 82, 106, 110, 138, 139
niche, 6–8, 10, 20, 21, 28, 57, 58, 62, 63, 65, 67, 69, 71, 76, 78, 88, 102, 105, 115, 117, 119, 135, 142–145, 147, 161, 179, 185, 191, 192, 198
niche marketing strategy, 142

O

open innovation, 19, 55, 60, 98, 117–119, 121, 122, 124, 129–137, 152, 154, 155, 197
outreach, 10, 11, 18, 20, 33, 34, 53, 54, 83, 134, 152, 165–167, 192

P

participatory market appraisal (PMA), 153
pedigree, 4, 67, 72, 73, 76
People, Accountability, Control, and Transformation (PACT), 60, 82, 83, 187, 188
PNS factors, 7, 20, 33, 43, 50, 54, 55, 78, 79, 83, 97, 121, 124, 126, 134, 136, 149, 154, 158, 167
poverty, 20, 172, 173, 194, 197
product design, 15, 29, 47, 57, 128, 135, 137, 138, 178, 187

proximity, 10, 11, 16, 18, 20, 41, 48, 53–55, 62, 64, 72, 78, 98, 99, 119, 122, 127, 131, 165–167, 174, 197
public policies, 59, 88, 95, 101, 102, 106, 165, 182–184, 194, 195

R
RACE factors, 43
rapid market appraisal (RMA), 153
relationship management, 27, 38, 56, 162
resilience, 75
resource utilization, 37, 154
reverse accountability, 18, 26, 82, 83, 85, 99, 124, 152, 188
reverse entrepreneurship, 93–103, 197
reverse innovation, 12, 20, 93, 96, 97, 101, 115, 145, 179

S
semantics, 48, 49, 52–54, 85, 121, 124, 128, 129
services ecosystem, 56
six-branched growth, 16
skills, 10, 18, 19, 23, 26, 27, 31, 33, 37, 38, 50, 53, 64, 67–69, 71, 72, 87, 88, 94, 97, 99, 101, 102, 113, 123, 132, 142, 144, 150, 157, 171, 172, 179, 194, 197
social business model, 38
social capital, 39, 41, 43, 60, 95, 97, 102, 104
social challenges, 7, 19, 20, 194, 195, 197
social engagement, 56, 174–176, 191
social impact theory (SIT), 39, 40
social learning, 45, 53, 107, 119, 158
social media, 7, 10–12, 22, 28, 30, 32, 35, 37, 46, 48, 50, 52, 53, 57, 60, 74, 106, 113–115, 118, 119, 121, 124, 128, 129, 131, 132, 134, 148, 151, 158, 160–162, 165–167, 174–176, 184, 186, 191–194
social phenotype, 176, 184, 185
stage-gate model, 141
sustainability, 10–12, 19, 20, 38, 40, 41, 47, 49, 57, 58, 63, 82, 98, 101, 109, 164, 180–184, 191, 194, 195
sustainable entrepreneurship, 184, 191
synchronizing entrepreneurship, 196
systems thinking, 8, 142, 148, 177

T
transformation, 24, 25, 37, 74, 79, 103, 149, 158, 180
transformational leadership, 18, 59, 79, 81, 82, 85, 150, 194
transition, 3, 5, 13, 20, 75–77, 98, 99, 102, 119, 150, 155, 156, 191, 195, 197

U
urbanization, 95, 98, 107
user-generated contents, 22, 40, 48, 53, 56, 120, 122, 126, 128, 153, 158, 166, 187

V
value-based design, 178
value creation, 10, 11, 19, 87, 99, 105, 107, 119, 121, 122, 137, 147, 153, 160, 163, 164, 180, 183, 198

W
wisdom of crowds, 74, 117, 124, 128

Z
zero-based management, 16

Printed in the United States
by Baker & Taylor Publisher Services